FOOD AND FEMININITY IN TWENTIETH-CENTURY BRITISH WOMEN'S FICTION

For Ella Rose, my work-in-progress

Food and Femininity in Twentieth-Century British Women's Fiction

ANDREA ADOLPH
Kent State University-Stark Campus, USA

ASHGATE

Published by
Ashgate Publishing Limited
Wey Court East
Union Road
Farnham
Surrey, GU9 7PT
England

Ashgate Publishing Company
Suite 420
101 Cherry Street
Burlington
VT 05401-4405
USA

www.ashgate.com

British Library Cataloguing in Publication Data
Adolph, Andrea.
Food and femininity in twentieth-century British women's fiction.
   1. Food in literature. 2. Women in literature. 3. Mind and body in literature. 4. English fiction – 20th century – History and criticism. 5. English fiction – Women authors – History and criticism.
   I. Title
   823.9'14093564-dc22

Library of Congress Cataloging-in-Publication Data
Adolph, Andrea.
   Food and femininity in twentieth-century British women's fiction / by Andrea Adolph.
      p. cm.
   Includes bibliographical references and index.
   ISBN 978-0-7546-6734-6 (hbk)
   ISBN 978-0-7546-9457-1 (ebk)
   1.   English fiction—Women authors—History and criticism. 2. English fiction—20th century—History and criticism. 3. Food in literature. 4. Femininity in literature. I. Title. II. Title: Food and femininity in 20th-century British women's fiction.

PR116.A36 2009
823'.91093564—dc22

2009030054

ISBN: 9780754667346

Mixed Sources
Product group from well-managed forests and other controlled sources
www.fsc.org Cert no. SA-COC-1565
© 1996 Forest Stewardship Council

Printed and bound in Great Britain by
MPG Books Group, UK

Contents

Preface   *vi*
Acknowledgments   *vii*
List of Abbreviations   *viii*

Introduction: Long Division: Surpassing Mind/Body Duality   1

1   Regimentation of the Private: Hunting Down "Matter out of Place"   35

2   And the War Taketh Away: Female Embodiment and Sexual
    Excess in the Era of Austerity   69

3   Body as Text, Body in Text: Reader Response and the
    Consuming Body   105

4   Whole Numbers, Strange Remainders   151

Bibliography   *169*
Index   *177*

Preface

Over the several years of my work on this project, many friends, students, and colleagues have provided me with the small gestures and kindnesses that allow us to create and to progress both personally and professionally. I thank them all. I particularly thank those who have contributed to my passion for all things culinary—the chefs and waiters with whom I worked for many years, the friends with whom I have eaten meals both glorious and humble, and the writers who have paved the way for interest in a book like this one. Bon appétit!

Considerable thanks are due to Michelle Massé, whose faith in this project from beginning to end has been extraordinary. Her good questions, careful reading, and generous mentoring have all helped to make this book a reality. She and Devon Hodges also came forward with offers of child care at a particularly critical juncture in the life of this project.

Thanks are also due to those who have read and responded to the project at various stages. Panthea Reid, Elsie Michie, Pat McGee, Kate Jensen, Jayne Moneysmith, and Vi Dutcher have contributed to the ways in which I have thought about and shaped my finished product.

Jonathan Hackford contributed friendship and a place to stay during research trips to the United Kingdom in 2001 and 2003.

This work would not be what it is without the availability of archives and special collections, and I thank the staff members who have assisted me at the University of Sussex Special Collections (Mass Observation Archives and Monk's House Papers); the British Library at St. Pancras and its newspaper library at Colindale; the Women's Library at London Metropolitan University; and the BBC Written Archives Centre. The gracious suggestions and interest in my work that I have encountered during my primary archival and cultural research have nourished my thinking in untold ways.

A research trip to the United Kingdom during the summer of 2003 was supported in part by a Summer Research Award from the Office of Research and Graduate Studies at Kent State University. Prior to that, a Dissertation Year Fellowship from Louisiana State University provided support for an early version of this study.

My daughter, Ella Rose, offers me daily reminders of how rooted in the material world I am and should be.

Acknowledgments

A significant portion of Chapter Three was initially published as "The Reader's Body: Reader Response and the Consuming Body in Helen Dunmore's *Talking to the Dead*" in *Lit: Literature Interpretation Theory* 17.3–4 (2006).

Excerpts from *Jane and Prudence* by Barbara Pym used by permission of Dutton, a division of Penguin Group (USA) Inc., and by permission of the Laura Morris Literary Agency on behalf of the Estate of Barbara Pym. Copyright © 1981 the Estate of Barbara Pym.

Excerpts from *Talking to the Dead* by Helen Dunmore are used with the permission of A. P. Watt, Ltd., on behalf of Helen Dunmore.

The text of "Cookery Demonstrations" by Doris and Elsie Waters is used with the permission of Ms. Pamela Lorraine and with the approval of the BBC Written Archives Centre.

Quotations from unpublished work by Virginia Woolf are used with the permission of The Society of Authors as the literary representative of the estate of Virginia Woolf.

Material from the Mass Observation Archives, University of Sussex, is reproduced with the permission of Curtis Brown Group Ltd., London, on behalf of the Trustees of the Mass Observation Archive. Copyright © The Trustees of the Mass Observation Archive.

List of Abbreviations

JP   *Jane and Prudence* (Pym)

MHP   Monk's House Papers, University of Sussex

MOA   Mass Observation Archives, University of Sussex

Introduction
Long Division:
Surpassing Mind/Body Duality

The following pages explore ways in which aspects of the mind and the body have been brought together—to varying degrees and with varying results—by selected British women writers of the twentieth century.[1] Though the mind and body, as components of individual subjects, have been driven apart from one another since Plato, since St. Paul, since Descartes, seemingly since time immemorial, there also have been writers and thinkers who have worked, whether consciously or unconsciously, to rhetorically reunite these elements that actually are never far from each other. Throughout literature, philosophy, and other academic disciplines (as well as beyond the academy) there exist many voices who have sought to explain the ways in which the flesh and the intellect are indeed only components of a whole entity known monolithically as the "human being." In one mid-twentieth-century conversation about mind/body division that illustrates central aspects of this debate, Stanley Cobb refutes the idea that any further issue is at hand: "I believe that Freud's statement about the 'mysterious leap' from the mind into the body is today meaningless. There is no separation between psyche and soma [...] there is no leap at all for one who believes that mind is not a supernatural phenomenon but is *the active integration of the billions of nerve cells and hundreds of cell masses of the living brain*" (Deutsch 11; original italics). Henry M. Fox, however, is more willing to problematize this issue: "The dichotomy of body and mind represents a special case of the more general dichotomy of thing and thought. These dichotomies are misleading because they verbally allude to a split which does not correspond to the unitary nature of experience and of the living organism" (Deutsch 14). A grand difference between these two versions of a similar opinion—that the mind and body are indeed not separate entities, but

---

[1]   As I suggest throughout this introduction, language necessarily limits us in the ways we can define such entities as the mind and the body. Though I use the terms in all their monolithic glory, I do so self-consciously, and at the peril of discounting the experiences of some bodies altogether. Because the basis for my consideration is philosophical and seeks to rectify multiple divisions, however, I hope that the ways in which I use the term "body" or the term "female body" are more broad-based than exclusive, and that this work imagines an ontology that is in some small way shared—beneath markers of class, race, ability, age, et al.—by women who are products of Western or of Anglo-European culture. For the purposes of studying texts by English women writers of the twentieth century—women who have come from both middle- and working-class backgrounds—I necessarily locate my less philosophical, more cultural and sociological, discussions of women and their bodies within the contexts in which such writing has been produced.

exist as complementary parts of a whole—lies in Fox's identification of the role of language, of rhetorical construction, in this popular divergence of the mind from the body, a divergence that has proliferated and turned inward upon itself so that issues related to mind/body duality have become some of the more complicated additions to theoretical debates at the turn of the twenty-first century. While for some theorists any consideration of a dichotomy of mind and body is an intellectual gaffe akin to belief in a flat planet Earth, for others the concessions that must be made to the limitations of linguistic expression, and to the roles played by such limited language in the construction of and interrelations of human experiences, open the discussion to scholarly inquiry, even if such inquiry can never reach a point of finality or exactitude.

No actual separation of mind from body creates current troubles for theories of embodiment, of ontology, or of the ways in which discourse shapes epistemology. Rather, it is the long-standing *belief*—mostly in a culture loosely termed "Western," but that can for the purposes of this project be located more readily in Anglo-European traditions—that the mind provides the domain for an "essential" human being, while the body is merely a vehicle through which the mind can project a preeminent intellectual self. "We conceptualize ourselves," write George Lakoff and Mark Johnson, "as split into two distinct entities that can be at war, locked in a struggle for control over our bodily behavior. This metaphoric conception is rooted deep in our conscious conceptual systems, so much so that it takes considerable effort and insight to see how it functions as the basis for reasoning about ourselves" (13). As a metaphor for the "self," human intellect has historically borne the weight of human existence and experience, regardless of the necessary quantity of the body that is equally at work to act, to perceive, to explore. As Francis Barker explains, "From the spectacular semiosis of the Renaissance body [...] modernity fashions a new body" whose "passions are attenuated to a guilty residue; its status as a site of meaning is consigned to detritus. Depressed almost completely below the threshold of signification [...] the body disappears into the past" (vi–vii). This historical privileging of the intangible, whether that be a mind or a spiritualized "soul," at the expense of a more complete conceptualization of the self is at this root of the dichotomy of human experience, and until the body has been not only theoretically, but also popularly, reunited with the realm of intelligence (or of additional ephemeral qualities such as a conceptualized spirit), Western society will continue to be conflicted by the effects of this compromise. Until individuals have been encouraged through high and low cultures—through the media, the arts, and the daily newspaper—as well as through academic proclamations, to consider an equality of the psychological and the physical aspects of "being," the two will remain merely conflicting halves of a difficult binary in which one side must necessarily be asserted above its other half. Until the body can be viewed, as Maurice Merleau-Ponty describes, as "not itself a thing, an interstitial matter, a connective tissue, but a *sensible for itself*" (*Visible* 135; original italics), the division through which we as human beings are asked to conceive of ourselves will be at odds with the inherent connectedness of the mind and the body within human experience.

To understand how the mind and the body work together, one needs a model to express ways in which this functioning takes place. The "body image"—an intellectually projected version of the physical body as explained in discourses of psychology and neuropsychology—is a combination of physical and virtual components of embodiment and can serve as a model for examining not only how the mind and body are interdependent, but also how they relate to the text/ reader dyad (this is fully explored in Chapter Three). If the body—because of its reduced state in some contemporary discourse to a sort of inert surface made intelligible only as a result of cultural inscription—has become a questionable structure, then considerations of its projection/image rectify this reduction through an emphasis on the primacy of the connection *between* the physical body and its iterative image, rather than on either one or the other. The body image "attests to the necessary interconstituency of each for the other, the radical inseparability of biological from psychical elements" (Grosz 85) by displaying ways in which the body works through the psyche and the psyche manifests itself in the flesh. Merleau-Ponty explains, "[M]y whole body for me is not an assemblage of organs juxtaposed in space. I am in undivided possession of it and I know where each of my limbs is through a *body image* in which all are included" (*Phenomenology* 98). Beyond the fact of the body is the way in which we come to understand the body: the image of the body, of our own and of others', is the way in which we come to acknowledge and to understand that thing we call "the body." Paul Schilder, a neuropsychologist whose work *The Image and Appearance of the Human Body* looks extensively at the ways the body and mind work as one, defines the term:

> The body schema is the tri-dimensional image everybody has about himself [*sic*]. We may call it 'body-image'. The term indicates that we are not dealing with a mere sensation or imagination. There is a self-appearance of the body. [...] although it comes through the senses, it is not a mere perception. There are mental pictures and representations involved in it, but it is not mere representation. (11)[2]

The image of the body is like the physical component of the body itself in that it is three-dimensional. It differs from other bodily "images" of a visual or representational manner, however, because of its direct rapport with the material body that it describes and perpetuates within the human psyche. The body image is a predominant feature of the body's own epistemology. It provides the body with a method through which to know itself and its existence: its physical experiences of pressure, pain, and temperature sensations sorted out by the various nervous

---

[2]   Following Henry Head, Schilder also uses the term *postural model* when discussing the "body-image." Both terms indicate one's psychic understanding of his or her own physical body, as well as understandings of the bodies of others. I use the unhyphenated, more contemporary term *body image* rather than Schilder's, but I also discuss *body/image* as my own way to speak of the dual role of the mind and body with regard to such an intellectual projection of the physical body.

response systems. Recent scholarship on aspects of the female body, often dealing with female eating disorders and body-related self-esteem, has appropriated the term to such a degree that "body image" is now in common discourse related to body size and to one's perception of the width and girth of one's (most often female) body proportions. The image of the body created by the mind, however, is a much more complex designation of the term, and exploring this phenomenon adds to the conversation on the body itself and extends that conversation to better include mind/body connections. As a way to understand a "psychology of movement," Schilder posits the body image as the basis of all human movement: "undeveloped psychic knowledge [...] finds its development only during the performance of the action [...]. In this plan the knowledge of one's own body is an absolute necessity," but "intellectual knowledge is certainly, as pathology proves, insufficient" (51–2). Corporeal knowledge, then, is more than an intellectual understanding of the body itself. The image created as a guide to sensory and other responses is a visceral, embodied knowledge; it is a knowledge fundamental to motility and thus to human agency. The body image is the body's own trope: it is the narrative that explains the fact of the body and of its everyday existence. There is significant importance to literary study of this sort of embodied awareness, as Ina Schabert makes clear in her discussion of "new" texts that return to a sense of embodiment not typically seen since before the Enlightenment project that effaced human physicality. "Highly valued" in this literature, she claims, "are the ways of knowing peculiar to the body: body memory, corporeal habits, certainties which one has in one's bones, feelings which go under the skin" (101). These sentient capacities of human existence complicate the notion of a purely discursive subject that is all too familiar to many contemporary readers.

Schilder discusses the body and its movement, how it originates in time and space through the body image, as a "gestalt": "the whole which is more than the sum of the single parts" contrasted with "the 'und-' connection of parts which are added to each other" (11). Ontologically, the gestalt is systemic, complete only in and of itself; it should not be understood as a series of discrete parts. Western thought has moved toward dismantling such systems and an objectification of such parts that results in what I explore below as "auto-objectification," but indeed, if we are ever to understand connectivity rather than divisiveness, then a complete model must be understood as the foundation of anything such a dominant thought produces or creates. For Schilder, movement as a total experience is a gestalt, and as such it involves the entire moving being. Movement "develops out of inner motives" and "contains as parts its previous stages of development" (61). In other words, as a dancer lifts her leg up and onto the *barre* in order to stretch, that movement stems from an internal drive and desire to do so (impetus, decision) and is the sum of each point along the arc of the gesture: the foot moves from floor to *barre*; the hip rotates; the knee turns outward. Such "human action confirms us [...] in the idea that a gestalt has to be acquired and created and produced by inner and outward activities" (61), by the coming together, unconsciously, of the mind and the body. The materiality of the flesh, then, articulates the body's desire to move. Between desire and movement, though, ensuing motion is understood by the individual through the psychical image of the body itself, so that the *barre* can be reached without the aid of visual acknowledgment. Movements can be produced without conscious establishment of how and where and when, can be accomplished with eyes closed, with sight turned inward toward the image that is the psyche's guide to the outward nature of the body.

Together the mind and body create a gestalt—or, more precisely, develop *from* a gestalt—that should be encountered as a single sum of both its intellect and its corporeality. The gestalt of the mind/body combination, though, should not be understood as something fixed or regulated, but as a creation that shifts and flows, depending upon context: "a construction and destruction connected with the needs, strivings, and energies of the total personality" (Schilder 211). This continual building up and tearing away at the gestalt of mind/body totality is illustrated in the way that a body image changes as an awareness of physical surroundings changes, as individuals experience their lived bodies differently, depending upon motility, emotion, and other fundamentals of everyday life. "We expand and we contract the postural model of the body," Schilder writes; "we take parts away and we add parts; we rebuild it; we melt the details in" (210). Thus the cane becomes an extension of the body/image; the anorectic envisions a larger counterpart within the mirror than stands without; the "personal space" that we use to psychically protect ourselves shrinks and expands according to the identity of whomever sidles up beside us. The gestalt of the body/image (both the physical body and the image of the body envisioned from within) is a result of various equations and derivatives; it is a sum of its passivity and its resistance, its unknown surroundings and its recorded experience. As such, how can it ever be broken into fragments that maintain definition and refuse change? If the body/image is the result of "the continual activity, the trying out" (Schilder 211) of various states of being, then it can only be taken as the sum of its parts, as a whole structure, and not as qualities of the mental or the physical realm inducted into a hierarchy that negates the entire being by subjugating a selected stratum.

The body image stresses the interconnectedness of the mind and the body and presents individuals as gestalts of their physical and mental spheres. To discuss "the body," then, is to speak of more than flesh, but of intellectual activities of individuals as well. The flesh is the external exhibition, in many ways, of the "inner activities" Schilder mentions as part of the body's gestalt (61). To discuss "the body" is to implicate more than simply the physicality of some one person. The gestalt of the body is both inscriptive surface and intelligible text, both image and context, material and intellectual. Its textuality can be "read" as a site of culture and of biology. The body is the medium for all human expression and for human interpretation of the nexus of cultural and material experience. Michel Foucault delineates the body's textuality from its experience by suggesting two registers of embodiment: "a useful body and an intelligible body" (*Discipline* 136). For Foucault, the "two registers are quite distinct, since it [is] a question, on the one hand, of submission and use and, on the other, of functioning and explanation" (136). In this system of categorizing corporeality, Foucault asserts an important function of embodiment that is subject to cultural and social forces. The human body can be "used" by external forces, and in turn it can be— and is daily, as will be discussed in Chapter 3—analyzed and "read" by others as significant of cultural data. This scheme, though, creates a teleology that makes no room for exceptions, for shifting cultural values, or for simple resistance beyond the borders of this circular construct. Susan Bordo puts Foucault's terminology into play through analysis of anorexia and other feminine "disorders" (hysteria, agorophobism) and explains the intelligible body as the body symbolic: for example, "the nineteenth-century hourglass figure [...] representing a domestic, sexualized ideal of femininity" (181). The useful body differs from the symbolic through its relationship to praxis, in Bordo's case a feminine praxis: "straightlacing, minimal eating, reduced mobility [...] rendering the female body unfit to perform activities outside its designated sphere" (181). Cultural practices are joined to their resulting social and cultural significance at the site of the body. In this case, Bordo's analysis of the "intelligible body" illustrates how bodies are not either/or, useful or intelligible (but never otherwise), but are instead always both and always subject to the possibility of an existence beyond culture.

Though both Foucault's and Bordo's theories of the body are excellent lenses through which to begin to examine the body's textuality, the Foucauldian notion of "docility"—at the heart of his theories in *Discipline and Punish* and of Bordo's extrapolations from them—which "joins the analysable body to the manipulable body" (136), lends itself too much to an external/material image of the body and to that body's use value merely as a site of cultural inscription. Docility joins together only the materiality of bodily practices and their significance; Foucault leaves out the interiority of the body and the body's intellectuality. What can be viewed from the outside by another, in Foucault's terms, has nothing at all to do with the view of the body by itself through the extended body or body image. Though Bordo asserts the danger of "giving a kind of free, creative rein to *meaning* at the expense of attention to the body's material locatedness in history, practice, culture" (38), often her discussions of the female body, particularly of the anorexic body, tread closer to a fixed idea of docile bodies than her disclaimers might suggest. In her essay "Material Girl" (in *Unbearable Weight*), Bordo explains bodily effacement through examinations of the body's "plasticity": the body's ability to be reconstructed through plastic surgery, diet, and exercise. Though she acknowledges a cultural ability to efface the body if the body is viewed only as a site of cultural inscription and normalization, she still defines "the body" only in terms of its materiality. To trim away flesh is to affect far more than the body's shape and size; the shapes of body images and of psyches change as well with each developed muscle, shed pound, or Botox injection. Further investigations into mind/body totality should consider the potential plasticity of the brain and any resulting, lasting imprint upon the psychical component of the "self" that results from the ways in which bodies are constructed and reconstructed for cultural conformity. Growing scholarship in cognitive theories (beyond the scope of this project) can provide new models for understanding the extent to which the abstract mind and the actual brain are mutually dependent upon each other not only as functions of human experience, but also as signifiers for what it can mean to be human. Just as the body can change in size and appearance, the body image will change in order to account for lost or added physical dimensions, and phenomena such as phantom limbs experienced by amputees call into question a notion of that newer image as primary or as stable. Discussions of the body, if they are to take into account the body's psychical components, must include the more complex ways in which the body can be read as a gestalt of the mental and the physical.

This project began—as, I am certain, have many—as support for an agenda quite different from that which lies beneath the current study. A child of Western culture, of a United States so formed by multiple versions of the mind and the body (ethical, cultural, religious), I was no stranger to the metaphor (à la Lakoff and Johnson) that creatively fashions a self from the fodder found in the realm of the intellect. I was merely, until I had unearthed and interrogated a variety of theories of embodiment and of human subjectivity, unaware of the ways in which I have been complicit in my own separation of mind from body, and in which my own belief system had internalized the widely held mind/body binary that in turn had formed the intellectual basis for my initial scholarly pursuit of female embodiment in literature by women. As I searched for evidence of embodied female experiences in texts by women as a way to imagine whether women writers have an edge over their male counterparts when it comes to documenting and describing female experiences, however, I was as bound to the idea of a body divided from the mind as numerous others have been. Though I was discontent with the rationales of some ongoing debates—debates that tend to polarize between an essentialized privileging of the body and constructivist promotion of discursivity and intellect—and wished to examine them further so as to discover why such theories to me made little sense, until I began to follow not the trail of "the body" through literature, but instead a broader path trod by a more comprehensive female identity, I was unable to imagine the unification of mind and body that now is so central to my thinking in these many pages. My search for the body in these literatures, though an important step in the process of developing this study, was, I realized as I stretched my readings out into certain discourses of philosophy and psychology, not taking into account an entire female "self" that must be considered as a conglomerate of mental and physical modes of being and as a spectrum of aspects ranging from the intellectual to the physical, but mostly containing what lies in between. Interestingly, too, as I found through my chosen critical lens of food consumption those representations of embodied women that I had set out to discover, I also found, right there beside them, their theoretical counterparts: disembodied, discursive "sisters" who serve as representations of the mind that must accompany those of the body in order for an author to make some "whole" sense from our collective fragmented understandings of individual ontologies and subjectivities.

A thinking through of the ways in which the mind and the body can be philosophically reunited in order to promote new ways to conceive of the individual human being is, I think, particularly germane to feminist discourses, especially to those discourses that have sought to define female experiences as they relate to issues of sex and gender. In *Volatile Bodies: Toward a Corporeal Feminism* (1994), Elizabeth Grosz posits a notion of sexual difference based not simply upon biological facts or effects, but instead upon an interrelated mind/body continuum that can "avoid the impasses of reductionism, of a narrow causal relation or the retention of a binary divide" (210). In many ways, my thinking stems from her challenge in that work to feminist scholars and thinkers that we imagine new models beyond the binary for future thinking about women in social and cultural contexts, as well as for imagining embodiment beyond the narrow function of physical vehicle for the intellect. The binary of a cultural mind/body division is reflexively evident in the division among many of the theorists, as mentioned above, who have typically viewed the body as either primarily a biological system (and as the entity responsible for sexual difference) or primarily a lesser quantity when compared with the power of the intellect and its mutable responses to the effects of language.[3] If one can acknowledge the problems that a mind/body division can create for the ways in which we imagine the individual in society, then an extrapolation of such divisiveness from theory to theorist can in turn illustrate how such divisions of thought can be equally problematic, and certainly counterintuitive, for imagining those new models for feminist inquiry encouraged by Grosz.

At the close of the twentieth century, the body as a concept faced challenges more potentially terminal than simple subordination to the mental realm. Theorists such as Judith Butler, while working toward an important understanding of the ways in which language helps to construct individuals, also destabilized any previously understood *terra firma* of the body.[4] The idea of the body as "fact"

---

[3]   Grosz outlines three schools of feminist thought on embodiment (15–19): "egalitarian feminism," described in terms similar to what might be called liberal feminism, and in which the body, viewed negatively as something that "limits women's capacity for equality and transcendence" (15), is removed from the field in order to privilege the masculine concept of the rational mind; "sexual difference," a school of thought founded upon understanding the "lived body," in which Grosz includes thinkers as diverse as Judith Butler, Gayatri Spivak, and Hélène Cixous; and "social constructionism," theorists who work toward an understanding of the role of social codes in the body's experiences. Though this three-tiered model works well for Grosz's argument, I find that she lumps together theorists that in another context might be construed as at odds with each other. Grosz does not get underneath the very different types of lived bodies, for instance, that Butler and Spivak discuss, and the very different critical ends that make up such theorists' agendas. For the sake of my own argument, I prefer to consider the range of theorists at work recently on theories of embodiment as most easily divided into two groups.

[4]   Butler's work in *Gender Trouble: Feminism and the Subversion of Identity* (Routledge, 1990) and *Bodies that Matter: On the Discursive Limits of "Sex"* (Routledge, 1993), while important to the field of gender studies, is also problematic in its seemingly reductive handling of issues of embodiment.

or fixed notion has been called into question in a way that theoretically extends toward a negation of the importance of individual corporeal experiences and of personal contexts in order to privilege a notion of perception based upon "pure" discourse. In *Bodies that Matter: On the Discursive Limits of "Sex"* (1993), Butler, ostensibly defending her negation of embodiment in the earlier *Gender Trouble*, nonetheless continued to drive her spike between discourse and materiality. In a reading of the work of Julia Kristeva, who posits the existence of a pre-discursive subject through semiotics and an emphasis upon the maternal body, Butler allows that "[l]anguage and materiality are fully embedded in each other, chiasmic in their interdependency, but, never fully collapsed into one another" (*Bodies* 69). She argues beyond this point to nearly contradict it, though, when she returns to what reads like the primacy of discourse: "materiality is constituted in and through iterability [...] the materiality of the maternal body is only figurable within language" (70). While Butler's sociolinguistic approach to issues of sex and gender were revolutionary when written and allowed for new ways of conceiving the human subject, and while the ideas of socialization processes and cultural constructs lend much to understanding how sex roles and gender ideals become socially and culturally standardized, and in turn play themselves out in everyday life, the idea that individual experience itself is at the basis of political motivation and necessity has historically been foundational to feminist thought. If the body is reduced to a series of cultural and social interactions—with the suggestion that such contact is random and relative, a reaction to some previous interface—then the historicity of contemporary feminist theory is jeopardized as its theories become polarized, much like those other discursive models discussed above. To remove the ground of the body and of personal/physical experience as a relevant starting point for libratory thought is to turn from a vast amount of what has come to make up feminist thinking. But to simply embrace an essentialist definition of sexual difference is also a limited methodology; constructivist ideologies are an equally important part of the dialogue. As thoughts on the body have expanded to encompass a wider definition of "materiality" that includes the realm of the intellect, such a shift can only help to further not only philosophical inquiries into the nature of being and of embodiment, but also feminist inquiry itself.

To such ends, I have chosen to focus my examination of the novels included in this study—my newly defined quest for the mind and body together in literary contexts—through the lens of food consumption (and other relationships to food, such as its preparation and serving) in order to investigate issues of the body that are not defined exclusively through discourses of and representations of female sexuality, as those discourses in particular seem perilously close to endorsing an essentialist, biology-driven point of view. Discourses of food, too, are a site where mind and body intersect: prescriptions for the flesh that originate within a linguistic framework are powerful forces within the culture of the last century. Schabert traces literary foodways that are "savoury, pungent, heavily spiced, and to be enjoyed imaginatively by the reader" (102). Many women writers (and some men, too) have explored issues of female embodiment via themes of motherhood, sexual expression (activity, orientation), or sexual abuse. Female bodies, however, enjoy (and deplore) a multiplicity of additional physical experiences, most of which have been deemed less important than those "defining" female experiences that relate to female *genital* difference rather than to a more complicated idea of a sexual difference for which the center is not the vagina or the uterus. Female consumption can be considered as both a form of female experience and a direct aspect of the body and its becoming, moving the female body beyond those traditional ways in which it has been viewed. "For every act of eating," Marcy J. Epstein writes of performative, public consumption, "there exists a signifying reaction that tells us in no uncertain terms that *that body has just made* [...] *itself*" (21; original italics). A consuming woman exemplifies, in this way, her body and the potential agency housed within that body. In order to place myself in a critical position removed from an essentialist view of the body as primarily a site of sexual difference (instead of as a site of multiple investments), as well as a position firmly anchored in the "everyday" material world, I have chosen to examine physical activities that signify a female body that remains a part of the quotidian world that cannot be ignored if the body is to be considered with regard to the realms of experience and sentience. The act of food consumption, an act that must occur on a regular basis for basic survival, is a foundational activity for women as well as for men; however, as I will explore throughout this work, I believe that female consumption provides a basis for explorations of many aspects of female experiences and of constructions of femininity, and that the idea of a consuming female anticipates social and cultural anxieties about female empowerment and agency.

Perhaps ironically—and perhaps not—issues of female consumption and relationships to food that include domestic and nurturing processes, though removed from the literal field of female sexual and genital experiences, nonetheless implicate related ideas of motherhood and of female sexual experiences. Try as I might to remove myself from those fields of inquiry most directly related to female sexuality, the female body, regardless of its status and activity, has become so culturally loaded with sexual (and biological) significance that it has become impossible (and eventually, for my argument, undesirable) to ignore the ways in which the consuming female body resonates with issues related to an embodied female sexuality. Good examples of such a linkage among forms of female sexual functionings can be found in Sarah Sceats's recent work, *Food, Consumption, and the Body in Contemporary Women's Fiction*. Sceats's chapter titled "The food of love: mothering, feeding, eating, and desire" sums up aspects of female consumption and embodiment that are at once cultural imperatives and dubious traits. "For many people," Sceats explains, "the connection of food with love centers on the mother, as a rule the most important figure in an infant's world, able to give or to withhold everything that sustains, nourishes, fulfills, completes" (11). The connections between food and women are emphasized through representations of serving and providing as they are through consuming, but to different logical ends. Discourses of psychoanalysis (put forward by Freud, Klein, and others) have illustrated many ways in which initiations into realms of consumption in infancy create intimate and long-lasting associations between maternity and eating,[5] and certainly there can be positive connotations made between mother-love and the potentially soothing qualities of food consumption. Sceats notes the flip side to this mother-food nexus, however, when she speaks of "the maternal capacity to devour" (15) at the heart of Freudian castration concerns. The devouring woman, whether mother or not, is a source of potential cultural anxiety, for the devouring, desiring woman is culturally defined as a sexualized being and is an "other" with the potential to escape from the bounds of normative social restraints that govern sexual practices and other, often gendered, behavior schemes.

The female body in either of these relationships to food—maternal or sexual—calls forth the notion of a body that exists in direct opposition to the "image of a body in accordance with a tradition of ideal architecture [...]. That body is [...] that of an abstract, adult man, lying down in a horizontal posture with his arms open, his legs spread and stretched" (Marin 107). Louis Marin considers such a "classical" body (as expressed in the work of Bakhtin), even in such an unseemly posture that for a woman would be considered lewd, as representative of utopian qualities, different from the "abysmal cavity, pit, and orifice of the living body" (107). This spread-open male body offers up phallic "life" and poses no threat to patriarchal, masculine order, while an equally opened-up female body would beckon, would potentially devour, drown, suffocate. That living body of cavities and orifices most typically becomes, through elision based upon generations of cultural forces, a female body, one whose blood and milk signify the maternal and sexual female body that cannot mask itself as a male alternative and whose secretions threaten the social order apparent in that "traditional architecture" (noted by Marin) of social structures. While, according to Grosz, seminal fluid "is understood primarily as what it makes, what it achieves, a causal agent and thus a thing, a solid" (199), the fluids produced by the female body remain fluids, and such secretions are significant of what Julia Kristeva calls the abject: "What does not respect borders, positions, rules. The in-between, the ambiguous, the composite" (4). Though Kristevian abjection is very much an effect of embodiment, and read within the confines of masculine definition remains unchangeably connected to the realm of the flesh, the very status of the abject as in-between, and reliance of abjection upon systems of discourse in order to have rules to break, allows for considerations of its by-products (blood, milk), and of such bodily functions as consumption, to take into account the workings between material and discursive planes. The abject, neither subject nor object, is a hybrid designation. Though often relegated to the realm of biological function, issues of maternity and of female sexuality can complement investigations of those other physical experiences (such as food consumption) more removed from the traditional Western definitions of "woman," the parameters of which rely upon a lens of a fairly reductive female embodiment

---

[5]   See Kim Chernin, *The Hungry Self: Women, Eating, and Identity* (Harper, 1985), particularly her chapter on mothers and daughters, for a complex analysis of eating disorders and maternal influence.

for their stability. As Kelly Oliver writes (with regard to Kristeva), "the maternal body [...] provides the most fundamental and powerful example of the seam between nature and culture" ("Nourishing" 69), between what I have referred to as embodiment and discourse. By any nomenclature, such division provides a basis for a collective theory of the body that ultimately reaches an impasse when it does not take into account that "seam," that dynamic site of tension that should be considered in theoretical discussions that seek to move beyond the trappings of binary systems in order to find ways in which components of dualities work together and are mutually enhancing.

The female body, then, so culturally invested with Kristeva's "abject," cannot avoid the fact of its myriad abjectivities once any one of them—in this study, the abjection of food consumption as well as of other physical contact with food that women have when dealing with food meant for others—has been illuminated. Once any single signifier of the body's "horrors" is acknowledged, then the myth of a pure body—a masculine projection—must be confronted. "The body's inside, in that case," notes Kristeva, "shows up to compensate for the collapse of the border between inside and outside. It is as if the skin, a fragile container, no longer guaranteed the integrity of one's 'own and clean self' [...] gave way before the dejection of its contents" (53). If, as Oliver reiterates, "to set up your own clean and proper identity of a self, it is necessary to jettison certain threatening elements from your own identity" (*Subjects* 53), then inversely, opening the door to a threatening element, allowing something into the body that may indeed defile that body, can obliterate any sense of an identity that might conform to cultural standards for the clean and the proper, and of that "corporeal 'universal'" that "has in fact functioned as the veiled representation and projection of a masculine which takes itself as the unquestioned norm" (Grosz 188). Both abject seepages and internalized "threatening elements" are components of a body that is at the very least feminized, but that most often is strictly female. In her memoir *Bad Blood*, Lorna Sage writes of her mother's fear of food as a "fear of the outside getting in" (123), as an anxiety related to those uncontrollable natural forces that lay both outside her own front door and, certainly, that existed within her own body. Complicating a female body that has been traditionally codified as sexual and maternal with the problematics of consumption, of ingesting and internalizing that which is "outside" or "other," can allow for curious, exciting new ways to imagine female experientiality, both those experiences that have seemingly been exhausted in critical discourses and those that have often been overlooked. If "what is excluded at the overt level of identity-formation [the abject, the other] is productive of new objects of desire" (Stallybrass and White 25), then so is what is included, what is consumed. The consuming female, even as she necessitates reconsiderations of those more common conversations about the female body, invites new ways to imagine female subjectivity.

Barker's thesis in *The Tremulous Private Body: Essays on Subjection* establishes and supports a rise in the importance of the individual, discursive "subject" at the expense of the historical material body, and speaks of such a philosophical project as the "inception of bourgeois modernity" (88). The increasing division—from Enlightenment onward and through the present day—of the public world at large and the private individual, Barker asserts, is "a caesura running through—and, by division, instituting—other separations; between knowledge and the object, between language and the world, between the mind, soul or psyche and the body" (vi). To build upon this argument, regardless of the particular division that may have led the way, all such binaried divisions create a vast nexus of social and cultural forces that work together upon and through subjects that are individually composed of interdependent mental and physical aspects; more specifically, I consider through investigations of literary and cultural texts the crucial link between (female) subject formation and the treatment of the problem of the body by twentieth-century women writers. As with the circularity of debate over embodiment, debates founded upon the idea of a constructed subjectivity often find themselves with no way out: "A power *exerted on* a subject, subjection is nevertheless a power *assumed by* the subject, an assumption that constitutes the instrument of that subject's becoming" (Butler, *Psychic* 11; original italics). The subject is, in part, only a subject because of the social and cultural forces to which she is subjected. Rather than attempt any salvaging of one at the expense of the other (my own grappling with these issues is indeed no less circuitous than are the thoughts of others), in this work I hope to think through what can occur by and because of the connectedness, the circle within such logical circuity, what Grosz has exemplified with the continuous Möbius strip that has no top that is not also bottom, no inside that cannot be simultaneously construed as out.

Because diffuse mechanisms of forces and subjects working together at once, inseparable, are at the heart of much of the work of Michel Foucault, some of my theoretical bases (many of which are delineated in the first chapter of this study) rely upon his thinking, regardless of Daniel T. O'Hara's assertion that Foucault no longer matters, because of "the ritual passing" of "our 'postmodern moment'" (142). Perhaps, O'Hara suggests, we have as a culture out-postmoderned ourselves, and have designed a definition of a new social order so relative as to have no room left for an acceptance of those very theories that have helped to establish such a thing as postmodernity. "Such a culture," he muses, "may possess a morality, an imposed standard of public and customary mores, but it is not ethical, since there is no freely selected *rapport à soi* ["oneself"] possible, except in the modes of pure negation, such as absolute irony and radical parody" (156). In the realm of pure discourse, there is no way to salvage a subjectivity that carries with it any hope of integrity. The "self" without its physical complement becomes a figure of fantasy, or one of derision.

As I have emphasized, what is more potentially invigorating to these ongoing discussions than any decisive pull toward one end of a spectrum or binary for discussions of both the body and the subject is an investigation of the rhetoric used in such conjecture, as well as an examination of how these components work together. Our language allows for discursive constructs, but necessarily limits us in ways that draw us back to the center and to an acknowledgment of continua, to that "seam" where parts are joined and where the osmosis of ontology and epistemology occurs for selves who are subjects but who are at the same time subject to the external world, who are physically established individuals who possess established psychical capacities. Butler argues that for Foucault, "a subject is formed through the prohibition of a sexuality, a prohibition that at the same time forms this sexuality—and the subject who is said to bear it," and that "prohibition becomes" in itself "an odd form of preservation [...] a productive contradiction in terms" (*Psychic* 103). In this sense the sexualized self—an identity formation that implicates both subjectivity and the body—is both the site of yet another inescapable maze of inquiry and another context in which the formation of an embodied subjectivity can be considered. Because, as outlined above, the female body is defined so often in Western culture in terms of its sexuality, discussions of female sexuality are critical to establishing what might constitute female subjectivity, as well as to the potential ramifications for female subjects of an identity that is itself a "productive contradiction in terms": a mind and body joined together in such a way that is fruitful for the female subject, and in such a way that allows for further insight into both the lived experiences of women and the texts produced by female authors. Rather than the binaried Hegelian model of a subject formed in opposition to an "other," one that "requires hostility, alienation, dominance, servitude" (Oliver, *Subjectivity* 151), a synthesized model provides a productive way to imagine subjectivity—indeed, sexuality—beyond the limits imposed by the "other" who is defined by disconnection. "Subjectivity," writes Oliver, "is not the result of a dialectic jerking back and forth from self to other. Rather, if anything, self and other are [...] perhaps even the refuse of the continual process of intersubjective exchanges that nourish and sometimes threaten" (*Subjectivity* 151). This idea of interchange to which I and those theorists with whom I am in chorus keep returning is inherent within the construction of sexuality in that the self and the "other" (whatever or whoever is the projection of one's desire) are at the center of that phenomenon known as sexuality. Female subjectivity, in perhaps its most "productive" form, is at once the result of an embodied sexuality and of the sexualization of women in social and cultural discourses. In order to unsnarl the ways in which women as a group have been maligned by such sexualization, and to consider simultaneously how those forces shape the female subject who can be productively resistant even while under social subjection, further consideration should be given to the interactivity of a female subjectivity that is a product of mental and bodily activities. Consideration should be given, too, to the processes involved in joining together those components of the subject, as well as to the cultural and social fission that demands division of the whole subject.

According to Oliver, "Julia Kristeva suggests that we become subjects, more precisely speaking subjects, because of, and in response to, the primary pleasure of eating" ("Nourishing" 68). Both within the maternal, psychoanalytic context of Kristeva's thinking and in broader contexts, female consumption provides a strong lens through which to examine those links that exist among the interconnected qualities of female subjectivity, agency, embodiment, and sexuality. From a feminist perspective, consumption provides a context fraught with examples of gender problematics: eating disorders, body-image dysphoria, and social and cultural disempowerment. As an act significant of positive associations with the female body, however, female consumption can also subvert some of the effects of those problems of the body. Epstein finds that staged eating—which I will extend to include eating represented within a fictional text—"[situates] femininity itself as a residual, disembodying aspect of female bodies," and asserts that such a movement of the (sexed) body out from behind discourses of gender can be "awesome and potentially liberating" (23). Traditionally destined to produce and serve food, consuming women can call into question the limitations of those relationships to food that have been historically more acceptable. The consuming female body, then, is a productive site of female agency that is also complicated by social inscriptions, and examinations of consumption can allow for the significant potential of this female body to be included in ongoing conversations that importantly also must include those more disturbing effects of female embodiment. The consuming female, as a result of philosophical and cultural definitions of that monolithic "woman," lies at the intersection of subjectivity and embodiment so central to female identity.

Of course, in contemporary parlance, the word *consumption* produces economic as well as physically material connotations, and female consumption in many forms can affect the dynamics of female subjectivity, as well as the reception by the socius of the female subject. As Rita Felski points out, the "discourse of consumerism is to a large extent the discourse of female desire" (65), and female desire—female sexuality—is at the root of a number of cultural anxieties. At the turn of the twentieth century, shopping (and other forms of consumer consumption) "was seen as engendering a revolution of morals, unleashing egotistic and envious drives among the lower orders and women, which could in turn affect the stability of existing social hierarchies" (Felski 65). Consumerism—importantly, female consumerism and consumption—not only intersects with the problem of the mind and the body, but has also provided a means by which to examine the plagued concept of a modern subjectivity as it has expanded to accept into its folds women and other marginalized groups, such as the working classes. "Given a prevalent equation," Felski extrapolates, "of bourgeois masculinity with reason and self-restraint, it was above all through the representation of the consuming woman that writers criticized the vulgar materialism brought about by capitalist development" (88). The female of the species, who already bore the weight of a suspect sexuality as the object of desire, under growing social investment in a capitalist project became imbued with an uneasy subject status as a consumer with desires of her own. If consumption relations, like those of the subject/object dyad, take on this two-headed appearance, then women can never be accommodated within this version of a consumer culture.

In a discussion of Baudrillard's theories of consumption, Rachel Bowlby examines ways in which the consuming subject is further displaced within a system that already signals its demise: "the consumer citizen is *not so much the possessor of as possessed by* the commodities which one must have to be made or make oneself in the form objectively guaranteed as that of a social individual" (28; emphasis added). When consumption is a necessary practice, as it is within a capitalist social order, the consuming "subject" is at once a social agent and *subject to* those consumable items at hand and to cultural mandates to acquire them, much like that more general subject, discussed by Butler in *The Psychic Life of Power*, that is dependent upon the very power that constructs it. In such a culture, the consuming subject performs those central complications of historical divisions of intellectualized subjectivity from an embodied self. If there is "ambivalence at the site where the subject emerges" (Butler, *Psychic* 7), then consumerism and its ingesting, consuming subject together form a system of ambivalence that blurs those dominant definitions of social order and ultimately becomes a microcosm of that order: the system as a whole is played out through acts of consumption. But within this structure lies a latent ability to resist the norms of consumerism; beneath such ambivalence is the potential for resistance because of the existence of sentient interpretation that requires both intellect and embodiment. Michel de Certeau distinguishes between what he terms "strategies" and "tactics," both of which are germane to discussions of agency—perhaps especially to explorations of female agency—and are its necessary corporeal component. Certeau's premise that there is always resistance within interpretive acts, acts that can include consumption, is a useful way to emphasize the ways in which literary representations of consumption can indicate cultural subversion as well as compliance.

Certeau's "strategy" is a "calculus of force-relationships" (like Foulcauldian bio-power) that "assumes a place that can be circumscribed as *proper* [...] and thus [serves] as the basis for generating relations with an exterior distinct from it" (xix). Certeau's "tactic" differs in that it is "a calculus which cannot count on a 'proper' (a spatial or institutional localization), nor thus on a borderline distinguishing the other as a visible totality" (xix). The strategy is directional, goal-oriented, and acts upon an "other." Systems of social regulation are strategic; they derive their position through separation from the controlled subject. The tactic, however, is "the intellectual synthesis of [heterogeneous] elements" that "takes the form [...] not of a discourse, but of [...] the act and manner in which the opportunity is 'seized'" (xix). There is no specific sequence or syntax within the tactic, but instead it is the impulse itself to "do" beyond the bounds of strategy. Tactics are functions in themselves; they are not simply functions *of* the system in place. A synthesis of the defiant body with its intellectual complement will result in practices that lie just beyond the proper space of strategy, and thus will always be a little bit unruly, a little bit resistant to attempts to bind and to limit, as with household and bodily maintenance, which naturally defy the ideal but impossible standards set for them (this phenomenon is discussed in Chapter 1). Although the human mind might be programmable to an extreme degree, and thus prone to be a realm likely dictated to by the socius, the body is highly unlikely to conform without concerted and continual efforts and can undermine the project of systemic functioning. The more active the body becomes in a given tactical process, the more likely the system will be threatened or subverted on some scale.

Everyday practices that are by nature tactical, according to Certeau, include "talking, reading, moving about, shopping, cooking" (xix), all of which lie in the realm of "the *thinkable*, which is identified with what one can *do*" (190). Tactics consist of what is conceivable, what is imaginable, and therefore of what is possible. Such practices "intervene in a field which regulates them at a first level" (they are inseparable from the milieu), "[...] but they introduce into it a way of turning it to their advantage that obeys other rules and constitutes something like a second level interwoven into the first" (30). Activities that result from syntheses of mind with body, tactical by design because their synthetic natures transgress the monolithic binary structures of our culture, are practices that do not simply conform to external strategies, but redefine those strategies and subvert them in a way that becomes epistemological. Tactics are by nature interpretive through the knowledge of the body as well as of a purely intellectual understanding of a given situation. The sentient as well as rational subject is the arbiter of interpretation, and unique aspects of embodied analysis are located within acts such as consumption. Certeau's tactic is characterized by the idea of "use" and is what he calls "the labor of consumption" (30). Consumption, as a tactical mode of use, requires both passivity and action; it cannot be circumscribed by the system, but is in part a result of social values and cultural information. Consumers are receptacles, but also "carry out operations of their own," through which the facts of such use are "no longer the data of our calculations, but rather the lexicon of users' practices" (31). Though alone the tactic lacks syntax, the synthesis of the tactical practice and the larger system within which it is deployed and alongside of which it exists creates a particular linguistic structure, but this structure is idiosyncratic to its user as well as to the moment of performance. While strategies that serve the system can become routinized, tactics are wily; they need not be consistent.

The activity of consumption is itself a map of agency. Certeau illustrates his theory of consumption with the example of reading as a practice in which the consumer absorbs words chosen by another, but in which the act of reading depends upon what consumers "make of what they 'absorb,' receive, and pay for" (31). Interpretive acts that are a product of the tactical act of "reading" cannot be strictly enforced by systemic regulations, and in this way indicate the precarious nature of any ideology offered up to a normalized population. Consumption is "characterized by its ruses, its fragmentation [...], its poaching, its clandestine nature [...] in short by its quasi-invisibility, since it shows itself not in its own products [...] but in an art of using those imposed upon it" (31). The concept of an objective or literal interpretation is "the index and the result of a social power, that of an elite" (Certeau 171), but shifting, interactive "poaching" of information—taking up and using what one needs from the confines of someone else's field of knowledge or from the product of another's labor—is a threat to that elite power structure. Via the physicality of such actions, the body itself is always poaching, always reconsidering, reinvesting itself as it moves through a variety of climates, cultures, and situations that demand from the embodied subject tactical acts of reading, interpretation, consumption.

Once redefined through an interaction between the strategy and the tactic, the system can be understood as partially a product of the agent who deploys her own "mode of use" (30) as she negotiates the system. The performance of such negotiations allow for the actions of the body to be interpreted by the intellect as they work in tandem. If one is to imagine a female agency that is in part engendered from the flesh, then that agency emerges as tactical, "an art of the weak" (37) that uses what is presented by the system/strategy, but simultaneously uses the system idiosyncratically. This agency will, if only in small ways that escape all but the closest of gazes, be a subversive agency, one that provokes the regulatory functions of the social system. The modern female subject, then, even though she is created by a system that does not cease to encourage through popular discourses aimed at women "a pursuit without a terminus" (Bordo 166) and that manifests as strategic projects such as prescriptions for weight control and body sculpting, is still subject to the physical aspects of her own subjectivity, of a subjectvity that *does* and *uses* according to Certeau's theories. This sort of resistant response to social conditioning is central to the argument that I lay out in my readings of literary texts: while writers might make use of the well-known division between mind and body through representations of consumption and food-related domesticity, this binary is inherently unstable. The tactical nature of female subjectivity rises up in the texts examined to complicate the expected narrative functions of the female characters. Although such a tactical subjectivity can and does produce an ambivalent, anxious subject (literary examples of which are discussed in Chapter 4), it also emphasizes the liberatory aspects of a renegotiation of mind/body duality into a spectrum that runs a gamut from one to the other and that engenders multiple mutations of the two as interactive and synthesized. When the physical aspects of "self" are necessarily a component of subjectivity, the subject can never be viewed as simply a blank slate awaiting social conditioning, as didactic theories of social construction might suggest. When the historically chronic emphasis upon an embodiment that is divorced from constructions of subjectivity is allowed to define our relationships between the components of our "selves," the psychical damage that results will leave its mark upon both human subjects and their cultural production.

One result of this division of the physical self from those less tangible qualities of the subject, a problem complicated by the blurring of the subject/object duality consolidated by a consumer culture, is what I call "auto-objectification": the objectification of one's own body through alignment with an ideology that prioritizes a transcendental, purely discursive and intellectualized "self." Although those who have become acculturated to understand the body as separate from the mind are likely to exhibit some effects of auto-objectification, female subjects—already so strongly affected by social and cultural objectification and sexualization—exemplify this result of this particular cultural phenomenon. Women have historically been limited to a realm of embodiment (as opposed to that privileged masculine reason that has been historically allotted to male subjects) while at the same time encouraged through social and philosophical doctrines to turn away from their bodies. Under capitalism, participation in which is almost impossible to escape, women have become further challenged by this paradoxical social inscription: while female agency has increased with the rise of economic freedoms and participation in consumerism, women have simultaneously been subject to increasing levels of figurative and actual commodifications. The ambivalence of subjectivity and of consumer capitalism has in turn invested both men and women with ambivalence toward their physical selves, but for women, sexually objectified and culturally allocated to a field of embodiment, such an ambivalence is magnified. Countless volumes that outline beauty and bodily maintenance, as well as the periodicals that suggest monthly, even weekly, the necessary prescriptions that will enable life in perfect modern harmony, augment through mass culture what divisions of gender have long emphasized. Examinations of the cultural texts with which women have been inundated for at least a century provide a clear map of the forces that have divided female subjects, and reading them alongside literary texts that demonstrate the impact of auto-objectification illustrates the ways in which such messages have become ubiquitous and have permeated both high and low culture. The hiding away of the body behind discursive trappings of gender that Epstein discusses in her performance theories has led to an elision of the feminine with the female and has enveloped the process of auto-objectification into social normativizing gender ideals that affect all women, including women authors and the characters whom they create. The auto-objectified body has not been returned to the realm of a "whole" subject, but has instead become a thing at once a part of and separate from the individual, an object to shape and bend at will in attempts to conform to (and occasionally, to refute) social and cultural standards for behavior, for cleanliness, for beauty. Modernity has moved the unconscious shaping of social and cultural forces into more deliberate and directed practices, and during the twentieth century, these ideas became markedly perpetuated and in turn became ideals to be consumed via mass media such as periodicals and cheap tracts aimed at a growing consumer population.

Even as those artifacts of such acculturation sometimes give credence to a concept of mind/body totality, contradictory information about a unity of mind and body has often been expressed in manuals of standardization, thus further complicating the dividing line.[6] A "Society Beauty" interviewed in 1902 for *The Art of Being Beautiful* appears rather prescient in her insistence that "the intellectual and the physical must be wedded if you would have general and durable beauty" and that "the absurd idea which has crept into fashion that mental and physical charm cannot go hand in hand is both pernicious to happiness and derogatory to

---

[6] Similar contradictions have long been present in women's magazines, with advertisements and rhetorical content often at odds with each other. Articles on women's careers or physical fitness, for example, can be dichotomous next to advertisements for cosmetics or other products that feminize and sexualize women. Such a problem was part of the reason for the cessation of publication of *Ms.* magazine in the late 1980s; in order to avoid the conflict, *Ms.* reorganized and began publishing without ad content a few years later.

the sex" (116). The impetus for this discussion, however, is not a search for some organic unity, but is an indictment of the growing number of women who were seeking education and employment at the turn of the twentieth century. The "Baroness," as the Beauty is slyly referred to, begins her series of dialogues with a dismayed discussion of "the class of clever women that is becoming more prevalent day by day" who "withdraw from their physical bank to pay into the mental one, and, of course, lose in the translation" (19). She quotes from a speech delivered by Lord Salisbury to the Royal Academy, in which he deplores that a "'few years hence, those who are then alive will see all the principal ladies of their acquaintance as Aldermen and Common Councillors. How do you imagine that they will dress themselves?'" (11). "Is not this picture true and terrifying?" asks the Baroness. "It shows that there are people who really cherish the hideous!" (11). The hideous nature of the intellectual woman lies not in her state of disassociation from her physical body in any philosophical sense, but lies instead in the lack of standardized beauty that this masculinized creature projects through her dress and appearance. Though the idea of synthesis with which she begins her instruction is interesting to find in this otherwise didactic conversation, synthesis, thus situated within such a context and surrounded by other, more imperative prescriptions, is only a fleeting contradiction, one that loses its way in the forest of standardization.

Later, at midcentury, Jill Adam's 1940 *Beauty Box* similarly presents readers with dichotomous ideals for a unity of self. Just as she deplores Hollywood's beauty standards while at the same time presenting others that are just as rigid, she begins her treatise on beauty with an extended metaphor likening a whole woman to a flourishing tree, a tree, however, that is inaccessible to those caught up in the prescriptive elements of the rest of the text. She explains:

> In order to have a flourishing tree of life, it is necessary to have wholeness. [...] civilization has made it possible, for the first time in history, for the woman to be a whole tree herself. Yet so far she hasn't quite managed it. The traditional 'wife and mother' attends only to the root [...]. The modern 'worker' woman forgets about the roots and concentrates her energy upon the branches [...]. The 'kept' wife or mistress [...] is often a poor dry stump, no good to anyone, and quick to rot. [...] the tendency in modern life to specialize has made us lose sight of the fact that the human organism is a complete whole, with each part—mind, body, spirit—interdependent and related. (5–6)

On its own, this sounds much more like the contents of a contemporary women's magazine or self-help book, one of the genre that hopes to guide women back out of late-twentieth-century ideals of superwomen who could bring home the bacon and fry it up in a pan, among other ideal feminine qualities. As doctrine from 1940, Adam's musings are provocative, and like the Baroness, she seems to prophesize rather than to fall into the same mode of prescription as her contemporaries. Within an illustrated book of beauty and diet advice that neglects both the intellect and the spirit once her opening admonishments end, though, this advice does little but provide readers with problematic and contradictory information, and even if those readers do not stop to critically assess the dissonance, seeds of the problem will be sown by the time the text has been completed. On a cognitive level, there will be some understanding that not only are there prescriptions for physical beauty to be adhered to, but that there are also additional elements to consider on the road to a "real" beauty of wholeness. In order for women to have strong roots and leafing limbs, further ideals must be sought after, further standards deployed. Here, too, morality is meshed with standards for physical "housekeeping," and beauty (or its lack) seems to stem as much from the gender role one performs ("wife and mother," "worker," mistress) as it does from any other regimen. Adam reinforces the social functions and moral policing that underlie dicta for cleanliness and for physical maintenance, illustrating through moralizing over the "poor dry stump" of the sexually transgressive female how a division of mind from body actually serves the system, is a primary aid in the regulation of individuals within society.

The result of this regimentation of the body and of a division of the dynamic factors that constitute an individual result of what I have called "auto-objectification": the objectifying of one's own physicality by the intellectual, "subjective" component of the individual woman. While early in the twentieth century some women may have been less likely than others to come into contact with conduct or etiquette manuals (especially those women from poor or working classes, or those who resided outside of urban areas), by the onset of the World War I, books on beauty and other aspects of physical maintenance (not to mention the variety of housekeeping and other manuals) were mass-marketed by publishers such as C. Arthur Pearson (a publisher of mass-produced books on self-improvement and other topics) and appeared as readily to the reading public of those first decades as do the multitude of pulp diet and exercise books that await contemporary shoppers on line at the supermarket. Escaping this particular consequence of the prescriptions laid out in these texts was not always, perhaps rarely, possible. Much has been written about the objectification of women by men, by masculine discourses and conventions, and by the male "gaze" effected within visual and performing arts (painting, photography, film, television, video). Though I do not mean to discount either that work or the real social and cultural effects of these mechanisms, a more damaging, more foundational objectification originates within one's own cognitive experience, for auto-objectification lays psychical groundwork for some outcomes of other, secondary objectifications. Once a "self," an individual's epistemology of being, is divided by an array of social and cultural practices that function to contain an individual within the limits of an existing system, the dynamic process of production and connection breaks down.

Though women have historically been disenfranchised from the realm of reason and intellect, a morality-driven social system invested so heavily in the idea of intellectual primacy will still privilege a disembodied sense of femininity above a transgressive female body. Judith Butler notes that "there appears to be no 'one' without ambivalence" (*Psychic* 198), but once a dynamic ambivalence of the "one" is converted to a static, dualistic hierarchy, the individual female subject, especially under the beauty and other regimes available to her, is apt to objectify her own physical being; the body has become something to manipulate, to exert one's will upon in an effort to standardize and to normalize the self to a variety of social codes. The auto-objectifying agent is simultaneously caught by the forces of a system that negates its inherent resistance and by its very ability to act, even if that act is only a manipulation of the physical self at the expense of its intellectual counterpart. The more objectified her body becomes from her own vantage point, the more effective are those regimental processes delineated in cultural texts such as beauty manuals, as well as in those from similar genres. Kristeva suggests that "dietary prohibitions" (though her argument is based upon the religious literature of Leviticus, do not books on beauty and femininity themselves garner a fanaticism akin to religion?) might be a "screen in a still more radically separating process [...] an attempt to keep a being who speaks to his God separated from the fecund mother" (100). Prescriptions that dictate laws for eating and that codify what enters the body aid in the distinction between the materiality of the female body and the discursive qualities of the intellect. If the body is little but an object separate from a self understood, through divisive strategy, to be an inner, ephemeral self unconnected to the flesh, then the body is vulnerable to damaging behaviors and self-imposed strategies. The rise in physically altering behaviors such as eating disorders and plastic surgery, and in more commonplace processes such as dieting and body piercing, is proportionate to the distancing of the modern psyche from its physical self, often when these behaviors appear as effects of conscious choice or individual agency.

Sciences such as neuropsychology (further examined in Chapter 3) and those that investigate cognitive processes have already discovered the necessary connectedness of the mind and the body, but theoretical and other discourses continue to perpetuate this division and to aid in the distancing of the mind from the body, even when seeming to seek liberatory truth in the space between the two. But the body is a component of one's mode of being; it is necessary if one is to access that rational thought so privileged by most modern societies. "Because our conceptual systems grow out of our bodies," assert Lakoff and Johnson, "meaning is grounded in and through our bodies" (6). Our bodies, along with our minds, are the bases of epistemology, of processing the information so rapidly produced in a world that has been sped up exponentially over the last one hundred years. This unity, as a fundamental element of how an individual knows the world and her position within it, is therefore foundational to what proceeds from that knowledge and to individual initiative based upon how a given environment is perceived. Split asunder, the divided mind and body limit the quantity and the quality of experience that can be processed by the individual, and limit as well any action that can proceed from that experience. The mind/body split fostered by a regimented and normativizing society, then, poses real consequences for an understanding of individual agency. A "freedom of the will" is "based on the more basic notion of freedom of action" (Lakoff and Johnson 190), and without a dynamic and fully integrated "whole" that benefits equally from the flesh and from the intellect, any freedom to act is truncated; individual will is compromised.

Once private regimentation dismisses the importance of the body to the function of the individual, auto-objectification in turn diverts activities toward the primary object of the self (the body), thus limiting actions that involve the world beyond the individual and limiting tactical responses à la Certeau. That is not to say that there is no longer agency, action, or resistance. Though social regimentation establishes the parameters of the system within which most social and cultural activity takes place, there is still dynamism inherent within the structure of the individual, if to some (and sometimes large) degree modified by the effects of social inscriptions. The lines that circumscribe behavior are permeable, and whether through everyday "tactics" or more sweeping gestures of transgression, there will always be at least the potential for an agency that issues from the exchange between the mind and the body, and not from the strategic mechanisms that work to drive wedges through the connections that structure complete individuals.

Conformity of all into a very few molds is central to maintaining any but perhaps an anarchic social system. Auto-objectifying practices lie at the heart of such social maintenance, and the rhetorics that have been produced as a way to dictate what one should be, wear, and look like provide interesting examples of dicta for adhering to such standards, even as those prescriptions change and evolve seemingly arbitrarily.[7] The first chapter of this study explores the cultural rhetoric of both household and bodily maintenance in order to illustrate the ways in which auto-objectification and its related quest for physical perfection are part of the modern project and central to manifestations of the mind/body duality so prevalent in Western culture. While these texts provide cultural context for the literary works addressed in later chapters, these volumes of regimentation are also texts in and of themselves that exhibit concerns identical to those identified within their fictional counterparts. Fiction and nonfiction together showcase a range of concerns that women readers throughout the twentieth century (and beyond) have had to negotiate as auto-objectified subjects. In Chapter 1, I explore a sampling of cultural texts that have provided models of domesticity and femininity for women of the twentieth century. Through examinations of the rhetoric of household manuals that provided housewives with standards for a general maintenance of the private sphere of the home, I explore the ways in which issues of cleanliness and order that began with the system of the English home ultimately extended to those individual subjects residing within. Elizabeth Langland finds that in the nineteenth

---

[7]   Other critics have used extensively the literature of conduct manuals for their studies of eighteenth- and nineteenth-century texts, but by the later nineteenth century, those manuals were much less popular than the housekeeping and culinary manuals, as well as the beauty books and other mass culture, that I find important to studies of twentieth-century culture. For discussions of earlier texts, see Nancy Armstrong, *Desire and Domestic Fiction: A Political History of the Novel* (Oxford, 1987); Nancy Armstrong and Leonard Tennenhouse, eds., *The Ideology of Conduct: Essays on Literature and the History of Sexuality* (Methuen, 1987); Helena Michie, *The Flesh Made Word: Female Figures and Women's Bodies* (Oxford, 1987); and Elizabeth Langland, *Nobody's Angels: Middle-Class Women and Domestic Ideology in Victorian Culture* (Cornell UP, 1995).

century, such manuals were "aimed specifically at enabling the middle class to consolidate its base of control through strategies of regulation and exclusion" (24), but as the twentieth century began, and as newly invented household aids allowed for middle-class domestic standards to become the gold standard for the "English home," manuals that provided rules for maintenance were not simply aimed toward a middle-class audience, but reached women across class strata. Books like those written by Mrs. Beeton, which outlined ways in which the middle-class housewife might ensure that her household staff could keep order, were joined by mass-distributed volumes that targeted all women who ran households, both those who kept servants and those who swept their own floors and did their own washing up. Standardization may have initially galvanized middle-class endeavors, but eventually the need for an eradication of dirt knew few class boundaries.

With English homes thus brought into similar order, the individuals inside those private doorways themselves became the subjects of a proliferation of manuals that addressed the health and well-being, as well as the physical appearance, of English citizens. Nancy Armstrong notes that by "the mid-nineteenth century authors of advice for women accordingly found it unnecessary to articulate the whole body of the woman [...]. A fragment [...] could represent the whole" (16). The growth of medical science and the identification during the nineteenth century of germs as the cause of many diseases also added to such literatures a rhetoric of health that became a basis for both home and bodily maintenance. Under the guise of health and medical certainty, too, manuals aimed at women that were actually no more than prescriptions for physical beauty added to the imperative tone of the rhetoric of bodily maintenance. As with the English home, the prototypical English body, which began as a middle-class entity, eventually became the broadly accepted, and widely expected, form. Women's bodies, so long kept hidden beneath layers of clothing and locked away during periods of confinement, in the twentieth century became the focus of a tremendous amount of discourse that stipulated acceptable weights and appearances for English women as middle-class standards became the standards for all. That emphasis on moderation and morality at the center of the standards found in nineteenth-century household manuals reappears in these beauty manuals that explain to women of all classes those appropriate standards of femininity demanded within a particularly circumscribed English social system. Lorna Sage, whose post-World War II working-class childhood was nevertheless filled with middle-class standards, explains what was expected of her as a "fifth-form debutante": "discreet mouse make-up; a pastel coloured frock; *small* heels [...] no straps showing, but lots of straps (even if you'd hardly any breasts going bra-less was unthinkable, it would have announced you were some kind of retard, a lack of elastic armour was a sign of moral idiocy like being cross-eyed and slobbering)" (211; original italics). Properly bound, Sage represents the image of respectability necessary if one is to be accepted into what once was strictly the domain of the middle class.

Prescriptions such as those found in housekeeping, health, and beauty manuals exacerbate the effects of auto-objectification. The literature that has been produced (and still is produced) to codify what it means to be a modern female subject, as well as what it means to be a female consumer within a culture driven by innovation and change, provides a foundation for ways in which a philosophical mind/body duality can materialize and become exhibited in all its ambivalence. When the flesh is little more than an object to be maintained to code, it is difficult to reconcile the physical component of the subject with the intangible qualities that have long defined the subject in its entirety. Although the "self" is an entity comprising both physical and intellectual or spiritual components, the material self has, through a process of acculturation, foundered in the "domination of the object-world" by the privileged intellect (Barker vi). Manuals that outline ways to efface dirt and other "matter out of place" (detailed by Mary Douglas in *Purity and Danger* and here in the first chapter of this project), as well as ways to diet, sculpt, colorize, and exercise the body into proper form, all add depth and breadth to the schism that has been maintained between the psychical and physical selves. Such tracts, too, provide certain ammunition for the impossible task of "dominating" a physical world that includes a physical self.

The chapters that follow my cultural history of such rhetorics outline, in different ways, the effects of auto-objectification on the creative processes of women who, as subjects within a culture that demands such division, have produced written texts that bear witness to that mind/body duality inherent within the culture from which they have been derived. Formal aspects such as characterization, narrative voice, and genre development, in the texts that I explore here, exhibit the ambivalence of the divided mind and body, as well as the discomfort that stems from impossible social and cultural mandates. Though subjects are handed prescriptions for maintaining their homes, their families, and themselves, the irreconcilability of such a duality supported by maintenance literature with the actual makeup of human beings creates a cognitive dissonance that finds its way into the creative products of writers whom I discuss here—Barbara Pym, Angela Carter, Helen Dunmore, Helen Fielding, and Rachel Cusk, among others—writers whose texts provide a host of varying examples of the narrative effects of dividing the mind from the body. Lakoff and Johnson explain that "the very way that we normally conceptualize our inner lives is inconsistent with what we know scientifically about the nature of the mind" as embodied (268). Through grammar (the "I" who attempts to control the physical world, including its body) and metaphor (the "inner self," etc.) we all are locked into a conflict between what we think, conceptualize, and perhaps ultimately transmit through the written word, and the "fact" of science or of sentience, of experience.

The concept of an "empirical philosophy" proposed by Lakoff and Johnson may seem to be a contradiction in terms, but such a term encompasses, in essence, the sort of writing explored in this study. When the body and mind are separated, even lexically, there will be some form of resistance, potentially on the parts of both the author and the reader, whose own embodiment—a combination of mental and physical aspects—belies the separation of these components. Whether writers use this duality as a trope for other divisions or self-consciously play upon this well-trod duality, its appearance signals the cognitive register of a subject, of an author who understands, if only on an unconscious level (what Lakoff and Johnson call the "cognitive unconscious"), the problematics of mind/body division. Internalized as what I call auto-objectification, this division can result in unstable, difficult to categorize characters and in narratives that fragment, split off, rupture, and suggest a desire to reunite the two parts of a female whole, even when there may not yet be language enough for, or metaphors consistent with, such a being.

In his recent *Narrative Bodies: Toward a Corporeal Narratology*, Daniel Punday questions the agenda of a narratology that negates the "what" of narrative in order to make primary the "how": "the body appears in such studies usually as one of many 'things' that a narrative might describe—in the same category as chairs, desks, and rocks" (3). Such division of the "what" from the "how" echoes the division of the fact of the flesh from the culturally preeminent intellect, and as with those faulty divisions, in narrative such separations are often difficult to integrate into an understanding of a textual world that ostensibly represents a "real" world in which embodiment is central to existence. In the works that I examine within this project, the "how" of the narrative is exactly the "what" of the body: the body is the vehicle for the narrative of each text and is the site of narrative articulations of social forces such as sex/gender and social class. The use of the body—in the cases presented, of distinctly female bodies complete with attendant cultural baggage—as a mode of characterization is primary to literary works that are implicated in the effects of auto-objectification. The ways in which an author chooses to utilize embodiment in order to grant readers insight into a character can vary, and does, in the fiction examined in following chapters, but that embodiment always emerges as a central path toward an understanding not simply of character or motivation, but also of the narrative composite of a text. Seymour Chatman argues for an understanding of character that is more than semantic or linguistic, and indicates that, as with people encountered in everyday life, characters emerge as multidimensional beings for those invested in a given narrative. Individual aspects of characterization are not discrete under such a theoretical aegis, but allow for readers to extrapolate about characters and their relationships to plot in ways that expand an ability to enter a textual world. "Narratives," explains Chatman, "may not examine habits microscopically, but they do demand of the audience the capacity to recognize certain habits as symptomatic of a trait" (122), the latter of which is a more developed aspect of character. For each action, custom, habit, there will emerge a system of traits that themselves create character. The more physical the network of traits, the more "real" a character can become for readers whose lived experiences guide their reading acts.

The degree to which a literary character is embodied within a narrative determines in part the ways in which readers are asked to understand that character and suggests the degree to which characters might be considered sympathetic, or to which a character might evolve into a full-fledged protagonist. Punday notes that the "potential distance between body and character is an element of the interpretation of narrative" (66); the distancing of a character from her embodiment sets up the conditions under which we can "read" that textual individual. If a character is the result of gendered traits, for instance, traits that are socially constructed rather than material "facts," then such a character is left "disembodied," particularly when characterized in terms that oppose the narrative terms of other, textually embodied characters. Though one can assume with relative certainty that characters in fictional texts have bodies, those bodies are not always significantly present within the text. For a variety of reasons—social codes, narrative technique, limited observation—the physical body does not appear readily in many literary texts, Schabert's "literature of the body" notwithstanding, even in those texts of the later twentieth century, when the boundaries of acceptability grew wider and more flexible than they had been in the past. The mental, psychological aspects of character have become dominant, particularly in literature that might be considered "modern." When the physical body is represented, though, it is not always a site of characterization, but often simply of description and verisimilitude; the importance of embodiment is not always illustrated through its narrative functions. Punday has observed (as have others) that "usually we think of literary characters in terms of their contrasts to each other" (54), and the terrain of the body provides perhaps one of the most obvious manifestations of such oppositional characterization. Mieke Bal designates one method of discussing characterization through a use of "[s]emantic axes [...] pairs of contrary meanings," and continues to list a variety of axes: "*rich-poor*, or *man-woman*, *kind-unkind*" (86; original italics). The binary-centric language that we must use to designate character necessitates the use, in some examples, of a binary method of understanding how characters differ from one another. Bal adds, though, a way to further situate such definitions of character: "Such a selection involves the ideological position of the analyst and also points at ideological stands represented in the story" (86). The dominant ideologies that produce readers' perceptions of such divisions will mandate the ways in which such binaries can be understood, with one aspect always granted primacy over the other. In the case of embodiment, the opposite aspect—the intellect—has long been privileged. It is difficult to understand a contradictory method of knowing the body as an equally sound and positive aspect of character.

What Punday describes as "differential embodiment," or "the creation of central, relatively disembodied heroes or heroines, and more embodied peripheral characters for whom physiognomy is a far more important element of characterization" (14–15), is the process through which the binary opposition of characters generally occurs. In the novels that I examine in several chapters of this study, the manner of character opposition is a result of differentiated embodiment constructed via the effects of food, food consumption, and other gendered relationships to cultural practices that center on food. Because of the ways in which dominant Western thought privileges the intellect over embodiment, the characters more aligned with their physicalities are generally cast as suspect. Typically, Punday explains, the amount of authority granted to a narrating subject in a text (or to the dominant character) is directly related to the distance of that character from his or her embodiment. Because through narrative "the world must be made visible [...] we must find some way to position ourselves in relation to that object" (154). If subjective narrative authority is to be granted to a narrator or to a character, then that entity must be placed on the proper side of the subject/ object binary; the object status understood as a condition of embodiment must be avoided in order for a character to emerge as a protagonist, or for a narrator to be viewed as reliable. "Disembodied" characters thus have been privileged in our literary narratives, perhaps especially in novels that have sought to explore the relationship between the individual subject and the society at large. If, as Mary Douglas suggests, "the physical body [...] is polarized conceptually against the social body" (*Natural* 101), then on a narrative plane the social codes of that social body can be found in characterizations that lack specific connections to physical existence. Narratives might use "different degrees of disembodiment to express the social hierarchy. The more refinement, the less smacking of the lips when eating, the less mastication, [...] the more controlled the signs of anger, the clearer comes the priestly-aristocratic image" (Douglas, *Natural* 101–2). In this way, then, female characters who are represented as a conglomorate of socially discursive, gendered traits are usually more sympathetic, more elevated within the narrative, more important to the narrative than are those represented women whose embodiment is central to the ways in which they are drawn. Authors who are aware, however, even unconsciously, that the divisions and dualities that negate the importance of the physical body actually belie what can be understood as lived experience often find ways to thwart this time-honored privileging of the intellect. The literary texts explored in many of the following pages are examples of this resistance: the resistance of authors who cannot fully understand mind/body division because in all actuality, there is no real division beyond our linguistic frameworks. The socially codified body is rarely the same body that is a part of everyday life.

A textured and evocative method of foregrounding the importance of the body within a text calls for the crafting of a character from the actions of his or her body, often from its most manual, rote activities. Not only can such a focus upon the common actions of the everyday provide a means for reader identification and response; it can also allow the idea of the body to push through layers of language and landscape and to engage a reader's own body scheme during the process of reading and explicating another body's textual terrain. The use of food imagery, when connected to representations of consumption, is one way such a foregrounding of the body can occur. Because images of eating and of other sentient relationships to food can signify the human body, fictional characters whose representations revolve around food can easily invoke the idea of the body, thus allowing for a more intimate and sustained interchange between a reader and the bodies within a text. When eating and food are central to the makeup of a fictional character, issues of embodiment, power, and subjectivity should be considered essential to character creation. As a biological necessity, eating is not among the list of activities that can be ascribed to the praxis of a Foucauldian "useful" body. Certain eating habits do complement certain cultural prescriptions, but eating as a basic practice transcends (or, rather, rescinds) the trappings of culture. Though Certeau sees cooking, rather than eating, as an everyday and therefore resistant activity, eating is even less a product of cultural mandate than is food preparation. Eating is action; it is central to the creation and sustenance of life. Eating is one of the few processes that all bodies have in common and, as a process that defines a body as active, and therefore as a site of other potential activities, eating signifies a body's potential for conscious agency beyond a social network. Motility, which extends to include the idea of agency in its active sense (and not to agency that only designates a nexus of cultural responses), is dependent upon its own image and is not simply a result of or a response to external influences of society or culture. There is an internal, psychical will to movement, toward agency, and eating-as-action contains within it the body's resistance and propensity for unique, subjective experience.

In novels examined in Chapters 2 and 3, the mind/body split is represented through divided characterizations of women aligned, through represented relationships (sometimes negative) with food and with eating, with either the realm of the intellect or with that of the flesh. Though similar divisions of women have occurred in texts by both male and female authors, most often in what might be called the "madonna–whore" division of women characterized as oppositional through sexuality and, occasionally, maternity, in the texts explored in this study, the authors chosen demand a move beyond such an old and troubled definition of "woman." In ways that echo Certeau's theories of tactical resistance, these authors complicate the notion that women can easily be put into one category or another. In each of the works examined, the construct of the sexual versus the asexual, feminine woman is dismantled and is illuminated as a construct incompatible with women who are more than bodies and more than the gendered expectations set forward in beauty books and women's magazines. The divided protagonists (divided between two characterizations, rather than within one)[8] found in these works exhibit, through authorial use of mind/body duality, the very fact that such a duality provides an ineffectual way to define female experience.

Interestingly, too, within the consumer-based modernity of the twentieth century, the authors whose works are examined in these chapters weave food—eating, preparation, production—into their narratives as a way to make prominent the separation of the body that consumes from the ephemeral self who does not. I do not examine these texts for pathologies related to food, such as eating disorders, although those have been important issues for feminist scholarship. Instead, I look toward conflicting, multiple ways in which food signifies within these texts: as body, as feminine, as sexual, as female caregiver. Food has long been a daily part of the feminine, domestic domain; however, in the twentieth century, it has also become a referent laden with signification beyond the culinary or gastronomical. Likewise, as modern psychology and philosophy expanded popular notions of subjectivity, the notion of mind/body duality emerged (via Freud and others) as fodder for serious intellectual investigation. While such duality can easily be

---

[8]   For examinations of single female protagonists who are themselves divided, see H. M. Daleski, *The Divided Heroine: A Recurrent Pattern in Six English Novels* (Holmes and Meir, 1984), and Nancy Armstrong, "Occidental Alice," in *Differences* 2.2 (Summer 1990): 3–40.

located throughout literary history, writers began to interrogate these ideas in early twentieth-century works. One example of this emergent strand of thought is the work of Virginia Woolf, who argues across her literary canon for a balance of what she calls, in her essay "The New Biography" (1927), "granite" and "rainbow": those seemingly irreconcilable entities of human material experience and human psychology. As she approached the final years of her life, Woolf continued to explore new ways in which to bring those two realms together, with regard both to the individual subject and to the larger social order. In a related article entitled "Luncheon at 'The Leaning Tower': Consumption and Class in Virginia Woolf's *Between the Acts*," I read together her last novel, *Between the Acts*, and an essay of 1941, titled "The Leaning Tower," in order to imagine that novel as an extension of Woolf's search for the society that she imagines in the pages of her essay: one unimpeded by social class and free from the sorts of social divisions brought about by differing levels of access to education and other forms of cultural capital. Woolf's novel illustrates how narrative investigations of mind/body duality provide a language that articulates other inadequate social structures, such as class and gender.

In *Between the Acts*, Woolf characterizes two of her predominant female figures as oppositional through food consumption and, by extension, through the signification of the class status of each of those women. The fleshly, vulgar Mrs. Manresa, an upstart in the older society represented by her opposite, Isa Oliver, is a woman whose materiality and consumer capacity are out of place in the English traditions of quiet country estates and quaint village pageantry. Class mobility—though the subject of her concurrently written essay, a phenomenon with which the middle-class Woolf had some difficulty—provides one source of the novel's tension, and although the theme of community is important to the novel and has been the subject of much critical attention dedicated to the text, the characters who stand on different sides of the dividing line between tradition and social change mark the ambivalence of the narrative. Wolf characterizes Isa and Mrs. Manresa in part through constructions of embodiment (and lack thereof) that parallel the divisions by social class, and she does so through a deliberate use of the characters' relationships to food and food consumption. "Real" and cultural capital—in the forms of consumable goods and language-based knowledge—are awarded to Mrs. Manresa and Isa, respectively, with the cultural ultimately presented as the more desirable form. Pierre Bourdieu suggests a strong link between cultural capital and "ascetic consumption in all areas"; excessive consumption is "'vulgar'" and is "close to that of the working classes" (185). With the realms of the tangible and intangible, the material and cultural, so linked to consumption in the novel, representations of class division are essentially linked to consuming practices and, in turn, to those who consume and who are embodied vis-à-vis that consumption. Isa is a creature driven by the language of poetry and by the access that she has had to cultural and material wealth; Mrs. Manresa, who has arrived in the middle class by marriage to a tradesman, is cast as a figure of difference and scorn. Her sexuality, called into question by her embodied nature and her consumption practices, is the type of sexuality long associated with women of the working classes. Regardless of Woolf's determination to imagine a collective new society for a future England, her creation of Mrs. Manresa is telling of the limitations within which Woolf was able to envision a dissolution of class structures.

Auto-objectivity, complicated by the contradictions of consumption in the same way as subjectivity, becomes, I argue, more apparent as the modern project grinds on. Early in the century, writers such as Woolf approach the binary with ambivalence, but their narratives do not seem to struggle as directly with mind/ body duality as do those who write later in the century, when the idea of modernity has become second nature and the effects of an alienating auto-objectification become standard modes of being. Each of the postwar writers examined here, however, grapples self-consciously with such a construct and attempts to make it a malleable one in her hands. As social and gender constructs in general were challenged, particularly by women, in the postwar world, those earlier, easier divisions of women into sexual castes were targets of the feminine pen; however, dismantling a duality that lies at the center of social and cultural divisions is a difficult task. Though some attempt to create, and some come close to creating, a female character whose mind and body are combined in equal parts, none of the writers whose work I examine in these chapters is fully able to concoct a version of woman that defies mind/body duality or its resultant auto-objectification. Though the separation is made evident, and is deplored, it cannot be completely discarded. It has become far too ingrained into a collective "cognitive unconscious."

Chapter 2 begins my examination of literary examples of how women writers have used this mind/body duality to express concerns with issues of gender and class, as well as how their writing suggests those tensions that result from the unnatural request that we deny part of the subject at the expense of another. This chapter moves forward, into and beyond World War II, and considers the effects of food rationing upon the already problematic consuming female subject. This period of British austerity (rationing began in 1939 and for some items continued through 1954) produced an abundance of cultural materials that provide an interesting way to foreground my reading of Barbara Pym's novel, *Jane and Prudence* (1953). The war brought with it much social instability for England and, as men left to fight across the Channel, British women left their homes and learned to take on new roles and new skills as they battled the war from the homefront. The English home, however, still beckoned to those women when their shifts in the public sector ended. Women's culture produced during this period maintained codes for female conduct and for domestic and bodily maintenance that were perhaps more strict than that which had been enforced before German bombs began to fall on English soil. Standards for female sexuality, and for female consumption, became mingled in the rhetoric of wartime cookery books, women's magazines, and BBC-produced programming such as serialized novels and daily spots produced by Britain's Ministry of Food.

Pym's novel, written between 1950 and 1952, is a product of its time. For those living in the rural vicarage that provides the setting for the novel, the continuation of food rationing has created a shortage of food, and the war has left the village with an equally short supply of eligible men. Into this world, the realm of vicar's wife Jane Cleveland, comes her younger, attractive friend Prudence Bates. As with Woolf's earlier oppositional characterizations, Pym's dual protagonists are sharply divided by their respective relationships to food, both its consumption and its preparation. The sensual qualities of food become eroticized with respect to Prudence, who, as a single woman working in the public sphere, blurs the line between the home and the world beyond. While Prudence is adept in the kitchen, and enjoys such exotic (for the time and place) items as smoked salmon and fresh garlic, Jane can only open a tin or escort her husband to the local tea shop when mealtime arrives, and little more. Unlike Woolf's Isa and Mrs. Manresa, whose character opposition falls along lines that conform more closely to those older methods of aligning women as either physical or mental/spiritual, however, Pym's Jane and Prudence are difficult to pigeonhole. Examinations of additional fiction of the period that adheres to a more typical relationship of food to femininity—Noel Streatfeild's *Saplings* and Mollie Panter-Downes's *One Fine Day*—allow the playfulness of Pym's narrative to emerge. Pym tinkers with the traditional conventions of and expectations for using mind/body duality as a method of characterization and trades the domesticity that might more typically belong to a housewife such as Jane for the intellectual ambitions she continues to nurture, years beyond her academic life. Jane, too, dares to imagine equality for men and women, at least when it comes to the division of the meat that arrives in the village in such sparse quantities. While Pym sets up what looks like a traditional opposition of mind and body, she problematizes those limited roles for women in a way that illustrates the changing social roles that existed for postwar British women and that complicated the structure of postwar British society.

Chapter 3 examines more formal narrative effects of mind/body duality. In this chapter I look at two novels together: Angela Carter's *The Magic Toyshop* (1967) and *Talking to the Dead*, by Helen Dunmore (1996). Each of these novels uses particular generic conventions (gothic and mystery) that necessitate construction of tension through a withholding of information, and each foregrounds an embodied, consuming female character in order to maintain its narrative secrets. Through an elaboration upon theories of the body image as developed by Paul Schilder, as well as upon other theories of reading and of imagining, I explore ways in which the extratextual embodiment of readers serves as a catalyst for reader identification with those embodied characters within these texts. Because the body image has social and interpersonal, as well as personal, qualities, I consider how the bodies within the texts—in these two cases bodies that are necessary to sustaining the separation of overt and embedded narratives—call upon readers' bodies in a way that results in an interactive reading experience.

In the final chapter I investigate a selection of literary and cultural texts in which women writers have attempted to combine in single characters the mental and physical aspects of female subjectivity. For Virginia Woolf, the modern world offered little in the way of that wholeness she was in search of when she ended her life in 1941. In an essay published shortly before her death, Woolf identified the historical figure of Ellen Terry, a popular Victorian actress, as her best example of an embodied female intellect. At the end of the century (and into this one), though, contemporary writers battle with such constructions, and, though several fictional and actual women represent well such attempts to correct the unnatural duality that troubles female subjectivity, the lasting effects of auto-objectification cannot be erased from either the female figures or their critical receptions. Along with cultural texts, in this chapter I pair recent works by Helen Fielding and Rachel Cusk in order to conceive of the types of female characterizations that can result from a more decided movement away from mind/body duality and its attendant auto-objectification. In these novels the writers have attempted to combine in single characters the mental and physical aspects of female subjectivity. Such a creature, however, is still an uncomfortable, often troubled, sometimes parodic individual.

While writers attempt to construct "whole" women from both the physical and the mental realm, and while philosophers and theorists call for further considerations and combinations of the mind and the body, the results of such constructions—which do not fit into any secure, known mold—are ungainly in a culture that still demands moderation and adherence to standardized norms. As women who are simultaneously intellectual and educated, physical and sexual (and auto-objectified) beings, Bridget and Agnes both embody the ambivalence with which our culture responds to women who defy the binaries that shape their lives. I suggest in this final chapter that while in these novels there is evidence of a movement toward representations of women that contain the spectra of female experience, such experience might lie beyond the language with which we currently must create such textual subjects.

Chapter 1
Regimentation of the Private:
Hunting Down "Matter out of Place"

As a society, we seek to reach goals that, when it comes to constructed ideals based upon faulty dualisms, often work against the grains of our lived experiences and visceral comprehensions of the world at large. Households that can never reach sparkling perfection are nonetheless toiled over as if the ultimate is possible; bodies that will defy sculpting and rigorous dieting will still be subject to ideals of beauty and health. One result of this separation of mental and physical components of the human subject is the "auto-objectification" explored in the introduction to this project: the objectification of one's own body and the epistemological contradictions that create complex issues for a "whole" being who has learned to grant primacy to the intellect at the expense of the flesh. Though logic will often provide us with a basic understanding of the limitations of such dichotomies, we most often will continue to adhere to the standards of acceptability provided by external forces, even when those standards are not consonant with our everyday lives. Processes of internalizing these forces of culture and of making second nature our responses to anomalous objects or behaviors eventually allow us to override our less-than-socially appropriate instincts in order to survive within the public sphere. We are, however, as subject to culture within the "private" domain of the home as we are without.

Anthropologist Mary Douglas places her foundational study, *Purity and Danger: An Analysis of the Concepts of Pollution and Taboo*, within a broadly defined definition of "culture," and through examinations of several tribal communities draws conclusions analogous to those that can emerge from an analysis of English (indeed, of most Western) cultural maintenance, both private and public. Like much of the makeup of any general culture, the idea of order—or of its absence—is a relative one. More specifically, "dirt [is] matter out of place [...] is never a unique, isolated event. Where there is dirt there is a system. Dirt is the by-product of a systematic ordering and classification of matter, in so far as ordering involves rejecting inappropriate elements" (Douglas, *Purity* 35). Dirt, or a desire for its expulsion in the quest for cleanliness, is only apparent in the face of an ordered system that defines the acceptable, normative level of grime that might pass undetected in the home (an amount that has been drastically reduced over the course of the twentieth century). Discovery of and reaction to dirt is a direct result of specific processes of acculturation, and the collective discourse of dirt and how to rid one's home of "matter out of place" is the result of similar phenomena in the acculturation of individuals to matters of their own hygiene. The discourse found in the literature of domestic maintenance, however, complicates the boundaries between the public and the private person by emanating from an author's position within a system while at the same time speaking of the actual public nature of issues regularly perceived as private and as most appropriately relegated to the realm of the private home.

To adopt the viewpoint of the housekeeping manual, which perpetuates a single standard set by one more overarching, is to privatize and, by extension, to internalize widespread cultural standards for the daily function of one's household, standards that set the stage for resulting auto-objectification in its members. Within the pages of a multitude of volumes of maintenance literature lies a code not only for the upkeep of the home, but also for the maintenance of those within the home, their physical as well as moral lives. If the relativity of dirt is accepted, however, "cleaning then becomes a personal [...] activity, having [...] everything to do with how we define ourselves and our surroundings" (Horsfield 11). Our relationships to dirt and to our idiosyncratic definitions of household maintenance are at once subject to the public standards of culture *and* intrinsic to the construction of each individual subject who cleans, cooks, or scrubs, of the subject who mediates culture and its standards as they become manifest within the home. The domestic setting, then, with its need for maintenance reflecting back the cultural standards of an external and public society, is a site that is dominated by those constructed standards while it concurrently provides them with a paradoxical challenge. For dirt can never fully be gotten rid of, and germs defy eradication; therefore, a high standard of physical maintenance, as it increased from the mid-nineteenth century and as it continues to increase (note the recent expansion in the market for merchandise labeled "antibacterial" as we continue a vain attempt to conquer the microscopic world), guarantees resultant practices that defy a defined norm. What is desired can never be achieved.

While the middle-class housewife at one time was less involved on a physical level with the day-to-day cleaning and maintenance of her household, she was nonetheless responsible for its management. Increasingly the "servant question" of the later Victorian age gave way in the twentieth century to a push for servantless households. By the turn of the twentieth century, very few households could maintain more than cursory domestic help, if any help at all could be afforded, and women's periodicals lauded women who, like the *Girls' Own Paper*'s iconic "Margaret Trent," diligently toiled away to maintain lovely homes. And the numbers of those who did benefit from domestic help continued to dwindle, particularly during periods of war: "By 1947, 94 per cent of [British] women had no help of any sort in the home" (Hardyment 185). Increasingly, domestic manuals were written not to quantify and explain the duties of the household help, but were instead aimed toward the growing number of domestically involved housewives of the middle and working classes, many of whom first learned the rules of housekeeping in an educational system that was integral to the codifying of domesticity and femininity. Ideologies of masculine and feminine social and cultural responsibilities for most families emerged divided, and with each separate realm arose a separate discursive tradition founded to maintain the order of a new and rapidly shifting society. The structure of public discourse, however, hardly surpasses that of its domestic counterpart in either specificity or complexity. As efforts to control what are essentially fluid and relative social apparatuses, the languages of law and of laundry, of public and of private, seek to regulate and to maintain some definitive measure of social and cultural norms, some prescription that would enable the home and the office, the scullery and the shop—and thus the larger English society in general—to hold together like a good steamed pudding or a finely wrought injunction. An examination of the language that provides order for domestic chaos illuminates just how much the public and private arenas have in common and underscores the formative nature of the domestic with regard to what has typically been thought of as a separate sphere of masculine influence. The contents of household manuals and the rhetoric of receipt books provide a map of English social mechanics as telling as many of the public texts more traditionally venerated and as foundational to the constructions of twentieth-century attitudes toward mind/body duality that had solidified by midcentury.

As discourses of housekeeping and housework suggest, rules for living within the walls of the private home are dictated by societal and cultural constraints as much as public regulations are. These rules, too, are just as circuitous and as flawed logically as the binaried social system from which they stem, and thus are just as resistant to any definitions that are rooted in the imprecision of duality. Housework, a systemic activity that helps to affix most women to domestically defined roles, is also a site at which the system's own logic breaks down. If, traditionally, women have been associated with "nature" and men with its flip side, with "culture," then housework, as a process of acculturation and social normalization, doesn't quite fit the social schema. Though Simone de Beauvoir may hold that a "healthy young woman will hardly be attracted by so gloomy a vice" as housework (426), women of all age groups find themselves compelled to take on the role of housekeeper in the name of social order, and this social training is a powerful thing. The image of the domestic zealot is often parodied: "Fictional heroines who enjoy cleaning are frequently the targets of innuendo. Their mental health may be questioned, or their sexuality, or both" (Horsfield 16). Beauvoir writes of how "the rage for cleanliness is highest in Holland, where the women are cold," and champions instead (albeit in a rather racist manner) the sexualized women of southern Europe: "If the Mediterranean Midi lives in a state of joyous filth, it is not only because water is scarce there: love of the flesh and its animality is conducive to toleration of human odor, dirt, and even vermin" (426). But cleanliness and sexuality are not always treated oppositionally. Although women are labeled, in a broadly stereotypical way, as inherently and transgressively sexual, they are in turn held almost exclusively responsible for the perpetuation of culture and of normative social behavior within the household. The propriety of the household and that of its inhabitants are clearly bound together within the codes of femininity, even as female nature is loaded down with paradoxical attributes. While Margaret Horsfield correctly identifies fictional women who, through an overidentification with household maintenance, "are at least laughed at, occasionally humbled, often scorned, sometimes even killed off" (16), ironically (or perhaps not so), sexualized women also meet with these exact fates in a number of fictional texts. While social definitions seem to hold citizens to a level of conformity, on one hand, they also contradict themselves and create circular processes in which no singular identification can resist interrogation. How does one maintain a balance between cultural expectations and cultural nomenclature, between gender roles defined by tradition and by contemporary political ideologies such as feminism?

Cleanliness and Morality in the English Household

The domestic realm and its housekeeper are not without elements that resist such constraints and contradictions, and that call into question the definitive status of all those assumptions and agendas so easily enfolded into the psyche. One still has the potential to interrogate constructs, and because of this cognitive ability, those constructs must develop and strengthen if they are to survive, though certainly (thankfully) not all do. Douglas suggests that "any given culture must confront events which seem to defy its assumptions. [...] we find in any culture worthy of the name various provisions for dealing with ambiguous or anomalous events" (*Purity* 39). Most of the tribes she explores respond to such ambiguity through rites and rituals of religious worship. Western traditions influenced by Christianity follow this pattern, and even when religious practices are not present, the idea of a secular, widespread moral code accomplishes the same task of socially aligning individuals and their various cultural practices. The state of the spirit or, in lieu of religious inclination, of one's integrity or intellect, has been regarded most highly in post-Enlightenment Western societies, and to jeopardize this "higher" nature of humanity is perhaps the greatest transgression of the moral codes of the West as they have evolved over several hundred years. Furthering one's psychical life from a material existence has been rhetorically necessary in order to maintain this division, and such a division has left its dividing mark upon Western culture. Risking the prized ability to reason or to commune with a higher power (depending upon one's spiritual or intellectual foundation) is considered the ultimate danger to a continuation of the societal standards of "morality." Regardless of whether those codes are a standard idea of moral right and wrong or a more elliptical question of ethics, according to Douglas, "Attributing danger is one way of putting a subject above dispute [and] helps to enforce conformity" (*Purity* 40). When anomaly threatens a social system, it can be more easily contained if the perceived danger is a great one, because few will argue with those who only seek to correct an agreed-upon impending danger. The extent to which such systemic maintenance occurs is one important way to measure the efficacy of that system, and so failure to maintain the system is indeed dangerous. Danger from anomalous organisms or occurrences within a system or a society is not as dangerous as the danger that stems from the lack of maintenance of or lack of complicity with the system itself: the social order is only as strong as those who serve it allow it to become.

Following the Wesleyan adage that equates cleanliness with godliness, the housekeeper, through her responsibility for the abolition of household dirt, is also responsible for the moral maintenance of those who reside therein and for the social projection of the morality contained within the household, or at least for the projection of the moral code that a household hopes to represent to the outside world. A lack of household dirt can denote purity within, and an accumulation of matter out of place can in turn signify excess: gluttony, intemperance, lust. Because of its importance to the maintenance of a society, when the moral or ethical fabric is perceived to be at risk, the threat of danger grows exponentially. In order to guarantee as much as possible the continuance of a given system of moral codification, its elements must appear within society in a diffuse manner; they must be an integral part of a majority of the systemic components. There are many aspects of a social order in which the idea of established morality resides, and thus many areas in which the survival of the social system can be perceived of as being in danger, which in turn provokes reactive moves toward stabilization and conformity. The social order is maintained from many sides, and neither the public nor the private arena is without its moral or ethical investment, for only by preserving both spheres equally can the total survival of a moral status quo be achieved. Within the private, domestic agenda of housekeeping and household maintenance lies a fundamental "moral" aspect of the home itself, because "[u]ncleanliness or dirt is that which must not be included if a pattern is to be maintained" (Douglas, *Purity* 40). The maintenance of the system relies upon the foundational maintenance of home and hearth.

Dirt becomes a way to further divide society within lines already drawn by class and caste. Morality, or subscribing to at least the outward expressions of the social order, provides for shades of gray within more extremely segregated territories. In her memoir, *Bad Blood*, Lorna Sage presents the vicarage where she lived during her formative years in post-World War II Britain (her grandfather was an Anglican vicar in northeast Wales) as "a secret slum" (14), and the vicarage dirt was "almost a point of vicarage principle, a measure of our hostility to the world outside and separateness from it" (12). Her grandfather was a pariah within the region because of an adulterous and intemperate nature, and Sage plays with the notion that although their dirt was symbolic of the fetid moral code perpetuated from within the symbolic purity of the vicarage, no one was allowed inside to see it. By masking the state of their household morality with a closed front door, the family was able at least to practice socially acceptable roles, and were thus never fully abandoned by the local congregation. Though her family was genteel only through its association with the Church and lived in a state of impoverished squalor, Sage wryly muses, "If other children were dirty, that meant they were common, their parents were neglectful and slummy, you could catch things from them. [...] I mustn't play with dirty children. So there were two different kinds of dirt, theirs and ours" (12–13). The offense here is not the actual dirt, but the social transgression of showing one's dirt, of not having the sense—the "class," if you will—to adhere outwardly to public norms. Douglas notes this connection between practice and expression: "Pollution ideas can distract from the social and moral aspects of a situation by focussing on a simple material matter" (138). A good show of cleanliness can exalt a household—even one defiled by direct exploitation of the accepted code of morality—beyond its social and economic realities through simple distraction. If the rules of the system's game are followed only as rigidly as will prevent a disclosure of other habitual failings, then the game, it seems, has been won.

According to Mary Poovey, the 1842 *Report on the Sanitary Condition of the Labouring Population of Great Britain* is "probably the most widely read government document of the Victorian period" (116). It is also likely one of the more telling documents with regard to this nexus of social class and normative social behavior, and its findings extend themselves well into the twentieth century and contemporary conflations of social propriety and proper household and bodily maintenance. Its author, Edwin Chadwick, a "tireless agitator" (Horsfield 78) for the cleanliness of Britain and for sanitation reform, does not place the blame for slovenly behaviors directly upon the heads of the working classes, but he does find that questionable morals lurk within the same corners and crevices as do dirt and disease. The conclusion of his report, which helped to fuel the Public Health Act of 1848, stresses that "the removal of noxious physical circumstances, and the promotion of civic, household, and personal cleanliness, are necessary to the improvement of the moral condition of the population; for that sound morality and refinement in manners and health are not long found co-existant with filthy habits amongst any class in the community" (424–5). Likewise, Chadwick finds that "conditions of the population, of habitual personal and domestic filth, are not necessary to any occupation; they are not the necessary consequence of poverty, and are the type of neglect and indolence" (316). An important aspect of Chadwick's conclusions about class and dirt is this idea that dirt and disease are the result of individual will, of a desire to neglect the "'proper'" state of domestic affairs, which the report defines as "moral and sanitary" (Poovey 119). By studying working-class life almost exclusively within its domestic arena, rather than at work sites or in shared social spaces, Chadwick's study "produced ideological effects that had a strong moralizing—and, ideally, regulative—component" (Poovey 119) with ramifications for ensuing definitions of a domestic ideal. The report does place certain responsibilities with the British government, but at the same time the idea is clear that regardless of one's physical circumstances, enough desire to effect change should allow the true state of the household to emerge *if indeed the true state of the household is a moral one*. Such an assumption is a strong incentive to participate in maintaining the status quo if one is to be assured of a place in the social order.

With enough ingenuity to ensure cleanliness on a material level, proper inner cleanliness should out under such a theory. Because Chadwick "generalizes the domestic values of the middle class to society as a whole" (Poovey 126), he assumes a "combination of self-denial and susceptibility, [that] women of all classes presumably shared," creating this particular female ideal as a domestic one, and assumes the theory that "working-class women could be counted on to transport middle-class values into the working-class home" (Poovey 124–5) through a normalizing domestic ideology. To such an end, the national educational curriculum was eventually changed based upon notions such as "the only way to improve laundry-work in the masses of homes would be by teaching it as a school subject to girls in the public elementary schools" (Sillitoe 63). The institutionalization of courses in the domestic sciences—cookery, needlework, laundry, household management—came into vogue initially as a way to educate the working classes by way of bringing their standards for hygiene and homemaking into line with those typically associated with the middle classes. Ruth Whitaker notes that "public opinion, educated by Chadwick and by Public Health Commissions into a realization of the appalling standards of life and food in the homes of the workers" (22), embraced this notion of teaching to children skills and standards that they could then carry back with them into the slums that they most likely inhabited. Kelsall explains that "[n]eedlework was the first of the domestic subjects to be introduced to school children [...]. Its practical value was self evident, and the necessity for cleanliness in handling the materials used provided a vehicle for teaching the elementary principles of personal hygiene" (1). The emergent educational system at this time codified a strong link between the maintenance of the home and the upkeep of the flesh. Connections that drew heavily upon the link between dirt and immorality became transposed from the domestic realm to the more private sphere of the individual body, and these cultural assumptions continue today within auto-objectifying behaviors.

The constructed relationship between the dirt on one's floorboards or the cleanliness of one's body with the degree of morality that can be attributed to an individual (as well as the link between class and morality) is hardly unique to the period when Chadwick patrolled urban slums to assess England's sanitation needs. In 1951, a report by Mass Observation made it clear that working-class British women whose primary work was within the home spent most of their time attempting to bring those homes up to culturally defined standards, likely in an attempt to avoid the blatant judgments of neighbors like Lorna Sage's grandmother. The bulletin, entitled *The Housewife's Day,* for which working-class housewives were polled and interviewed, states what many engaged in domestic labor could long before have confirmed. Mass Observation's statistics show that the average British woman's day in 1951 filled fifteen hours, of which eleven were spent specifically engaged in domestic duties. The theory that women's work is swift and their leisure time ample was discredited by the results of this study, but this "new" information was naturally not without its detractors. After reading an advanced copy of the bulletin, James Benson, of Kemsley Newspapers (whose *Daily Telegraph* announced publication of the bulletin on 11 July 1951), responded to the Mass Observation offices that perhaps a more intelligent class of housewife (read "middle-class") might be better able to use their time more efficiently than did their working-class sisters.[1]

---

[1]   Regardless of her class status, the housewife provided, and continues to provide, a vast amount of unpaid labor. In 1960, Mildred Wheatcroft, Chairman of the Council of Scientific Management in the Home, calculated that if "we estimate the value of this work at 3 s. per hour, which is a rate commonly paid for domestic work, we find that the home industry is contributing a potential of some £4,500,000,000 to the national productivity. This corresponds to about a quarter of our gross national product, and is a great deal more than the total of wages paid in the manufacturing industry" ("Home" 14). Imagine what that amount equals nearly half a century later.

The assumption made by Chadwick in his 1842 report is echoed here by Benson; however, his rhetoric includes a different twist. Simple sloth is not the only element that brings about excessive dirt and an increase in the amount of time needed to clean it. For Benson, "intelligence," as well as will or "industry"—attributed in a de facto manner to the middle classes—figures into a woman's ability to maintain an adequate household. The same morality erroneously linked to superior cleanliness is here implicated, through the ideal of the British household and its devoted housewife, as a by-product of the ability to reason and to think critically. Benson's letter illustrates the connection made previously between a morality generated by organized religious influences and the more rarefied morality of the superior and rational mind, as well as how the two are reflected in standards for sparkling domesticity. As Carolyn Steedman recalls of her own working-class childhood during the years following World War II, "there are people everywhere waiting for you to slip up, to show signs of dirtiness and stupidity, so they can send you back where you belong" (34). Again, the idea emerges that a gap between the social code for cleanliness and the actual state of the private sphere will be perceived as moral shortcoming, and for Steedman, this gap is compounded by her socioeconomic class. In order to become socially mobile—the path widely encouraged during the twentieth century—one must adequately perform the legible attributes of middle-class morality. Without constant vigilance, the home (or the bodies within the home) can become damning proof of one's inability to uphold other, more socially troublesome values. The self-policing aspects of auto-objectification, through this conflation of morality, cleanliness, and an individual's social worthiness, are brought into stark relief.

With standards for household cleanliness firmly in place as a method of representing the moral hygiene of English citizens, the "pollution belief [...] can have the effect of aggravating the seriousness of the offense, and so of marshalling public opinion on the side of right" (Douglas, *Purity* 133). What is defined as morally "right" within public discourse implicates one's will to maintain certain domestic and moral standards, as well as a level of reason or of intellect necessary for the adoption of such standards. This method of maintaining cultural morality is a reflection of the efficiency of mass acculturation, in this case, of the ability of a middle-class moral and ethical standard to superimpose itself over a multiplicity of moralities and codes for behavior perhaps better initiated on a local or regional level than from any nationalistic prescription, such as those emanating from household manuals that beseech their readers to scrub away for the sake of English pride. In *The History of Sexuality, Volume One*, Michel Foucault suggests that one effect of the eighteenth and nineteenth centuries' "incitement" to an increase in the discourse of sexuality was "a centrifugal movement with respect to heterosexual monogamy" in which the "legitimate couple [...] tended to function as a norm" (38). This normalization of the monogamous (and most likely married heterosexual) couple results in two social phenomena germane to this discussion thus far, aspects of social and cultural conformity that are foundational to an understanding of separations of public from private and of the mental from the corporeal, attitudes that result in a schism, in an auto-objectified subject. The first is a dependence upon the family unit, upon the household, as the primary venue for an enactment of normative morality, and the consequential need for maintenance of the household through a particular regimentation that leads to specific behaviors. Without this basic domestic structure, individual behavior can come into question; the maintenance apparatus of the household is particular to the legitimized norm. Without the sanction of domesticity, the individual can be viewed as an anomalous element, as not only a source of social pollution, but as pollution itself.

The second result of this movement toward a legitimate domesticity is the idea of an inherent security and privacy in such a model. For Foucault, this stems from a turning away from any examination of the sexuality of monogamy in favor of an exploration of whatever might deviate from that norm: the above-mentioned "legitimate couple, with its regular sexuality, had a right to more discretion"; "[e]fforts to find out its secrets were abandoned" (38). Such an abandonment of the domestic realm in a search for (sexual) deviance from the accepted norm has never been permanent, however. The myth of a privacy granted to the (monogamous, heterosexual) household underlies the notion of a division between public and private, and assists in our definitions of masculine and feminine as each realm is gendered, but its structure is no more private than is any system that lies outside the home. Once granted this sense of exemption from public scrutiny, the "private" domain simply becomes subject to more insidious power schemes and regimentations, and the self-policing subject becomes an unconsciously auto-objectified entity. Though from this exclusion of the private domain from much of overt public discourse comes the clean, scrubbed vision of the nuclear family, the degree to which that family is scrubbed becomes social and cultural ammunition against any relief from the vigilance of domestic maintenance. Dirt or other evidence of pollution, representative of the moral standards maintained within the home, becomes its figurative language, and the public eye will revert back toward the private world when that world appears in representative disarray. The discursive qualities of cleanliness become a domesticated mode of representing and of interrogating the morality, and thus the sexuality, of those who reside within the thin walls of the private home.

Douglas also outlines a methodology of power that she finds in "the interplay of form and surrounding formlessness," between the system and its polluting dirt; her theories parallel those of Foucault. She summarizes: "first, formal powers wielded by persons representing the formal structure and exercised on behalf of the formal structure: second, formless powers wielded by interstitial persons: third, powers not wielded by any person, but inhering in the structure, which strike against any infraction of form" (*Purity* 104). Both the structure and those who are complicit with it are active parts of its maintenance. For Foucault, power "is not something that is acquired, seized, or shared, something that one holds onto or allows to slip away; power is exercised from innumerable points, in the interplay of nonegalitarian and mobile relations" (*History* 94). His "bio-power," a network "bent on generating forces, making them grow, and ordering them, rather than one dedicated to impeding them, making them submit, or destroying them" (*History* 136), is the same systemic power that normalizes both human sexuality and its representative cleanliness. Moral codes, particularly codes for normative sexual behaviors, become a site where the syntax of household maintenance becomes synonymous with the ways in which the physical body must present itself to the world at large. Though there is no sense of immanent destruction attached to breaking the codes of such power (as opposed to codes that carry with them the certainty of severe punishments or of death), there is at once an opportunistic and an ethical interest in maintaining one's position within the structure itself, both of which work as deterrents to subversion of the structure.

Foucault's theory of regimentation stresses a "double system: gratification-punishment" that, through ascribing "opposing values of good and evil" to observance and nonobservance of social order, encourages complicity in the system through creating a desire for reward (*Discipline* 180). Such regimentation reinforces the ways in which our binaried codes play themselves out within our culture, as well, reminding us that only one option within a given duality will bring gratification of an acceptable kind. "The chief function of the disciplinary power is to 'train,'" notes Foucault; "[...] It does not link forces together in order to reduce them; it seeks to bind them together in such a way as to multiply and use them" (*Discipline* 170). Under such a power structure, the domestic realm functions as a site of linked forces. Proper maintenance of moral codes and of social norms for sexual and other expressions becomes inscribed indelibly onto one another, so that what matters is not the actual state of household affairs, but instead the total function of the household as a discreet unit within the larger social scheme. The twentieth-century British housewife, caught up in a system of private maintenance for a public "penal accountancy" (Foucault, *Discipline* 180), must devote herself to a regimentation of that by which her household and its conformity will be defined and judged.

A large component of Foucault's exegesis of the regimentation and rise of information regarding sexuality is the aspect of confession. "Western man," he notes (and, for the sake of my argument, let's include Western woman, as well), "has become a confessing animal" (*History* 59). The discourse of the power structure is not only that which is formulated about its subjects, but is also the information that those subjects relay about themselves. Through a desire to add points to the positive side of the moral column log, atonement or purification is sought as a corrective, but a major result of this corrective process is the further implication of the individual with the structure and its moral codes. "The obligation to confess," states Foucault, "is now relayed through so many different points, is so deeply ingrained in us, that we no longer perceive it as the effect of a power that constrains us" (*History* 60). As moral subjects within a system, we readily, indeed, compulsively confess when we find that we have transgressed the boundaries by which we are circumscribed. Perhaps no one confesses more compulsively, or more often confesses for sins not yet identified, than the modern housewife. Enter her home (or mine, or your own) and you are more likely to hear something similar to "Oh, goodness, the place is a wreck; I haven't touched the floor in a month!" than a list of triumphs, domestic or otherwise. Her fatal sin—that of sloth or of a lack of intelligent will to achieve middle-class order against all odds—is as much attached to her status in the social order as are her sexuality and sexual expression. Her home, which lies within a nexus of social functions and expectations, is a vehicle for a domestic expression of the moral conduct of herself and of her family.

Cleanliness has become, in itself, her confession. Housework—the concealment of dirt—is a necessary part of the ultimate fact of transgression. Because dirt defies even the most devoted of housewives, they live under a constant threat of discovery. Even the vicarage family of Sage's childhood would not publicly flaunt its dirt, but instead shunned visitors who would have assessed the household accordingly. Later, Sage's mother, untrained for the expectations of "the advertisers and the social psychologists" and of "the people who'd planned" their newly built council house full of "light and hard, washable surfaces," continued the tradition of guarding "her genius for travesty when it came to domestic science" (119). The homemaker without ready ability to maintain her household to acceptable standards is in cultural "drag," and in such travesty can only survive social mediation through a carefully constructed ruse. "Women neighbours were never allowed in," Sage recalls, "nor were their daughters, who were suspected of being [...] household spies who'd run home and tell their mothers we didn't clean behind the sofa" (120). More usually, even when one is primarily a lackadaisical housekeeper, housework is the norm prior to entertaining guests, and most of us hope that unplanned-for guests will at least phone ahead. Whether dirt is all but removed or simply swept beneath the proverbial rug (or, in my case, up against the baseboards for later effacement), the woeful nature of sin itself—try as one might, there is always some sin to account for—is the domestic bottom line within a dualistic system that Beauvoir labels "Manichæist," the essence of which "is not solely to recognize two principles, the one good, the other evil; it is also to hold that the good is attained through the abolition of evil and not by positive action" (425). Compulsive confession serves as a way to atone prior to discovery, to ensure that once one's dirt is found out, it will already have been neutralized by the act of confession. Domestic confession acts as a private version of public sacrifice: the social self is expected to compensate publicly for failing to maintain the system to its optimal specifications, and this act increasingly removes the "self" that is responsible for acts of maintenance from the physical aspects of subjectivity that must be watched over with diligence.

Modernity and the Evolution of Housework

Washing machines, vacuum cleaners, and other products created to make the housewife's occupation more appealing may also have created a sense of guilt rather than one of leisure and may have added to the impulse toward moral concerns and domestic confession. "It is possible," suggests Elizabeth Roberts, "that some women felt almost guilty about the easier life the new machines brought and that therefore jobs had to be done more often to compensate" (32). Certainly the frequency with which houses were cleaned increased after the advent of domestic appliances. Horsfield queries, "Did a desire for cleanliness create new products, or did new products create an increased desire for cleanliness?" (139), and, though advertisements might appear to answer some loud cry for new conveniences, it is doubtful that already overtaxed housewives desired an increase in the standards they were expected to maintain. "I liked the new vacuum cleaner at first," Steedman recalls of the chores she performed while growing up, "because it meant no longer having to do the stairs with a stiff brush. But in fact it added to my Saturday work because I was expected to clean more with the new machine" (36). In this way mechanization, modernity, infuses the domestic training of each generation of young women, and each wave of "improvements" brings with it new lessons in regimentation and subsequently in the importance of separating the mind from the body in order to maintain the social order.

Though for many years only the relatively wealthy could afford items that came onto the market, eventually household "mechanical servants" appeared regularly in homes of all classes. The rhetoric of household maintenance reached not only middle-class women, but also women of the working classes who, though they largely had left service as an occupation, were unable to escape the cultural demands for clean English homes. Even as the twentieth century progressed and with it came the introduction of more women into the workplace and beyond the traditional sphere of domesticity, cultural rhetoric continued to bind women to their homes. Books from the 1970s that seemingly turn on the traditional do so through parody and often via cartoon drawings rather than depictions of actual women in defiance of the norm, but still admit to the place of women in domestic routine. "Until someone comes up with a mechanical Sarah Jane, *someone's* got to do the dirty support system work," sighs Shirley Conran in 1977. Although, she reminds us, "[n]o one's going to strangle you if the mantel-piece is dusty" (4), one also must keep in mind that "you have to be efficient if you're going to be lazy" (2). Even when in contemporary times some women can laugh at standards, many often find themselves bound to them, the cord invisible, seemingly uncuttable. Efficiency demanded of mechanical women is expected of those who in the flesh continue their battles against matter out of place.

The modernization of the household has not only disassociated "work" from the reality of household maintenance; it has also removed women from the physical reality of their everyday lives. Woman has been modernized right out of the natural world of the physical body that both biologically and culturally defines her. For a housewife to accept the rhetorical stance that housework, with the assistance of modern technology, requires little manual labor is for her to accept a de facto disassociation of herself from the activities she performs. Through a negation of the physicality of the activities that take up most of the housewife's day or that take up a good portion of the time spent at home by women who work beyond its front door, the information that assists women in building beautiful homes also disassociates them from a basic connection with their physical bodies, a process that assists in the development of an auto-objectified female subject. Without a rhetoric of the ways in which the practices of housework make use of the body, one of women's fundamental social and cultural roles divides them between two worlds: the physical world in which these functions are performed, and the intellectual world in which the value of these functions is constructed, a world into which the female of the species has only grudgingly been accepted. The domestically defined role for women—for those whose primary labor is housework, and for those who perform double duty as laborers outside of and within the home—is one that engenders ambivalence: for the role itself, for the housework involved, for the domestic realm, and for the physical body necessary for keeping up with the increasing standards demanded by a modernized world.

Along with the gap between the housewife and her housework, modernity has resulted in an increase in the gap between expectations for domestic achievement and the actual ability to perform such feats. With the mechanization of the household, imagined as the "substituting [of] machines for servants" (Hardyment 39), the housewife has had to incorporate levels of precision that before were expected only of machinery. The equation made between servants and machines expands to incorporate the housewife herself, though she has ostensibly evolved beyond the former and is more cheerily domestic than the rumbling latter. Even early in the twentieth century, prior to the proliferation of household appliances, Mrs. J. N. Bell chided that there "are an almost infinite number of appliances and machines, cookery-books, etc., in the market, but no automatic mothers or housewives. And although we might be clever enough to use all the first, and to repeat by heart all the second, nothing but personal effort will ever turn theory into practice" (12). The Hoover is not credited or blamed for the removal of carpet lint, but instead the (female) individual who pushes the appliance must assume responsibility for the performance of the machine. Her "personal effort" is the source of her household's cleanliness, and therefore of its moral fiber. And as this machinery decreases the amount of labor needed to complete a task, and as the expected frequency of performing those tasks mounts, the level of a housewife's personal investment also grows, bringing with it more guilt, more confessional apologies.

One thing these new products have done is to exacerbate the separation of the idea of "work" from the compounded tasks of housework, of the intellectualized qualities of household upkeep from the very physical, quite quantifiable aspects of women's everyday experiences. The implication of ease found (still) in advertisements for newfangled housekeeping aids negates the actual work—time and energy—it still takes to maintain even, or perhaps especially, a contemporary household. Again, the flaws in the logic of a system dedicated both to assisting the housewife and to keeping her social role intact become apparent. By the mid-twentieth century, when household appliances as basic to the contemporary kitchen as the refrigerator, the gas oven, and the vacuum cleaner were only beginning to radically change the way a home was managed, however, the idea of "work" had already been expunged from that of "housework." Adrian Forty details how, in the nineteenth century and in the earlier decades of the twentieth, there "was a danger that if the negative aspects of the work became too obvious, they would detract from the pleasure women were expected to derive from housework [...] housewives themselves avoided these contradictions by resisting making comparisons between housework and other kinds of work" (208). The dignity required of the house-proud woman, too, if she were to be the content specimen that she was expected to be, had to be disassociated from the dinge of the work done by paid servants (Forty 209). But the more predominant household appliances became, and the greater was the cleanliness expected of housewives, the more actual work resulted, and not all chores can be adequately accomplished by machine. For some jobs, the housewife continued to use that "spare" time to maintain high standards better than the machine could do. In 1962, Mrs. Kennedy, a working-class woman included in Elizabeth Roberts's oral history, acquired a washing machine and yet admitted, "'I always washed the nappies by hand. [...] I gave them three or four rinses and I boiled them once a week'" (33). Even with two children in nappies, Mrs. Kennedy put her pride in her own abilities before her desire for leisure. What Forty calls the "idea that machines could turn housework from laborious drudgery into a few minutes' pleasure" (207) may have caught on with advertisers, but in the wake of their four-color offerings for labor-saving devices were left women expected to do more and to be like machines—divorced from their embodied experiences—and who were working as much if not more than they would have in a simpler household.

The expectations for women that arose from the advent of modern invention were further compounded by the "sciences" that proliferated after the World War II and that were central to the creation of numerous rows of postwar housing for families seeking suburban achievements and middle-class lifestyles. Household management was moved rhetorically, and increasingly in reality, from the hands of housewives into those of engineers, scientists, and time-management specialists. Even as psychologist C. A. Mace accedes that "the need for carbohydrates" and "the need to love and be loved [...] are mixed in fact" (19), pages later in the volume *Housework with Satisfaction*, his contemporaries advocate in contradictory terms. The proper height for kitchen countertops (three feet), the amount of room that a family might need in order to experience comfort (a whopping postwar prescription was a thousand square feet per family), and the training of the housewife's body in "correct key factors in basic movements" (Anderson 39) were all part of schemes that not only continued the process of middle-classifying the vast majority of Britons, but also regimented households spatially and temporally. Even the location of the kitchen with regard to communal living spaces within the home became scrutinized: between kitchen and dining room "the middle-class woman prefers a hatch because it does not disclose the disorders of the kitchen and is a better barrier for smells; she puts up with the greater amount of drifting from room to room in exchange for the amenity" (Bennett 42). In 1955, *Meals in Modern Homes*, published by the Council of Scientific Management in the Home, suggests "that the main equipment in the kitchen should be arranged in the order work surface / cooker / work surface / sink / work surface" (40), in essence to allow for streamlined activity during meal preparation, but simultaneously making even the smallest of actions in the kitchen fairly routinized from home to home. Whether the reduction in motion that resulted in such mechanics ever helped housewives, however, remains unknown but unlikely.

Standards for domestic order have unarguably risen along with the proliferation of modern conveniences, but the expected dividend of time does not often materialize. The women polled in the 1951 Mass Observation study had not gained any additional time in return for reliance upon modern machinery, nor had their middle-class counterparts. "The assertion that middle-class homes could be kept clean all the year round without the help of servants," Hardyment argues, "was hailed as one of the triumphs of the twentieth century, instead of being recognized as a tyranny just as great for the once proud managerial housewife as that formerly exerted on her hard-working tweeny" (89). Even in 1960, the ritual of *daily* cleaning espoused by Phyllis Davidson, Senior Lecturer at Battersea Training College of Domestic Science, was an involved process even for the simple bedroom: "Ventilate the room. [...] the bed should be stripped [...]. Remove old newspapers, ashtrays, waste-paper baskets, flowers needing attention and generally tidy the room. Make the bed" (116). According to Davidson, appropriate strategies for household maintenance would allow the housewife "to look after the needs of the family with the least possible expenditure of time and labour so that [she ...] may have time to live a full life in other ways" (115). Her plan of work, if followed to perfection, would hardly allow for a life full of much else aside from a clean and maintained home. In 1982, housekeeping professional Don Aslett comforted another generation of still overtaxed women: "Most women are barely managing, meeting daily crises and demands" (10). The housewife became house-proud through her ability to maintain without assistance the level of domestic order previously accorded to those who managed the home only with the help of a retinue. The ideal household predominately became—and remains—that which is self-sufficient.

Discourses of Health and the Regimentation of the Body

For housewives, the quest to rid homes completely of germs became part of their investment in the English standard: with the right products, "not only was it possible, it was their bounden duty" (Horsfield 92). As scientific advances in germ theories, developed during the nineteenth century, furthered the search for domestic perfection, science itself likewise served as a model for the systematic study of household management. "Domestic science" is a phenomenon that changed not only the way in which household work was approached, as well as the manuals and periodicals that carried its message to women, but also the ways in which domestic education took place both in and outside of the home. The Education Act of 1870 had a singular impact upon the ways in which a cross section of Britain was educated, and the emphasis on health and cleanliness, particularly in the context of cooking, became a large part of the domestic-science agenda. While the government continued through the early part of the twentieth century to support the training of domestic employees in countless institutions throughout Britain, women were also trained through cultural media that domestic science was an important aspect of their futures as keepers of their own homes. In the early twentieth century "evening classes for factory girls were started" that assisted would-be wives in the art of cookery (Kelsall 6). Ursula Bloom (beauty editor in the 1930s and 1940s for the weekly periodical *Woman's Own*), in *Me— After the War: A Book for Girls Considering the Future* (1944), stresses that training in professional cookery is an education "that you can take forward with you" into marriage; "remember that," she advises (18). In writing from the 1960s, Phyllis Davidson emphasizes the importance not only of such an education, but of continuing education in the sciences of domesticity: "The modern housewife must keep abreast of developments [...]. Domestic science training gained in her schooldays will stand her in good stead; attendance at adult classes, broadcast talks and feature programmes and articles in good types of women's magazines are all of value" (192). Though training in vocational domestic arts continued to be offered, most women, it appears, were more interested in gaining knowledge that would enable them to create their own homes in the image of traditional English comfort and were encouraged "to make a study of the subject as complete as one does of any other branch of education" (Bell 8). With this kind of training moved from the private sphere of the home and into social institutions vis-à-vis state-sponsored education, the imperative of regimentation becomes a message that is most difficult to escape.

Domestic science became a movement for the broad dissemination of principles of sanitation and disinfection, insisting that "every woman in charge of a house must inform herself about the spread of disease and the importance of hygiene" (Horsfield 94). One president of the British Medical Association agreed with his sisters in "science" that "the housewife [...] was responsible for stopping the spread of disease in the home" (Horsfield 96). Once the threat of germ-carried disease enters the already crowded picture of domestic expectation, housekeeping stakes are further raised. "The slightest deviance from perfect cleanliness was a cause for social anxiety," notes Forty, "since the invisible passage of germs could put the health of the family, companions and even the entire nation at risk" (169). The social conditioning of domestic rhetoric, along with its attendant guilt, is multiplied when issues of health make housekeeping literally a matter of life and death. With dire consequences attached to transgression from these norms, the impulse to self-regulate and to maintain the order set forth by the socius is a powerful one, and the result is an individual who is always on the lookout for matter out of place and who is thus naturalized into a world in which materiality has little or nothing to do with conceptions of subjectivity.

As the meeting place for issues related to health, embodiment, well-being, and domestic normativity, the kitchen is one critical household center where disease must be battled for the good of the family: "A clean kitchen is, in nine-and-three-quarters cases out of ten, the criterion of a clean housewife and happy household" (*Household Management* 184). The housewife must work to ascertain the cleanliness of her kitchen and to avert any contamination of the food prepared within in order to maintain domestic equilibrium. The first items listed in the 1909 edition of Mrs. Beeton under "Advice for the Kitchen" stress the impact of less than three decades of germ theories on beliefs about kitchen hygiene: "Cleanliness is the most essential ingredient in the art of cooking; a dirty kitchen being a disgrace both to mistress and maid. Be clean in your person, paying particular attention to the hands, which should always be clean" (19). The passing of germs from one individual to another, rather than from random accumulations of decaying, miasma-producing matter, worked to implicate the housewife (or the cook, if applicable) as a source of disease. Not only must a kitchen be clean, but the hands of the individual must also be maintained to bacteria-free specifications. Of course, people do pass along disease, and the washing of hands is still considered to be the easiest and most common way to combat transmission of germs between individuals. This personalization of disease transmission, however, and the culpability of not the germ but of its messenger, only add to the level of social, moral, and familial accountability with which the housewife must contend. The housewife, a central cog in the machinations of modernity, not only had to maintain her home in response to cultural mandates, but also grew increasingly responsible for the upkeep of the flesh—that of others but, importantly, of herself—as the physical body came increasingly under the scrutiny of modern ritual. The human body is an extension of the home from which it comes, even though it might seem more logical to consider the home—built and maintained by the individual human subject—as an extension of its residents. The history of discourses that govern the home and its maintenance indicates that standards for upkeep of the more visible aspects of domestic life grew more insidious, more invested in the human forms within as the project of social and cultural regimentation took stronger hold and as the twentieth century wore on.

Though works like Mrs. Beeton's cookery and housekeeping manuals provided a wide readership with household instruction, for years the same sort of information was passed among groups of women and through generations of housewives and housekeepers. Household receipt books, kept by maids and ladies both, were forerunners of the mass-produced manuals, and their instruction—perhaps without the emphasis on disinfection perpetuated by germ theories of the late Victorian period—served on a local level the purposes of regimentation that those later texts made widespread. While later, printed works grew specialized with regard to the particular expertise emphasized, these earlier writings—preserved mostly in manuscript, though a few have been edited and published for contemporary audiences—are a jumble of household, medical, and culinary recipes that indicate the varied knowledge expected of a domestic manager. Before the publishing industry partitioned off the entities within the home, creating discourses of home maintenance separate from ideas related to the upkeep of the family within, handwritten documents passed from housekeeper to housekeeper rhetorically bound together notions of homemaking with issues of the human body and its maintenance. One such document, the *Receipt Book* compiled by a housekeeper of Gransden House in Huntingdonshire during the early nineteenth century, provides instructions on subjects as varied as how "To Salt a Tongue for Roasting" (11b), "To Make Leather water proof" (27a), and for "Easy and almost instantaneous cure for the Ague": "take a new-laid egg in a glass of Brandy and go to bed immediately" (29b). Care for all material items—both animate and inanimate—that lay beneath one's roof was the clear domain of the housekeeper.

The cures and remedies for ailments both domestic and corporeal in these early household-maintenance texts are combined in a way that rhetorically indicates an equation of a household's goods and its embodied inhabitants. Though certainly the lady of the house might value differently a piece of broken china and a family member down with the "Hooping Cough" (23a), advice on the maintenance of both appear together, indiscriminately, on these directive pages. A "Receipt for a Cough" (15a) lies between instructions on how "To Dress Cods" and "For Curing 2 Hams," perhaps mirroring the ways in which a woman had to (and often still must) move readily between domestic routines and those more attached to the physical health of others around her. The nurturing role relegated to women in most cultures is not limited to the role of mother/caregiver, but encompasses all aspects of a synchronized household, including its leather goods and crockery. Because of the broad-ranging duties of the housekeeper (duties that increasingly became the sole responsibility of the homemaker herself), the individual within the household was implicated in its general maintenance and established as yet another aspect of the home to be maintained. The family members, like the physical house surrounding them, have long been part of a household's rhetorical representation as well as of its internal, systemic functioning. The body is another item to maintain to the codes determined by the ideologies of a given time: its appearance, size, shape, and health are all part and parcel of what Jackson Lears has called "The Perfectionist Project." Writing of twentieth-century attitudes in the United States, Lears suggests what is evident in parallel British rhetoric: "a largely secular project [...] the creation of human subjects whose bowel movements were as effectively regulated as their performance in the office or kitchen" (162). Regimentation was not simply a project that would ensure a sparkling kitchen or a well-scrubbed lav. As Susan Bordo notes, "In place of God the watchmaker, we now have ourselves, the master sculptors" of what she terms "cultural plastic": bodies that we work into representations of modern society in our "disdain for material limits" (246). The language that supported the dawn of a new era—discourses of science, medicine, technologies—increased popular engagement with the notion of the body as material object at the mercy of a higher "self" that had been socially and culturally removed from its physical ontological qualities.

Once the discipline of medicine took stronger shape in the later nineteenth century and cures such as coal boiled in milk for cough or consumption (*Receipt Book* 26a) gave way to more scientific remedies, maintenance of the body, like that of the general household, became largely affected by processes of modernity.

As basic levels of health were more easily accomplished than they had been prior to the growth of medical sciences, and as mortality rates declined in proportion to the rise in sanitation and in disease control, the discourse of bodily maintenance expanded to encompass a wide range of practices. Along with the proliferation of household manuals during the mid- and late nineteenth century came an increase in discourses on how to maintain the human body at its optimum potential. Volumes that provided advice to women on how to maintain their physical appearance followed on the heels of those that gave them advice for keeping a clean and tidy home, and at the turn of the twentieth century, the mass-marketing of this type of publication was in full throttle (never, if current availability of these manuals is any indication, to slow down). As with domestic information, which began as part of familial or local ideals that were passed on orally or via receipt book, information for personal hygiene and for physical upkeep was moved from the private to the public domain as printing became an inexpensive endeavor and as mass production allowed for a majority of women to come by this advice. It would have been (and remains) difficult to escape from this avalanche of prescriptive tracts. With the basics of health care given over to medical science, more frivolous prescriptions for maintaining a proper body began to enjoy popular positions within British culture.

To a degree, this new emphasis upon the appearance and hygienic maintenance of the bodies in all of England had much to do with the sort of superimposition of middle-class values over the entire English population. Mary Poovey notes that for mid-Victorians the "sanitary idea constituted one of the crucial links between the regulation of the individual body and the consolidation of those apparatuses we associate with the modern state" (115), including the moral apparatus of the state, and this link continues in contemporary society. The appearance of the physical body, as well as the mysterious inner workings of the body, became increasingly regulated as the need to control shifting, socially mobile populations increased. As Michel Foucault's theories outline, this sort of regimentation eventually becomes self-regulated as the subject becomes increasingly a part of the system, a project that "becomes more elusive as it becomes more pressing" (Bordo 202). With more opportunity to become a central subject within the growing middle classes, an individual who had previously been marginalized could, Bordo explains, through an ability to "master the body," become a "symbol of successsful aspiration, of the penetrability of class boundaries to those who have 'the right stuff'" (195).

Dress and personal toilette have historically been significant of class status, but once industrialization was firmly in place in England, and once English citizens in turn began to experience greater possibilities for class mobility, social and cultural emphases on the external conditions of the body increased. As Mary Douglas writes,

> The body is a model that can stand for any bounded system. Its boundaries can represent any boundaries which are threatened or precarious. [...] We cannot possibly interpret rituals concerning [the body] unless we are prepared to see in the body a symbol of society, and to see the powers and dangers credited to the social structure reproduced in small on the human body. (*Purity* 115)

Douglas's notion of "matter out of place" extends beyond the hearth and the home to the individual citizen, and in order to exhibit a consistent social code, including an attendant morality or code of ethics as ordained by the dominant voices of a given social order, the body is expected to conform, to illustrate in the real world the desires of the socius for stability and orderly behaviors. Julia Kristeva's theories on abjection comment precisely upon the type of symbol that the body can be, the type of body that properly symbolizes society: "The body [...] must be clean and proper in order to be symbolic" (102). The tiny social and cultural rituals of dress, appearance, and personal hygiene, then, should be viewed not simply as appeals to vanity, but as projections of social and cultural anxieties resulting from issues such as class and gender, as well as those anxieties stemming from the already documented intersection between codified morality and issues of cleanliness.

A rhetoric of health, so attached to the literature of household maintenance through standards set for the control of dirt and germs, is also present in much of the literature written on the maintenance of the body and of its physical appearance, especially in that literature directed toward women. Health science and subsidiary disciplines such as physical education flourished simultaneously with the field of domestic science, and by 1937 the British government joined the movement with its Physical Training and Recreation Act, which in part provided for "more and better educated teachers of physical education" (Bourne 110). Public awareness of advances in medicine made way for an evolution of fairly routine matters into educational disciplines and into "sciences," and the industries involved in the maintenance of the body—again, especially of the female body—adopted the languages of science and of medicine in a way that helped to legitimize claims made for physical improvement and for control over the body's natural processes. An example of this combining of health issues with less pressing matters is the Women's League of Health and Beauty, which had "membership running into six figures" circa 1939 (Herbert 180). Maintenance of internal and of external standards became equally important and, as a part of the domestic sphere, such conditions fell under the auspices of the household manager.

Body Maintenance and Auto-objectification

While the housewife was expected to maintain her domestic domain to rigorous standards, she was also responsible for assisting in the maintenance of the individual bodies residing under her roof for increasing periods of time as child labor laws were expanded and decreases in infant death rates established larger family units. This maintenance, too (beginning with that of her own body), is imbued with the same imperatives as is housework: "No woman, indeed, can be truly beautiful unless she is also healthy; and to be healthy, so far as we can, is a duty to ourselves, and to our husbands and children, if we are married and mothers" (*Art of Beauty* 1). As with that "bounden duty" to keep up a clean and moral household, women became increasingly duty-bound to maintain their own flesh to standards as exacting as those prescribed for floors and windows. The receipt books of earlier times had helped to keep the household body running smoothly for generations, but as scientific and other discoveries helped to shape unique, specialized discourses of cookery, cleanliness, hygiene, and beauty, the rituals involved in managing each individual body within a household multiplied. Information available to a growing readership flourished; contradictions ensued. Domestic science perpetuated the ideal of housekeeping as increasingly scientific, and its demands of perfection and rhetoric of life and death kept (and keep) housewives compliant through fear and guilt. Likewise, the increasing number of books devoted to the female body and its appearance also borrowed liberally from science, and the insidious result has been strikingly similar to that found within domestic practices: feelings of fear, guilt, and shame resonate with socially produced moral structures and have kept generations of women occupied with concerns about the maintenance of the body's outer boundaries. Standards for beauty and appearance, like standards for dirt and cleanliness, have become invested with the larger issues of the social system, and as representative effects of the system must be maintained to code.

The first generation of mass-marketed volumes on bodily maintenance contains advice that is as dogmatic and as geared toward regimentation as were their predecessors of domestic ingenuity. In *The Art of Being Beautiful: A Series of Interviews with a Society Beauty*, the "Beauty" entices both her interviewer and the book's subsequent readership with rhetoric that makes no attempt to hide its quasi-medical ambitions: "The doctor does not diagnose a disease in a moment, and if he attempted in a moment to describe it we could not follow him. You must come to me often, and if you will take the trouble [...] you will be beautiful, admired, beloved as you wish to be" (15–16). The quest for physical beauty takes on a systematic quality based upon the professional dicta of medical and domestic sciences. Maintenance of all kinds requires specific agendas, executions, criteria for assessment. Advice books from this period forward specify quite particular (if conflicting) regimens for attaining that important element of beauty and rarely fail to imply the desirable outcome: admiration, devotion, love. This odd admixture of romance fantasy and the language of "hard" sciences has birthed a paradoxical and confusing set of criteria for women of the twentieth century (and into the twenty-first).

In *Health, Beauty, and the Toilet: Letters to Ladies from a Lady Doctor*, Anna Kingsford (in letters that originally appeared in *The Lady's Pictorial*) secures her readers' trust with her title of "M.D." She ascertains that "the demand for such instruction is universal, and, obviously, one who is both a woman and a doctor, competent to understand at once what is required, and the most efficient method of supplying it, is, from every point of view, the fittest exponent of the subject" (iii–iv). Though Kingsford may not have been a charlatan, her use of the title of "doctor" granted her, perhaps, more sway in some circles than did the status of the "Society Beauty." Both women, though, are a part of the social and cultural battle to reform the flesh, to present the body as something to be perfected and maintained rather than as a part of a "self" or as a vehicle for social agency. The project for perfection and for the creation of bodies that would mimic the "proper" social order is a manifestation of the alienation of the physical from the psychical self; the regimented body that results from such dicta belongs to a subject that has become auto-objectified in a quest to meet a normative ideal that exists, it seems, most fully only in the minds of publishers, advice-givers, and "lady doctors." The rhetoric of health that filled the pages of books such as Kingsford's and those by others presented readers with a fine line to tread. "Health" in these contexts not only meant "beauty," but increasingly also came to suggest particular levels of physical fitness and of bodily proportion. As interests in physical education and in regimentation of the body grew, calisthenics and other forms of exercise became popular in some sectors of the beauty industry—but always within the boundaries of proper femininity. Helena Gent's 1909 tract, *Health and Beauty for Women and Girls*, exalts the fact that women "will ride, walk, run, cycle, golf, hockey, skate and swim" (29) and provides photographic examples of exercises for women who wish to be "well developed and [...] finely proportioned, [...] brimming over with vitality" (25). Physical fitness, however, even in a book like Gent's that seems to eschew the usual fare of cosmetic and apparel advice, should only serve to heighten the femininity of woman; it should not compromise her attempts to be "woman 'womanly'" (25). Physical ability and agency are here parts of broader efforts of women to be attractive mates for their male equivalents.

In the twentieth century, women became increasingly responsible for their homes and related upkeep, all the while working diligently toward keeping their physical selves up to code. None of their activities, however, were meant to serve the woman alone, not even physical fitness. In the 1940s, Ursula Bloom provided additional versions of advice that combines personal and familial maintenance: "Household work is excellent for exercise. You can do breathing exercises whilst mixing cakes or puddings, you can practise keeping tummy and tail in, whilst you sweep. Mangling will develop the bust. If you want to reduce your hips, don't get down on your knees with a dustpan and brush, stoop to it" (*Housewife's Beauty* 142). Housework here not only helps to keep the household consistent with social and cultural expectations for the proper family abode, but also should allow for the woman who runs that home to maintain herself as a representative of the morality and conformity of her (and her husband's) home. Breathing, posture, and a bust that will simultaneously signify female nurturing and sexuality are all components of household maintenance and here rhetorically link definitions of women's sexuality with their social imperatives of homemaking and caregiving. Tied to roles—dictated by sex and galvanized by gender maintenance—that demand they define themselves in relation to others (family, spouse, children), at the turn of the last century and beyond, British women were mobilized but at the same time were curtailed in their efforts to surpass traditional boundaries of feminine ideologies. Even as many factors deny her leisure, she is encouraged never to lag behind in her attempts to be ornamental and convivial; even as she is asked to maintain herself for the sake of health, her beauty remains the underlying goal of these rhetorics.

Like the household whose bacteria cannot be eradicated, the body is a fluctuating biological system that resists efforts of normalization. It defies maintenance to standards of perfection like those advocated by Gent, as well as those implied more subtly by other authors and givers of advice. The late nineteenth-century "complexion specialist" Mrs. Anna Rupert defines beauty as "the union in woman of a pure complexion, firm flesh, mental delicacy, and refinement of bodily grace" (n.p.). The time and the effort that might be put into achieving these desired effects could certainly bring about stunning results, but the body, as a fluctuating system, cannot always be maintained to cultural mandate, regardless of the time and energy that one might invest in its upkeep. The fine complexion needs cleansing and toning and masquing and moisturizing, but even then the occasional (or even constant) eruption might occur. Firm flesh demands exercise, such as Gent proposes, but also will defy such conformity through age or because of certain genetic makeups (or, alas, upon the demands of gravity). Mental delicacy is easily within reach, one can suppose, of those women who spend a majority of their time pursuing those first two requirements, as is the grace necessary to balance out the effort expended on the hockey field or while riding a bicycle. Rupert continues, "If beauty were not a pleasure to God he would not have given it to woman" (n.p.), but if beauty is the result of divine gift-giving, then why must it take so much effort to maintain? Of course, Rupert here simply imposes upon the body's order the same identification of order with morality as found in housekeeping manuals: if beauty is God-given, then to let your own waste away is a sin as much as sloth, lust, or gluttony might be, though perhaps not quite as deadly. To become slatternly is to defy accepted standards of morality, and to wear such a disgrace upon one's person is even more transgressive than the disgrace of household dirt, which can be shut up behind doors and drawn blinds, a maneuver detailed in Lorna Sage's memoir. As beauty maven Helena Rubenstein echoes in 1965, "personal daintiness is premised on absolute cleanliness—even more, on absolute cleanliness other people can recognize" (258).

According to moral codes that also serve as measures for standards of cleanliness and appearance, going against the grain of accepted beauty standards is a sign of relaxed attitudes and careless habits. Unwashed hair or unkempt flesh—like household dirt—is matter out of place and as such initiates social responses to taboos of defilement, impurity, dirt. Rupert's invocation of high religion is an obvious example of connecting bodily maintenance with the function of a social order shot through with principles of Christianity. It is unlikely that many contemporary examples would contain such rhetoric, though secular zealotry for bodily maintenance is definitely still in fashion. Even a cursory look through works one hundred years beyond Rupert's 1892 pamphlet, however, will unearth attitudes that can produce similar responses. In 1965: "slimming is no sinecure. It is indeed something that calls for determination and considerable self-denial" (Cleland 8). The asceticism of the Christian faith is handed down in this advice for care of the body, and the shame, guilt, and ultimate confession (whether verbally or nonverbally, through the act of compliance) at the heart of normalization and cultural policing are reflexive activities in the world of beauty and of bodily maintenance. Kay Cooke remarks later in the century on such religious hyperbole:

"Strangling a few people is a sin. Invading East Timor is a sin. [...] I'm sorry, but eating doesn't quite make the grade" (23). By underscoring the sinful, criminal natures of going against a system that dictates the proportions of one's figure, however, these volumes create responses from readers that ensure the stability of that system. Even as some manuals begin to engender techniques for obtaining beauty based upon the non-Western religions that have become a part of our contemporary culture, the idea of the body replicating an inner, spiritual purity is evinced: "Set simple endurance tasks for yourself occasionally [...] Eat small, austere meals. [...] Take cold showers. [...] In this way, the spirit becomes taut, toned, tuned into the essential" (Leigh 23). Michelle Leigh's "'Zen beauty'" (14) sounds far too much as if it stems from the sanctuary of a convent than from some revelation of female empowerment via beauty regimen. Firm rules for the body's appearance and performance are necessary accompaniments to the regulations that order the broad social scheme, and greater comprehension of that bigger picture can be reached if it is seen as "writ small" upon the body, even within the smallest rituals of bodily maintenance.

The ways in which women have turned body maintenance into a religion of its own is more than evident in the countless tracts, periodicals, and how-to books that have confused and embittered woman for more than a century. This sort of social codification of women's bodies as representative of the finely tuned socius is rampant within women's popular culture throughout the twentieth century, and such messages continue to infuse current cultural rhetoric. Keeping the body firm and firmly in its place has become a critical, perhaps even a defining, component of being female in Western culture, even when these prescriptions are contradictory and hardly scientific. "Isobel"'s *The Art of Beauty* recommended a "slender, well-proportioned figure" in 1899 (32), and supplied additional cultural information as regards exact standards for female bodies. Though the quest to be trim is thought of almost always in terms of weight reduction (and, indeed, the number of pages in most publications devoted to that issue far exceeds those that address the underweight), "Isobel" cautions readers to avoid looking "'scraggy'" (39). This keeper of beauty secrets understands that "if, on reaching maturity, the figure still remains thin and undeveloped, it is natural enough that the woman should sigh for more ample proportions, and seek to use every legitimate means to ensure them" (39). This is no small undertaking, but resembles the sort of rhetoric that entices young men to join up and defend their country.

The use of "every legitimate means" is a battle cry, and the underdeveloped as well as the overdeveloped reader has been called upon to do everything she can in order to bring her proportions into an accepted range that remained narrow and difficult to achieve during the entire twentieth century. The underweight addressed here, though, are not falling behind a prescribed figure that is truly ample; the suggested weight provided for the woman who is five feet, six inches tall is 10 st. 1 lb. (141 pounds)[2]—a prescription that is hardly different from that which women would be handed one hundred years later. The standards have little to do

---

[2]   One stone is equivalent to fourteen pounds.

with actual health standards or with attractive qualities of beauty, but increasingly add to the regimentation of the private sphere on the individual level. Excess flesh, like dirt, like an unkempt appearance (and the sexual and moral transgressions that such things signify), is matter out of place, and as an element that transgresses the accepted boundaries of the system, the flesh is something that must be normalized if the system is to be maintained.

During the mid-twentieth century, writers such as Ursula Bloom controlled much of the discourse of beauty and body maintenance. Bloom was not only the beauty editor of the popular periodical *Woman's Own* for many years, with weekly columns running alongside ads for products such as Marmola Antifat Tablets ("It is folly to stay fat in these scientific times"), but she also authored countless books (how-to guides, romance novels, and histories under six separate *noms de plume*) that provided women with assistance for reaching desired cultural standards for the body and its appearance. "I put it on if I'm not darned careful," she empathizes, "and being a beauty editor I'm not allowed to waddle about like a tub. [...] I look yearningly after fried potatoes, and nice creamed cakes. But that's all part of the game" (*Me* 8). According to Bloom, "Perseverance is the latch-key to all true beauty" (*Wartime* 16), and with the various and often conflicting methods prescribed and treatments available at that time, perseverance, for the body as well as for the home, would certainly be necessary if one were to even come close to the ideal.

Though Kim Chernin hypothesized in the later twentieth century that "there is something precarious to this well-being" (29), the idea of feeling positive about oneself and one's surroundings has long been grounded in the idea of the perfected physical specimen. Such a specimen, though, is not necessarily derived from physical health, as Muriel Cox, in a manual published by *Good Housekeeping*, cautions against swimming to slim: "it tends to bulging muscles, which are no more attractive in a woman than bulging fat" (68). The ideal at midcentury is streamlined, the sort of figure that might fit effortlessly into the straight-skirted styles made necessary by the lack of available, affordable fabric during World War II and by the clothing promoted by the British government's wartime Utility Scheme. "The fat woman, more particularly now-a-days, is conspicuous, is worried about her condition and does not feel well," writes Bloom in 1941 (*Housewife's* 72), for whom the ideal weight of a woman five feet, six inches tall is 9 st. 9 lb. (138), just two pounds less than the ideal advocated in 1899. The physical component of a female "self" by this time has, in the eyes of the fashion-hawkers and beauty experts, become little more than an inert object that should capitulate to the will of the intellect, to its "willpower," and this attitude in turn is one that is easily internalized by a woman who learns through these dicta to view her own physicality as something merely to be maintained rather than as an integral component of her subjectivity.

Jill Adam, a contemporary of Bloom whose *Beauty Box: A Book for Women about Bodies, Faces, Make-Up, Let-Downs* was published in 1940, provides similar and even more paradoxical advice for her readers. She begins her book by lamenting the fact that "modern insistence on the desirability of the boyish figure has made women think that a natural, correctly proportioned feminine figure [...] needs slimming" (11). Her statistics for ideal proportions, however, are actually less than Bloom's; though she provides a range for weight rather than a single number, her 5'6" woman should weigh between 129 and 135 pounds, with the ideal weight given at 132 (13). The middle ground, by midcentury, is quite the narrow path. Adam, like Bloom and others, guides women toward a standard that continues to lose its feasibility because of its shrinking, limited range of acceptable standards. Cox suggests that "if you are more than six pounds over, or seven pounds under, your prescribed average, you should get to work" (61), which allows for very little leeway, and which prescribes a goal most unlikely for a majority of women.

While Cox does take into consideration some of the "subversive" bodily factors mentioned previously, such as age and genetic tendencies, she does so in a very limited and unsympathetic way. She assures some readers that she understands how this weight schedule is rather out of reach for some: "don't take it too terribly to heart, especially if you are the 'fine girl' type and Nature gave you a framework of good, solid bones to carry you through life" (61). Her words, however, lack a certain depth of feeling, and even the "fine girl" is left to feel remiss for not fitting into Cox's thirteen-pound range of acceptability. As for age, Cox takes into account that one will weigh more as one gets older, but lacks a real sense of knowledge about the factors involved in aging. At age twenty, her ideal weight is 9 st. 6 lb. for those standing 5'6"; at age thirty, this increases to 9 st. 12 lb. (61). Cox gives no weight suggestions for those over thirty, but Adam provides advice where Cox leaves off. "At forty and over which would you rather be?" she prods; "Fat, untidy, flabby, or angular, hatchet-faced, nervous? Answer is, why be either?" (77). The goal for a lifetime, then, is to avoid any standard but those that lie between these two sets of obviously undesirable qualities, which for a woman of average height seem to be found at above 135 and below 129 pounds, respectively. Though women should not desire excess in much of anything, especially of flesh, "there is a point where slenderness becomes plain skinniness, and good bones become sharp slates" (Rubenstein 185). Norms for female embodiment are rigidly regulated and, over the course of the twentieth century, remain relatively finite. By perpetuating customs that help to standardize both the form and the functions of the female body, this aspect of women's culture has worked (and continues to work) hand in hand with other strategies of social conditioning.

Though these prescriptions for female proportions are individually quite specific, many of the books available directly contradict each other. The images of women found within popular culture during this period also tend to differ from the bodies that would meet the height/weight ratios found within these charts, creating an even more maddening schism between real women's bodies and their ideas— gleaned from visual and written discourses—of what those bodies should look like. Weights given are not extremely varied, but change from year to year, from publication to publication, and were not always at all relevant to the bodies of actual women. Rachel Swift remarks that MetLife insurance charts, when first published in 1959, were based upon a study of policyholders, 90% of whom were male (63). Vascillating and questionable statistics did little but maintain a level of confusion and anxiety in women seeking to meet a norm that might change at any time. The 9 st. 9 lb. mentioned above is from Bloom's 1941 *The Housewife's Beauty*

Book; in 1943's *Wartime Beauty*, the ideal for a woman of the same height is listed as 9 st. 10 lb. (14). In *Me—After the War: A Book for Girls Considering the Future* (1944), Bloom again lists ideal weights for women, but this time suggests that one should (at 5'6") weigh 9 st. 8 lb. The discrepancies here are minor and likely are a result of shifting numbers released each year in government or insurance charts.[3] Bloom's weight prescriptions are telling, however, in their obvious arbitrariness and their reliance not upon a single, sustainable ideal nor even upon a real, lived ideal, but upon one that was handed down from some other, likely "official" source and disseminated via mass media to countless women across regions and class strata. The mandates of public-sector interests are heavily invested in by those within the private sector and ultimately are the foundation of private doctrine. The fact that in these volumes women are complicit with the system and its strategies for body maintenance only adds to the problematics of such a cult of femininity. Rhetoric of the beauty culture begins with the medical or political authority of masculine spheres, and in turn that authority becomes Bloom's or the domain of anyone who can properly adopt the tone and emphasis of public discourses. The result of feminizing the system's most overt apparatuses is the same type of control and regimentation found within the areas defined by science, law, and other public measures of standardization, making the private (female) body as subject to the regimentation of masculine discourse and patriarchal values as any other aspect of cultural production is.

These standards for female bodies do vary in a relatively arbitrary manner; however, they do not vary much. In fact, from the turn of the twentieth century and through the 1940s, published standards for weight changed very little, regardless of popular notions that idealize the early part of the century as a time when women were free from the stringent guidelines for contemporary bodies. From "Isobel"'s 1899 prescription of 10 st. 1 lb. to Cox's low-end 9 st. 6 lb. for the twenty-year-old woman of 1946, the standard deviates by only nine pounds. The dynamic body is reduced to a series of mathematical calculations, none of which might be appropriate for a given body. All of these regulative processes, however, encourage women to continuously evaluate themselves accordingly and to devote time and attention to their attempts to reach unrealistic ideals. Subject to the devices of the beauty culture, women are encouraged to further the mind/body duality that is always already present in Western culture; when the body is thus an object that is meant to be appropriately molded to fit the shape of a given culture, the "self" must deny its materiality in lieu of its plasticity.

While published standards for women's weight and body proportions changed little through the first half of the twentieth century (and really did not change all that

---

[3] A factor that further confounds the contradictory height and weight charts is the information in charts that prescribe caloric intake for women. The "Cover Girl" chart published in 1941 by a London Health and Beauty Bureau suggests a daily intake of 2800 calories for women engaged in the "light" work of six to eight hours of housework, and notes that the League of Nations recommended 2400 calories per day for the sedentary woman. Experience would likely be enough to create some doubt in most women that such intake could ever result in the body weights listed in the charts found in beauty books.

much during the second half), popular representations of the female form varied wildly from era to era. The late-Victorian and Edwardian ideal, when represented visually and not by charts of weights and measures, is fairly full figured (and presents a shape much enhanced by boning and lacing), as is one popular cinematic image of woman from midcentury, exemplified by British film stars such as Diana Dors and by images imported from Hollywood (Jane Russell, Marilyn Monroe). The 1920s, though, offered the leaner image of the flapper, a look again popularized during the 1960s, when very thin fashion models were touted by Sloane Square as one ideal for British women. This variance in visual prescriptions for female beauty only adds to the efficacy of a regimentation of the private sphere, of the body, as limitations for individual behavior narrowed and as rules for navigating societal expectations grew more rigid. There has often been a discrepancy between the published and the visual versions of the ideal, and this only increases the difficulty of most attempts to attain perfection. When readers of a periodical or those viewing a film are confronted not only with bodies that differ from their own with regard to size, but also with bodies that differ from the ideal weights listed in countless popular media, which version of the "ideal" woman should they trust as correct? The shifting context for female perfection only ensures that a woman will remain perplexed as to whom she should trust on matters of the female form, even when that person is herself. An auto-objectified subject will find it difficult to see these prescriptions critically, analytically, since these are foundational messages about the hierarchy that is central to the mind/body problem.

The existence of such a gap between these two versions of woman also increases the amount of effort expended in the pursuit of conformative perfection. For example, during the 1970s and 1980s published standards often suggested a standard for female weight that allowed for five pounds—to be added to a baseline of one hundred pounds—for every inch in height above five feet (the 5'6" woman, then, would be ideal at 130 pounds—9 st. 4 lb.—under such a prescription). At the same time, though, the average woman found on the cover of a glossy fashion magazine reached over 5'10" tall and weighed between 120 and 130 pounds. That visual standard has changed in more recent years to an even slimmer, often drastically unhealthy image (e.g., "heroin chic"), and yet in one contemporary article from *Woman's Own*, Lisa Pender happily reports, "I'm now down to 10st 4lbs and a size twelve, which is just perfect for me at 5ft 6in" (Hart 13).[4] Pender's image, though close to the range of published standards acceptable for much of the

---

[4]   For Pender and her millennial figure, weight training is an important part of her body maintenance. A major slant of this *Woman's Own* article is the fact that Lisa's husband is a personal trainer, and that she felt, when "a size 18 and rising," as if when she "was introduced as Tim's wife [she] could see the shock on people's faces. They clearly expected a Pamela Anderson clone" (Hart 12). The fact that her muscle mass will certainly push her beyond the limits of most weight charts, but will still be foundational to her contentment with her body size, is an issue rarely included in the rhetoric of women's body maintenance until recently, and charts for ideal weight still belie the fact that muscle toning will create a wider spectrum of height-to-weight proportions than would be taken into account if no muscle mass were added to the frame.

twentieth century, is far removed from the image of a rail-thin Victoria Beckham, found a few pages later in a pictorial on breast augmentation.[5] Which standard should readers trust? When the majority of fashion layouts rely upon what Kay Cooke mocks as "professionally-lit, re-touched photos of a size-8, six-foot-tall, 13-year-old aerobics instructor-model wearing a frilly baby-doll dress, platform thigh-boots and a terminally bored expression" (ix), and nearly half of all British women are a size sixteen or above (Cooke 9), a true problem ensues that extends itself dangerously into the realms of women's lived experiences. The number of women of all ages who are affected by anorexia, bulimia, and other eating disorders indicates that the desirable figure is more Posh than Lisa, but either way, the body is explained and understood as a thing to be changed, manipulated, controlled rather than allowed to represent the varying modes of embodiment that actually exist for women. The multiple hyphens in Cooke's ironic description of ideal feminine beauty represents on a grammatical level the very divisions and ambivalent reconstructions of female subjects who are at once granted more social power now than ever but simultaneously encouraged to maintain an ever-present vigil over their auto-objectified bodies. The confusion that results from the differing ideals presented within popular culture only multiplies the ways in which one must engage with the information. Because of the very confusion upon which standards for appropriate physical femininity are founded, these ideals encourage a certain level of conscious thought. The dichotomies actually engage readers as they attempt to sort through them rather than drive them away, leaving them with an impulse to standardize but with no clear set of standards to aim toward, a result of the strategies deployed by a system of maintenance upon women's bodies.

The gaps in this cultural logic also point to an issue that lies at the heart of the problem of mind/body duality. The problem is that a simple either/or understanding of these terms limits their meaning and ultimately ignores the variety of combinations that lie along the spectrum that runs from one term to the other. Because there is no true form that is ideal for the human body, its maintenance is an arbitrary language that cannot necessarily be deciphered across boundaries of time, space, class, race, or other markers of cultural identity. Even when a subject becomes auto-objectified and views her flesh as no part of herself, that body will defy a particular standard because it is a naturally fluctuating entity and, importantly, because it is always already a part of one's being. The body is as much a part of the "self" as is the rational mind that has been privileged for centuries. The data above shows the lengths to which women have been instructed to go to as they attempt to defy this reality. Also, in its radical inadequacy to truly explain the body, this maintenance literature actually expresses the futility of attempting to do so. Close examination of language that seeks to divide the attributes of subjectivity can often illuminate the shortcomings of such constructions. In this way,

---

[5]   Of course, the paradox of the simultaneously desirable small frame and large breasts only adds to the conundrum of bodily maintenance and adds cosmetic surgery to the already troublesome lists of diets, etc., that women use to control their bodies and bodily proportions.

the cultural artifacts examined in this chapter mirror the fictional literature that is examined in later chapters: regardless of the ways in which most of us have been trained to ignore the interconnectedness of mind and body, the ways in which the two are innately commingled often surface, even when there is no conscious effort to bring these ideas into ready light. The very nature of human subjectivity defies the language with which we attempt to define and describe it.

The Role of Consumption in the Regimentation of the Body

Because by nature it will defy such normalization, the human body is a site of potential unrest even as it is hypothetically representative of a social order. Even as regimentation tightens up, and even as rhetorics of bodily maintenance evolve to maintain currency across decades, there is never a point in time when the body—when anyone's body—can be counted on to find its own level of normative stasis. When there is the potential for resistance to the order demanded by cultural ideologies, efforts to bring the social agent out of its margins and back into the center of the social order will increase. As women began in greater numbers to move beyond domestic roles (whether as mistresses or as maids) during the later nineteenth century, the discourse of private maintenance, as I have chronicled, shifted from an emphasis upon domestic issues to one that elaborated this more personal maintenance of the body and, importantly, how that body might appropriately travel through public domains. As with the prescriptions for female bodies and their sizes and their shapes, the role of food consumption and of attempts to maintain the social agent through controlling her eating, is rarely absent from the maintenance literature of the late nineteenth century and increasingly is accentuated in the beauty and self-care texts of the twentieth. Not only are the effects of eating scrutinized (weight, proportions), but the ways in which women consume, especially within the public sphere, are subject to this narrow range of acceptable female behavior. Eating is not only standardized methodologically, but also with regard to quantity and to frequency. More typically investigated texts, such as etiquette or conduct manuals for women, certainly provided women with a set of rules for dining decorum, but their audience was predominantly limited to women from families with economic and/or social status. Nancy Armstrong explains that during the rise of the middle class in England, such material "set the standards for polite demeanor to which the prosperous merchant's wife or the daughter of a gentry family was supposed to aspire" (4). As class lines blurred during the period of the early twentieth century, when World War I and the advent of a strong Labour government initiated a destabilization of Britain's caste system, not only did conduct manuals begin to reach a wider audience than they had previously sought, but they also shifted from a discourse of manners to one that more firmly emphasized standardized behaviors, including food consumption, as a way to bring marginalized bodies to the center of normativity.

A 1928 offering, *Etiquette for Women: A Book of Modern Manners and Customs*, illustrates the ways in which expectations for women are not founded upon *how* one eats, but *how much*: "If everyone else has finished their course, and you are half-way through yours, it is much more polite to [...] let it be cleared away, than to keep others waiting while you finish" (Davison 66). The directive here advocates a denial both of food and of hunger that flourishes in later works, particularly in the genre of the beauty manual. Other directives seem to aim toward a correct manner of eating, but reveal a move toward limiting the amount of food a woman should eat, the better to maintain not necessarily her physique, but her conformity to social prescription.[6] For instance, the advice to "tilt your [soup] plate slightly, if you need to, but always *away* from you: don't try to scoop up the very last drop" (62–3) allows for a slight breach of high etiquette, which would suggest that the plate not be tipped at all. Instead, the amount of food to be eaten is the issue at hand. Similarly, the warning for dining on small game birds does not emphasize the method, but the outcome, the amount to be eaten: "you are expected to cut the meat only from the breast and the wings [...] even though this be but a mouthful. It is not correct to [...] try to get all the meat from the bones" (63–4). Eating in these discursive contexts is no longer an act of nourishment or part of a healthy regimen, but rather is solely a social act that evokes the connection between the social subject and the socius. By limiting the quantity and the potential quality of one's eating experiences, standards such as these work to limit the interpretive, subjective potential of food consumption, an aspect that I discuss below. A less prescriptive view of consumption would benefit the subjective consumer rather than society's stringent codes of manners and moderation.

The beauty manual, of course, differs from the conduct manual with regard to the rationale presented for personal and bodily maintenance, but when it comes to food consumption, the two genres are quite similar in their advice and their proposed results. The beauty manual does differ from the guide to etiquette, however, in that eating in this context is not simply a social act in and of itself, but is recognized more as something to be controlled in order to ensure proper proportions of the body. One beauty manual reminds readers that "everyone likes what is called a 'trim figure'" (*Beauty* 7), suggesting not necessarily that everyone desires to be trim themselves, but that the trim figure is the standard "liked" by "everyone." In order to be accepted, one should be trim, should conform to the very center of the range of physical appearance. This manual discusses eating in a way that utilizes the health-related rhetoric discussed earlier, but in ways that dictate the mode of consumption, as well as the effects of standardized behavior: "Eat plain, nutritious food, partaking very sparingly of highly-seasoned, savoury dishes, and rich pastry [...]. Eat abundantly of fresh, ripe fruit. There is nothing like it for purifying the blood and, as a result, the complexion" (7). To advocate for a healthy diet is far from a crime (and actually, the emphasis on fresh fruit is rather ahead of its time), but the directive to eat only plain food is one that certainly

---

[6]   Female alcohol consumption is referred to, as well as that of food. The following admonition is found in the 1902 manual: "Young ladies should not indulge in a variety of wines, nor in much wine. [...] do not empty the glass in one gulp—it is vulgar to do so [...]" (45).

undercuts any effects of a mode of consumption that might result from individual choice or agency. This admonition, too, is a part of the historical connection of women's sexuality to the types of food that they consume. Helena Michie has noted, "Sex manuals consistently equate food, especially certain types of food, and lust" (15). She points to late-nineteenth-century cultural literatures that prohibit the consumption of spices and of highly acidic foods because appetites for such edibles are in direct opposition to cultural norms: "Delicate appetites are linked not only with femininity, but with virginity" (16). The state of the female body *as signified by what the female body consumes* is a direct conduit to how the public can view her moral purity, just as with the application of moral codes found in attitudes toward cleanliness and hygiene. Through these equations, female agency is monitored and controlled alongside female sexuality, which is linked to consumption. Agency, though, is directly responsible for consumption and is literally the result of consumption: we cannot act if we do not eat. Under the guise of a succinct moral code for female sexuality, one that produces the effect of a "clean and proper" middle-class female body (Kristeva 102), a larger project of limiting female agency and subjectivity unfolds.

Like the proper household that cannot afford to signify excess or deviance from the moderate norm, bodies—for the purposes of this argument and within the already established context, female bodies—occupy a similarly rigid position when it comes to rules for eating, as well as for other forms of consumption. As a way to maintain and to survey an individual's position within the moral and cultural structures of society, these rules have moved from slightly fanciful directives to the upper classes and growing bourgeoisie toward a more and more insidious and everyday regulatory function across class boundaries. Like the middle-class ideal of moderation, characterized within the home by "'a good and plentiful table, but not [one] covered with incitements to gluttony'" (*Household Management* 7),[7] the body in its ideal is one that is neither too thick nor too thin and that draws little attention to itself through transgressions of the drawn outline of social inscription. The properly maintained body—in all actuality an impossible entity—would be the ideal Foucauldian "docile body," one that "may be subjected, used, transformed and improved" (*Discipline* 136) at the discretion of the system. Such a body is subject to the system and its structures, and is also the agent *of* those structures: the truly docile body lacks an integral or organic sense of agency apart from that required of it by the system. "Agency," suggests Molly Travis, "as defined in terms of individual performance, is not an intention but an *effect* that is always read in a social milieu" (6), and certainly any act perpetuated by a social entity must be interpreted within the context of a social system. I propose, however, an agency that lies beyond the system as well as inside it, that is, if not presocial, then perhaps contrasocial or, better, intrasocial. This agency is one that can initiate from the social mechanism but also from a mechanism that does not

---

[7]   *Household Management* quotes liberally on the subject of middle-class moderation from W. H. Grey, *A Few Words to the Wealthy on Household Accounts.*

always concede to the social: the well-maintained body whose biology (genetic, metabolic, endocrinal) subverts attempts to conform to social prescriptions for size or appearance, or whose agent-effect exceeds the limitations of social constraints of a given milieu. The body is not simply a vehicle through which a socially constructed subject performs the rituals of the dominant culture; it is not simply a vehicle used to enact willful subjective expression. As with all binaries that are cast as mutually exclusive but that are actually results of syntheses, the body is a part of an integrated system within and beside other systems, and without the body's role in the equation of agency, the subject would indeed be a docile being. Systems of maintenance that encompass physical, intellectual, moral, and other realms would not be necessary were the subject simply a nexus of social effects, because if it were, then the construct would maintain itself. On some level, the subject defies attempts at regulation in ways that go beyond reactions to that regulation, and thus the subjective apparatus requires forces of social normalization if the individual subject is to be maintained within proper boundaries. On the biological, corporeal level lie components of subjectivity that defy the social system and its regulatory measures and that work in tandem with the intellect to negotiate the will to conform that infuses everyday existence.

In the chapters that follow, I examine how literary representations of various forms of embodiment and "disembodiment" contain elements of this type of resistance to cultural formations of women. Each of the authors whose works I investigate tactically invest their writing with issues of food and of food consumption as a way in which to call forth our ideas about the female body and, importantly, to present those ideas in a way that questions the notion that any binary can adequately express the human condition. As the twentieth century waxed onward, the writers included increasingly and in a variety of ways responded to stereotypical conflations of female embodiment with transgression: sexuality, impurity, deviance. Consumption, when the subject of the act is female, will conjure up further images of female bodies, and of those bodies as potentially problematic when placed up against the social systems that must be kept running at a smooth pace if the social order is to proceed as it ought. These bodies are typically bound to the linguistic and cultural ways in which we have come to "know" female corporeality: as a part of a binaried structure, the opposite component of which is a highly prized mind. Although readers will respond to questions of embodiment in the ways that they have been taught to respond, the writers examined have complicated our abilites to reach such simplistic conclusions about female bodies. For embodiment that is conceived of only as a part of a dualism can never explain fully the lived experiences of women whose bodies, even when restricted by countless dietary, fashion-related, and health-based codes for conduct, are on some level resistant to the docility demanded of inert flesh at the mercy of culture. The narrative structures that run through the novels investigated in the following chapters resist—as the bodies within them do—the time-worn tale of psyche versus soma, and instead exhibit ranges of an embodiment that is infused with an "inner self" and with an intangible spirit that must acknowledge its debt to the flesh. The following pages outline how auto-objectified women comprehend on some level how philosophies and popular understandings of female bodies are often worlds away from the actual everyday experiences of those bodies. By foregrounding consumption as a method of characterization and as central to their respective narratives, these writers have invested their works with the body's tactical capacities as they seek ways to express what lies within the spectrum that connects the material and intellectual aspects of the "self," even as these women are bound to the insidious regulatory messages dealt to women in Western culture.

Chapter 2

And the War Taketh Away:
Female Embodiment and Sexual Excess
in the Era of Austerity

From the earliest days of confrontation and long past the final surrender, the Kitchen Front—so named by Lord Woolton, who headed up Britain's Ministry of Food—was one of the government's most important battlefronts during World War II. On the wireless and at the cinema, in countless newspaper and magazine advertisements, and through public cookery demonstrations and nutrition exhibitions, the Ministry attempted to reach all of Britain in order to ensure sound physical health and a secure homeland. Though nearly all who remained in Britain were affected by this program and by the rationing scheme that it helped to promote, British housewives were the target audience of Ministry efforts that merged the realms of public and private. One Ministry pamphlet illustrates the ways in which housewives were "inducted" into the war: "The line of Food Defence runs through all our homes. It is where we must always be on our guard. The watchword is careful housekeeping" (*Wise Housekeeping*). Control of consumption, typically an insidious endeavor, became a public duty of national proportions. "The general effect," the Ministry reported in *How Britain Was Fed in Wartime: Food Control 1939–1945*, "was to help the housewife to cope with wartime problems more confidently than would otherwise have been the case" and to make use of available rations in the face of "added complications: with the blackout, air raids, lack of fuel, and with the different members of the family demanding different meals at all hours of the day and night to fit with their duties in factory, Home Guard and Civil Defence" (50–51). While women were encouraged to serve in some public capacities (such as the Women's Auxiliary Territorial Service, or WATS), the rhetoric begun by the Ministry and propagated within popular culture indicated that women's most effective participation lay in their abilities to control the consumption of British citizenry.

In its quest to bring all of Britain under the umbrella of its food control, the Ministry launched a campaign equal in force to the domestic front already maintained by its housewives against matter out of place. Ina Zweiniger-Bargielowska reports, "Austerity altered culinary traditions and the kitchen front was central to propaganda on the home front. Sustained by a uniform propaganda message, housewives co-operated in the war effort and wartime food policy was generally popular" (*Austerity* 102). Magazines bore "Food Facts" advertisements that not only reinforced ideas such as the importance of the potato ("the splendid crop that saves our ships") to the British diet, but that also occasionally included brief recipes. A Ministry of Food ad in the February 1943 issue of *My Home* promotes "Viennese Fish Cakes": 1/2 pound of boiled, mashed potatoes; 1/2 teaspoonful dried eggs; 1/2 teaspoonful of anchovy essence; one tablespoonful of breadcrumbs; pepper, salt to taste. These are fried "fish" cakes, and the recipe is representative of those promoted during the rationing period. Perhaps the foreign nomenclature was an attempt to provide some added elegance to an otherwise poor relation to the real thing. Another Ministry of Food ad in the February 5, 1943 issue of *Woman's Own* lists "4 parts to the Potato Plan": "1) Serve potatoes for breakfast three days a week; 2) Make your main dish a potato dish one day a week—potato dishes can be delicious and satisfying; 3) Refuse second helpings of other foods until you've had more potatoes; 4) Serve potatoes in other ways than 'plain boiled.'" The January 1943 issue of *My Home* contains a Ministry of Food ad that calls upon British housewives to renew their dedication to the Kitchen Front: "You, and you alone, can take over from the Government, the vital work of keeping your family fit. The Government makes available the essential food. In your hands lies the rest! [...] You have done magnificently during the past three years. Let us keep working together and this year do still better." As the war drew on and food supplies continued to wane, it was necessary to increasingly give Britons, especially female Britons, encouragement to view imposed rationing and scarce supplies as part of a necessary national effort. Though women's periodicals such as *Woman's Own* and *My Home* shrank in size considerably during wartime because of decreases in paper supplies and in manufacturing capacities, they still maintained their prewar publication schedules and were one of the foremost vehicles through which the Ministry of Food reached its target female audience. Food Flashes at the cinema during newsreels, along with BBC radio broadcasts, reached a wider audience of both sexes, but women were still the main, and important, focus of Ministry attentions.

In morning broadcasts, well-known music hall actresses Elsie and Doris Waters (sisters who performed as "Gert and Daisy") helped to popularize food-related issues while speaking as official representatives of Woolton's Kitchen Front. As women who were popular with the working class, too, they were able to speak directly to those around whom a vast amount of Ministry discourse was centered: those whose health and nutrition were already in precarious positions because of the constraints of income and the related limitations of working-class cookery training. Their broadcast on the *Kitchen Front* program of 23 December 1940 pointed women in the right direction through song:

> Girls, girls go to a Cookery Class
> For you don't know all there is to know and it
> helps the time to pass
> If you're worried with your rations and you're
> slightly short of brass
> A shilling a day goes a very long way—if you go to
> a Cookery Class. ("Cookery Demonstrations")

Food-centered broadcasts over BBC airwaves were also aimed at schoolchildren, and the Ministry published *Food and Nutrition*, an official publication written for domestic scientists as well as for housewives until early in 1952, when the Food Advice Division was dissolved. Publications released by Woolton's office enabled news about changes in rations and in points values assigned other goods to be disseminated quickly. Along with Ministries of Agriculture and Supply, the Ministry of Food also printed and distributed numerous pamphlets outlining everything from "National Flour" to "Raising Rabbits for Meat." The Ministry cosponsored a competition that sought out Britain's best housewife in 1941, and chose Mrs. Miriam Branson of Nottinghamshire, aged 35, mother of ten, whose husband brought home £5 a week; Lord Woolton himself handed her the "diploma" (Brent). In order to maintain the support of its important female clientele, the Ministry of Food became its own little propaganda industry and endeavored to keep British citizens (both male and female) as content as possible for the duration of the rationing period.

Although wartime efforts meant for most that the activities of everyday life were foregrounded extensively and that material existence was by necessity prioritized above more ephemeral pursuits, the long-standing conflict of psyche versus soma did not recede during the wartime years. If anything, the division of mind from body, and the issues of control and maintenance, became underlying themes of the discourses that constructed British femininity and citizenship during the war and immediate postwar years. Although this philosophic duality was temporarily rearranged by necessity, it meanwhile became a part of what furthered the efforts to ensure that control and austerity policies remained firmly in place. The Ministry of Food was by no means alone in the effort to recruit British housewives for duty on the Kitchen Front. Ministry rhetoric that governed public opinion regarding the importance to the nation of the rationing scheme was abundant, too, in numerous areas of women's popular culture, from periodicals of the era to countless rationing-inspired cookery books. While control of consumption was no longer simply an issue of social and cultural prescription, its relationship to embodiment and to constructions of femininity continued to be a powerful force within women's wartime experiences, and separation of corporeality from rationality continued to be important to uniform participation in domestic wartime activities. In August of 1945, *My Home* contributor "The Man-Who-Sees" addressed the duality of female experience, what he termed the "worldly and unworldly" aspects of womanhood. The unworldly woman, he mused, "never goes to dances or to the pictures, rarely to parties. [...] does her duties [...] reads religious books, mostly; and poetry. [...] can go into raptures over a sunset or a flower-bell, but not over a new dress or a fine pudding!" (26) Her opposite: "Gay, bright, laughing [...] jostling, mixing, quarreling [...] knows which side of her bread is buttered [...] thoroughly enjoys her food [...] She wants to marry a man with enough money to give her a good time!" (26). This very distinct division among types of women—those who are aligned with the body and those who instead are natives of the intellectual realm—perpetuated in the magazine's advertisements as well as in its domestic agenda, is here approached from a philosophical point of view and by a male writer who assumes a peculiar omniscient authority. The same mind/body duality found prior to the war in maintenance literature once again surfaces here, at the end of the war but hardly at the end of the rationing period, in this Man's column.

Though the Man distinctly defines as oppositional these female archetypes, he also encourages an intertwining of the characteristics claimed for each sort of woman. He suggests that "we can try to *harmonize the two sides*" of ourselves (52), our fleshly selves-of-the-world and our ethereal, unworldly other halves. The unworldly woman, he writes in a phenomenological burst, "thinks that it is vastly more important to live on Beauty than to live on Porridge! But it is her body that mediates much of the beauty of the world" (52), while her worldly sister (whom, he despairs, the unworldly woman often connects "with the devil") must not neglect her "'inner life'" or risk becoming "a vast emptiness, a leaf lying by the roadside in the gutter" (52). His thesis—the transcendence of a mind/body duality that is harmful to "the happiness of a woman, as a woman, a *complete* woman" (52)—however laudable in its attempt at synthesis, is unfortunately undermined by the quite biased rhetoric he injects into his descriptions of womankind. Much like Jill Adam's allusion (discussed in the introductory chapter to this volume) to the woman who is sexual outside of marriage as a rotting tree stump, the Man-Who-Sees depicts the embodied woman without a developed intellect as so much trash, as the *excess* of the world. Status as a "vast emptiness" is quite different from that of one who merely "couldn't go into raptures over the beauty of a sunset if she had never seen a sunset with her bodily eyes" (52), as he says of the unworldly woman who forgets the importance of her physicality. This woman, however, simply needs to remind herself of her sensuality; the worldly woman must expunge her sensuality, and by extension her sexuality, in order to achieve a balance of inner and outer worlds and to avoid becoming a cast-off specimen by the side of the road. The Man on one hand supports a joining together of one ontological duality, but on the other states that in order to do so, the worldly woman should "have a cell to go into now and then, where she can be alone and make her Self" (52). The "Self," obviously, in this case is indeed *not* an entity of combined physical and intellectual qualities, but is instead an interior self that is encouraged to objectify and control her physical "self." Regardless of his explicit premise, the Man-Who-Sees only reinforces through rhetoric a mutual exclusion of mind and body, of intellectual and physical aspects of female experience. If an intellectual Self is still defined as primary within this duality, then the Man's initial descriptions of unworldly and worldly women do not serve merely as extremes to be tempered through adding together the flesh and the spirit, but instead serve as instructional devices. To be unworldly and without delight in matters of the flesh (such as food) is still to have a Self; however, to be worldly and without that inner life creates, by oppositional construction, a psychic void, a being without subjectivity.

Such a division of women via supposed allegiances to either the mind or the body—as represented not only in this *My Home* article, but also in numerous other venues—continued on as the cultural norm for women during the postwar era. With these widely available and popular women's magazines serving as a new form of maintenance manual, their edicts for female behavior became entrenched within the social discourse of a Britain that had conquered on one front, but that still battled to regain and maintain social order in the homeland. Again in 1944 domestic sciences were a part of an Education Act, and curricula for young women were proposed that "were linked by their applicability to the home"; popular fiction emphasized, among other issues, "the suffering caused to her family by a mother who had gone out to work" (Summerfield 61, 62). Along with the domestic agenda of women's culture and the move toward a normalization, once more, of the home as woman's sphere, came a retreat from avenues of female agency that ran concurrently with female sexuality. Embodied agency, "worldly" agency, is not the sanctioned agency of the domesticated, unworldly subject whose sensuality is acceptable only when it enhances her aesthetic sensibilities or her culinary prowess. The woman who "thoroughly enjoys her food" and who prefers Porridge to elements of natural Beauty embodies aspects of a female experience that imply decadence and excess. In this period of rationing and austerity, the excessive, worldly woman stands out as more than simply self-indulgent, especially when compared with representations of female self-denial, which was also heavily emphasized in the discourse of austerity. Women's proper, once-removed relationships to food center around their abilities to prepare it for others, and to "make do" as they create a semblance of a stable Britain. With the Ministry of Food guiding a nation's behavior toward food and toward consumption in general, and with rationing's foundation resting upon a strong sense of nationalism, the woman of excess signifies abhorrence on several fronts: sexual, national, economic, ethical. Hardly a creature of equal portions mental and corporeal, the consuming woman—especially during a time when asceticism is not only a mandate placed upon women by a patriarchal social system, but also a central notion to women's culture as defined by women *en masse*—is a fleshly, threatening entity whose lack of control and whose *inability to be controlled* signal the inherent instability of any postwar normativity attempted by British society.

During wartime, as before, a woman's proper relationship to food rested upon her ability to prepare and to serve that food, to nurture others through food rather than consume it herself and thus remind others of her potentially transgressive flesh. These traditional aspects of femininity were emphasized during the war as a part of the imperative of the Kitchen Front, and they continued to be part of the maintenance literature of postwar British women's culture, especially as rationing persisted well beyond VE Day. The role of women was bound to their ability to maintain domestic norms (or what might pass as normal) for the sake of the nation. Lydia Chatterton's *Win-the-War Cookery*, published on the heels of Ministry organization in November of 1939, prefigures the government agency's own pamphlets and propaganda. Chatterton, who "lived through the Great War [and] learned in home and canteen how to make a little go a long way," calls housewives to arms:

> [...] at home our workers are toiling to produce more food and on the seas our sailors are risking their lives that we may live. So we housewives must show our gratitude and admiration by making a firm resolve that nothing shall be wasted in our households, that, in fact, we should be proud for our sailors to see the emptiness of our rubbish bins. ECONOMY must be our watchword. True economy does not mean going short on food but using every scrap to the very best advantage, cooking it in a way that will make it yield the most nourishment. (1)

Here, at the beginning of a humble cookbook, she encapsulates what the public would hear for years to come from the Ministry of Food. The idea that the feminine role during wartime should include the maintenance of not only her family's physical well-being, but also the health of the nation itself, was not an idea simply perpetuated by the British government. This gendered concept had only lain in wait for the outbreak of war, and was presented in many guises from both public sources and from voices of peers, of women who took up the cause and hoped to bring their sisters along in tow, all the better to ensure the continuance of the country.[1] Cookery books served, during World War II, in the same capacity as those early receipt books and venerated tomes like those by Mrs. Beeton: as texts that provide information affecting the most intimate and basic qualities of human life. As a result of this quality of intimacy, the transmission, like the subject matter, takes on a personal tone. Nicola Humble discusses writers such as Josephine Terry, whose cookery book *Food without Fuss* is "full of zeal" and "positively celebrates the sacrifices the wartime housewife had to make" through "letting them into the secrets of her own great discoveries" (94). Like "the freedom of intimate gossip" that "assumes the importance of [...] relationship" (Spacks 43), or like advice from a confidante, the information provided by cookery books (as well as by the other sorts of maintenance manuals discussed in Chapter 1) is shared knowledge passed from one cook (in these instances, cooks are always assumed to be female) to another. The language of cooking and of maintaining the home during wartime scarcity is built upon shared resources, both literally and figuratively.

One clear implication of the language used in these wartime cookery books is the issue of solidarity. Chatterton is performing a feminine ritual of initiation, a sort of maternal ritual of training others, in this instance training women in those domestic arts that necessarily stem from want. Texts such as hers were a part of wartime women's cultural knowledge and provided knowledge based upon connection among women, what Mary Belenky et al. have termed "connected knowing," an epistemology that "builds on the subjectivists' conviction that the most trustworthy knowledge comes from personal experience rather than the pronouncements of authorities" (112–13). Though Chatterton speaks with authority, to be sure, it is not the authority of a superior, but rather of a woman who has gained experience from which someone else might benefit. Wartime women's popular culture encouraged a sense of community and continuity that strengthened the practices promoted by the Ministry of Food and other government agencies. When prompted by Woolton's publications, women responded as patriots, but when they involved themselves in the collaborative practice of sharing household

---

[1]   For a good investigation of the ways in which cookery literatures of the United States have affected gender construction, see Sherrie A. Inness, *Dinner Roles: American Women and Culinary Culture* (University of Iowa Press, 2001). For an account of the links between wartime domesticity and rationing in the United States, see Amy Bentley, *Eating for Victory: Food Rationing and the Politics of Domesticity* (University of Illinois Press, 1998).

information, they responded to that information as sisters united in battle. When Chatterton explains how to prepare a single kidney "cut in the thinnest possible slices and [...] placed in a hot pot between layers of vegetables," or recounts how "a supper of Jerusalem artichokes boiled, then fried in egg and breadcrumb and served with [...] anchovy sauce, kept everyone guessing what kind of 'fish' they were" (1), she is passing along the elements of a culture not often documented as part of the war effort, but a culture that was, indeed, a large and well-choreographed effort affecting British women from all walks of life.

This sort of cookery—that made necessary by wartime rationing and the culture of austerity created through national denial—is representative of what Michel de Certeau calls "'making do'": tactical responses to the materials at hand, "*ways of using* the constraining order of the place" (30, original italics). Cookery, as a tactic that subverts the rigidity of the governing system, "must constantly manipulate events in order to turn them into 'opportunities'" (xix). To such an end, Certeau extrapolates, "in the supermarket, the housewife confronts heterogeneous and mobile data—what she has in the refrigerator, the tastes, appetites, and moods of her guests, the best buys and their possible combinations with what she already has on hand at home" (xix). Interestingly, Certeau's rhetoric precisely parallels that used by Britain's wartime Ministries, which asked women to "make do and mend" their way through the war, and this tactical premise is almost identical to the culinary admonition found in the frontispiece blurb of the Good Housekeeping Institute's *Fish, Meat, Egg and Cheese Dishes* cookbook (1944):

> [...] difficulties are a challenge; and now, in wartime, the housewife has an opportunity she may never possess again to learn the real art of cooking. For the art of cooking consists not of putting together many sumptuous ingredients in the most expensive possible way. It consists of taking the ingredients at hand and using them with wit and imagination and skill [...] of being alive to suggestions, ready to try out new dishes [...] above all, of being more ready to get up and try something new than to sit back and grumble about the lack of variety. (n.p.)

Like Certeau's suggestion that opportunity lies within the confines of restriction, this cookery book identifies as an opportunity the challenge for housewives that exists within the culture of rationing. Making do, for the wartime British housewife, consisted of putting together sometimes meager, often disparate ingredients in order to provide her family with balanced and varied meals. Rationing, on paper, supplies each individual with the same quantity of food, but the quality of that food and of its preparation is left up to the cook and to the *bricolage* of meal preparation under extreme circumstances. Note, too, how this book asserts that the *proper* way to cook is the very method suggested for austere times. Correct cooking, it implies, is engendered by such a culture; only an ill-equipped chef will allow for a diet of mundanity to invade the lives of her family, regardless of how limited her choices might be.

In the context of this wartime culture, the idea of "making do" lends itself to what amounts to culinary trickery, and cookbooks from across the period exemplify Certeau's notion of everyday tactics as subversive. Turning Jerusalem artichokes into "fish" with a bit of anchovy paste, as Chatterton blithely suggests, is the sort of counterfeiture that stems from a culture that limits the scope of cookery while at the same time demanding variant excellence from those in the kitchen. This tactic, however, surpasses the sanctioned versions of "making do" that the Ministry of Food propagated with such stoic recipes as "Woolton Pie" (carrots, potatoes, and rutabagas, all wrapped in flourless pastry). The multiplicity of "mock" foodstuffs that the cookery books present goes way beyond the rhetoric of Kitchen Front cooking, which prioritizes duty over taste. Such practices are what Certeau discusses as "*la perruque*" (wig), a method of deception by which "order is *tricked* by an art" (26, original italics). The practitioner of *la perruque* "cunningly takes pleasure in finding a way to create gratuitous products whose sole purpose is to signify his own capabilities through his *work* and to confirm his solidarity with other workers or his family" (25), as does the housewife who refuses the lowest common culinary denominator of Ministry-advocated potatoes and carrots, and instead opts to reinvent the ways in which limited supplies of food can be thought. As a way to signify her own ability, as well as her identity as a proper cook and not as one who would allow the challenges of the day to control the quality of her products, the wartime housewife uses artifice as a way to transcend the parameters of the ration book. Of course, not all of her products are particularly transcendent. *Good Housekeeping's 100 Recipes for Unrationed Meat Dishes*, for instance, explains how "*[l]iver, lights* [lungs], and *heart* [...] often sold together as lamb's or pig's fry, sheep's pluck or calf's haslet" can become "Mock Goose," a layered casserole-type dish (32, original italics). "Mock Crab" (Chatterton 7) is about as appealing, and contains little to relate it to the real thing, but instead is sliced tomatoes doctored with a bit of grated cheese and served on toast. The strange combinations that result from such kitchen trickery are not the important aspects of these recipes, however. Instead, what is notable is the refusal of wartime women to admit defeat, to go without duck, without crab, as a matter of course. Life as usual, regardless of the scarcity of raw materials, is a strong message of both state and cultural rhetorics. The role of the housewife includes the maintenance not only of household order, but of normativity, if only its semblance. Zweiniger-Bargielowska notes that women "did most of the queuing, contriving and making do in order to preserve, as much as possible, customary culinary traditions and domestic rituals" ("Housewifery" 154). If the housewife is to rise beyond mere competency and perform her role to its utmost, then she will put to use what Certeau calls the "mobile data" of her grocer's bare shelves and create not only tasty, nourishing, and varied meals for her family from those meager stores, but also an essence of peacetime, an element of Britain's prewar comfort and its postwar potential.

Although the charge contained in many wartime cookery books was to transcend humdrum fare and to "make do" in innovative ways, not all housewives were adept at this form of culinary performance. In particular, middle-class women who before the war were household managers, but not directly involved in the minutiae of housekeeping and cookery, had more to learn than how to turn unrationed meats into something that passed for duck. Many women had for the first time to actually learn to cook at all, and the new wartime restrictions made the most basic lessons difficult to learn. While the Ministry placed a special emphasis upon reaching working-class women in order to ensure a healthier citizenry than had emerged from World War I, middle-class women, too, were in need of assistance. Laura Marshall, the protagonist of Mollie Panter-Downes's 1947 novel *One Fine Day*, provides a literary example of how this phenomenon played out both during and immediately following the war. In the kitchen, Laura moves "with the slowness and slight stiffness of the performing poodle who had learnt the routine too late in life" (62). Without the hired help that had made her prewar existence one of relative ease, Laura must now work from scratch not only to create meals from the scarce supplies available to her, but also to create interesting and substantive dishes for the sake of British normativity. Mrs. Prout, a village woman who helps Laura to maintain her home, assesses her as "a vague one, ever so dreamy, always forgetting to order more salt, letting the fish go bad, letting the precious milk boil over on the stove" (19). Laura Marshall is middle class, raised to entertain guests with food prepared by others, and she is also a child of the mind. Her dreamy qualities are foremost aspects of her characterization; her hands-on work in the material world, in the world of the kitchen, is a necessary detour that does not come naturally. Regardless of her affinity with the psychical side of mind/body duality, the facts of wartime and postwar life force her to come to terms with the dailiness of the physical world.

Prescriptions for feminine behavior guide Laura in her quest to meet the demands of postwar living. Even if her class status and her intellectual makeup are at odds with her new role of housewife, Laura is socially and culturally bound to certain gender criteria that manifest within her kitchen. Her forays into cooking are uncomfortable affairs:

> She began to move pans back and forth off the stove. She used the colander, the grater, wooden spoons of various sizes, and a small army of basins. Her cheeks became flushed. Would the sauce bind? And lo, it bound, while her heart did likewise. But with a hiss, something else had boiled over disastrously, so that the cat, who knew Laura, got up and withdrew in prudent haste. A sad brown smell invaded the cluttered kitchen. (61)

Necessity and duty reinvent Laura, and her daughter, Victoria, raised during wartime scarcity, learns to mimic her mother's valiant attempts to make do in the kitchen: "the dead slab that she would disguise as something or other" (61). During the war, Victoria thinks, "[f]ood was queer, but interesting" (150), and when she takes a turn at food preparation, that "dead slab" could be anything—the culinary practices engendered by austerity efface food's particulars. "'I've put something in the oven,'" she reports; "'It looks like fish'" (170). Her father sees in her "the flushed and triumphant air all women wear when meeting a sudden emergency, as though drawing from it a mysterious source of pleasure" (171). Victoria has incorporated cultural mandates to make do—to make whatever her mother bought at the butcher's into fish for her father's evening meal—and to exhibit proper feminine capabilities.

While the housewife's wartime role mandated a particular use of imagination with regard to the meals she might present to her own family, it also centered on a certain amount of self-denial. Denial has typically been a part of an ultra-feminine construct of woman; however, in the context of austerity and of wartime rationing, that denial is based far more upon on reality than upon an ideal concept of a self-sacrificing female. In Panter-Downes's novel, Laura Marshall exhibits the kinds of self-sacrifice that wartime women's culture propagated: "All those years she had existed on a nursery plane of conversation, domestic gossip over the boiled egg and the Ovaltine" (16). The sparse quantity and infantalizing selection of foodstuffs are highly feminized. Austerity has made Laura a self-professed "greedy woman" (35), but she withdraws from overtly indulgent consumption and feels guilt at accepting cake with her coffee: "the flesh was weak, the flesh craved the filling wad of starchy substance" (32). The gendered nationalism that asked that women not only give of themselves for the good of their households and families, but also for the greater good of the country, is embedded in Laura's approach to her own consumption. As women like Laura were increasingly asked to turn to traditional values and to uphold the cultural and social integrity of Britain, the equity suggested by Woolton's Ministry of Food and its propaganda was at odds, however, with real gender divisions. Though the Kitchen Front effort cast women as incredibly important to the sustenance of a British way of life, those men fighting on literal fronts, both within the country and overseas, emerged as most important. Regardless of marital status, the acceptable role of all adult women during the war period included the care and feeding of Britain's male population.

As the war effort demanded more of women in the workplace and in the day-to-day efforts of wartime, the rhetoric of femininity became increasingly pronounced within traditionally feminine strongholds such as women's magazines. "What a test of affection," gushes one *Woman's Own* writer in the September 14, 1940 issue, "to lay down your sugar ration for your husband-son-boy friend! Yet who wouldn't if it meant he was going to get a really good package from home." Who wouldn't, indeed, lay down her rations for those soldiers who lay down their lives for those at home? When it was commonly understood, though perhaps irrationally, that "the wholesaler [...] has to let the troops have 85% of all the chocolate he has" (MOA TC 67/2/B), the added suggestion from this "insider" source within women's culture that denial is optimum incites its audience to an extreme feminine impulse to caretake through self-sacrifice. Unlike the cookery books, whose intimate rhetoric helped to solidify a community of women battling scarcity, these other sources of wartime "advice" for women reinforce those limited roles typically ascribed to the feminine realm. Advertisements from the same period contain similar, if muted, language of feminine self-denial: "Make up for the rationing of butter and meat by giving your family extra large helpings of this rich, creamy custard pudding—Cremola" (*Woman's Own*, April 27, 1940).

The exclusive emphasis here on the family and the erasure of the female self who prepares the custard is a reminder that the care and feeding of *others* was stipulated as the paramount concern of British women during World War II. The objectified— by self and by others—female subject at this time was often completely effaced in the wake of her role as caretaker for her family and for the welfare of the state via the individual bodies of which she was in charge. While the products of her labor were praised, the woman exerting herself was often forgotten.

When Chatterton suggests, for instance, that it "is possible to live on potatoes and milk alone" (31), it is highly doubtful that she is suggesting this diet be offered up to the entire family. The rest of the family is worthy of Cremola, of sweets, and requires meals of balanced variety and nutrition. *Hard-Time Cookery*, published by the Association of Teachers of Domestic Subjects soon after Chatterton's own cookery book was published, lists a number of food items that "the housewife should try to include for each individual member of her family" on a daily basis. The list is fairly diverse, though precise: "1. 1 pint of milk daily. 2. An orange, *or* half a grape fruit, *or* a tomato, *or* a helping of raw salad daily. The salad should, if possible, include watercress. 3. An ounce of butter or vitaminised margarine daily. 4. Cheese. 5. Eggs *or* some sort of fatty fish, *e.g.* herrings, sardines or canned red salmon. To this list carrots and potatoes would be useful additions, and *some* at least of the bread eaten should be wholemeal, if possible. Not less than 3 pints of water, or beverages made from it, should be drunk daily" (9). "The present situation calls," they write in 1940, "even more insistently than usual, for a sound knowledge of the principles of diet so that meals may be well planned and well balanced, even when some foods are scarce" (3). In contrast to this suggestion, Chatterton's advice has more in common with the popular "bread and butter" diet than with the sorts of meals advocated by professional agencies such as the Association of Teachers of Domestic Subjects and the Ministry of Food. Those balanced meals, however, like the bodies that those meals would nourish, seem to belong more to those within the household than to the household manager herself. Within the atmosphere of self-sacrifice that women were called upon to heed, the female form was rhetorically effaced, even as the female body was still very much a part of women's popular culture of the day. Zweiniger-Bargielowska explains that "the flexibility of female consumption standards served as a buffer in the family economy," as women often allowed for others in the family to consume the woman's own meager rations ("Housewifery" 155).

Such self-denial did not go unnoticed by others in those households, however. In 1940, early on in the rationing period, one man remarked to a Mass Observer, "it'll af[f]ect my wife more than me" (MOA TC 67/2/B), and nine years later, another husband echoed that thought: "Strongly suspect wife of going without a lot of things" (Mass Observation, *Our Daily Bread*). In keeping with these concerns of men that women were not benefiting from the public emphasis on health and nutrition, some women reported how they made do on very little. One woman from Slough wrote to Mass Observation in 1948, "Potatoe [*sic*] ration: 3 lbs. a person a week. Don't think that I ever exceed this for myself alone. I often consume much less" (MOA TC 67/5/D); there is a note of pride in her explanation that is in keeping with the ascetic ideal, though it appears she lives alone and her sacrifice would thus not be for others' direct benefit, but for a national good. This attitude is mirrored by another Mass Observation respondent in 1950, who writes, "I found that a small tin of meat was enough for three days. A smoked haddock was also enough for three meals, useful, as the fresh meat ration was not enough for two days" (MOA TC 67/5/E). Of course, not everyone agreed with these two women; in 1947, a woman remarked on the decrease in potato rations to three pounds, "I don't think it's going to be adequate" (MOA TC 67/5/C). Although the number of people reporting that they were not getting enough food rose from one-fifth of those surveyed in 1941 to two-thirds in 1946 (Mass Observation, *Future Outlooks 1946* 4), and certainly that number includes men as well as women, it may well be that the number early on included those women who were encouraged to send their rations to men overseas and to serve others before they served themselves, and later grew to include a wider cross section of British society.

While women were asked to maintain cheerful and patriotic attitudes in the midst of austerity, and while they were challenged to rise above scarcity and to "make do" daily on the Kitchen Front, they also were persuaded through the arena of popular culture to maintain appearances and demeanors as close to that of "normal" peacetime femininity as possible, all the better to ensure that postwar beauty would be continued fluidly. In *Wartime Beauty*,[2] the ubiquitous Ursula Bloom challenges her readers not to waver in their quest for beauty: "Looking lovely in wartime is not as easy as looking lovely in peacetime, but not one whit less important" (2). An attractive appearance, as well as an attractive attitude, was defined by some areas of women's culture as part of women's wartime effort. The idea was made clear in any number of media that after the war, one must be prepared to return to traditional roles, and that when that time would come, one's appearance would play an important part in Home Front reconstruction. Meanwhile, too, women were encouraged to remain attractive in order to bolster the morale of servicemen and of those men who stayed home to work in factories and in other war efforts within Britain. Bloom's win-the-war rhetoric added to the militaristic flavor of the Ministry of Food's ads and publications, but called women to a battle of a kind different from that waged on the Kitchen Front: "It is our duty to do the best that we can by ourselves. [...] It is your duty to eat your full fat ration because this is necessary to health. It is your duty to get proper exercise [...] If you can do exercises on rising, remember that they [...] will have you ready to face the day in full fighting trim" (2–3). Like prescriptions for physical proportions and for household cleanliness, the more abstract gender-based role for women directly following World War II is one reached only through precarious balance: there is

---

[2]   This title is part of Bantam's "Home Front" series, which includes titles such as *Gardening: How to Use Manures and Fertilizers*. As with the early receipt books discussed in Chapter 2, series such as this one combined the human body and its care with the care and maintenance prescriptions for any number of things.

little room for deviance from the norm suggested in these women's magazines and cookery books, and the same suggestions are echoed in countless voices of women who saw their future within the pages of such texts. Lorna Sage describes "the model family of the 1950s ads: man at work, wife home-making, children (two, one of each) sporty and clean and extrovert" (89), and the postwar era as "the time when married women, having been sent back home en masse, were encouraged in every possible way to stay there—first demobilised and then immobilised" (119). With new council housing like that occupied by Sage's family making possible a "middle-class" lifestyle for a greater percentage of the population than existed prior to the war, more women than ever came under the edicts handed down through women's culture. Even though opportunities for women had been pried open during the war years, cultural as well as personal rhetorics maintained that the best way to live one's (female) life was that way depicted in the adverts and colorful centerfolds of women's periodicals. Women were, for the most part, asked to cook well and with inspiration, to look good, and to retreat to a traditional domesticity as soon as their duty to Britain became one of solely domestic proportions. These prescriptions were not perpetuated by any Ministry, however, but could often be found within the culture of women's programming and women's periodicals, typical modes of information-gathering and components of leisure for women. Mass Observation reports in *The Housewife's Day* (1951) that "relaxation from domestic demands took the form of [...] sitting and reading—books, newspapers, magazines—listening to the wireless, watching TV [...]" (13). "By the 1960s," Penny Summerfield claims, "five out of six women saw at least one magazine per week which urged upon her the virtues of new discoveries such as the delicatessen and the avocado, advised her on furnishing and household gadgetry, and encouraged her to become a home decorator" (61). The ways in which such women often chose to retreat from their domestic duties ironically tied housewives, as well as other women, even more tightly to the mores of the home and to the roles for women strongly encouraged during the postwar era. When they were not actually performing the feats of cooking and cleaning and caretaking, women were often engaged in reading about such activities, and about how to better perform those activities once their too brief leisure time was up.

"She could cook like an angel and looked like one. What more does a girl have to do to get a man?" reads the caption above Steve McNeil's story "She Knew What She Wanted," which ran in the July 6, 1950, issue of *Woman's Own*. Popular fiction appearing in magazines of the postwar era represented women's roles in much the same manner as did the advertisements beside them. In McNeil's story, Sally Hannegan seems at first to want nothing but golf lessons from good-looking pro Jimmy Vernon, but ultimately wins his heart by the proverbial way of his stomach. Under the guise of taking lessons only to impress a spectral near-fiancé, Sally, in the name of thrift (a virtue in this time when British staples such as tea and meat were still rationed), packs enough lunch for two and wins over the "slender young man with intense blue eyes, and hair which, when the sun caught it, looked as blond as overripe wheat" (9). After one meeting, Jimmy recounts the credentials of this "long-legged, slender creature with a pert face [...] blue eyes and hair the color of Turkish coffee": "She can cook, she can sew, she can speak foreign languages, she loves children, and she looks like an angel. [...] She can sail a yacht and play tennis. She can dance, she has a sense of humour, and in her old age she won't run to fat" (9). Though this list is one put into Jimmy's head by Sally herself (with the exception of that last prediction, which is all Jimmy's own), and is a superb list of accomplishments, it is Sally's cooking that wins him over. When she lays out their first "impromptu" luncheon, Jimmy "sipped his coffee. It tasted like ambrosia. [...] The strawberry tart tasted like strawberry tart that Grandmother used to make if she could have made strawberry tart that tasted like the one Sally made. The chocolate fudge melted in Jimmy's mouth, and his heart melted along with the food" (34). By the time Sally remarks, "I am completely without guile, believe me. Lots of women would bring a big lunch out here just to show you that they can cook, but not me" (35), readers have their doubts, but Sally's veiled guile is justified by her superbly proper domestic nature. Her sexuality, though it flares once when she "put one hand on his cheek [and] put up no defence worthy of the name" when Jimmy kisses her (35), is subdued by her appropriate relationship to cookery and, by extension, to domesticity, to marriage, to prescribed roles for British women in that postwar time period. When women's relationships to food fall within proper boundaries, it is less likely that their sexuality will be called into question.

Sally does not entice Jimmy to think thoughts impure; instead, he explains how she "is the only one I ever saw who makes me think of paying a grocery bill and looking at furniture advertisements" (9). Sally's expertise in the kitchen not only wins over the man, but also ensures her continued position as his nurturer and as a woman who fulfills her duty to Britain. A product of the scarcity of war, and a woman who has to make do with what rations might be available to her, Sally fits Bloom's standards of a woman who can also keep up her appearance and attract a mate. Her self-denial is abandoned only as far as it must be in order for her to gain this appropriate companion; any other excess on Sally's part is avoided. Her characterization relies upon the food in her picnic basket: she can create food, she can improvise, she can be thrifty, but she also is the agent *of* the food and not its primary consumer. The food that melts in Jimmy's mouth, thus melting his heart, does not touch Sally's lips from a textual standpoint. The feminine relationship to food, as represented here through the character of Sally, is one removed from its actual consumption. Sally's food contains elements of nationalism, of the feminine, and of the promise of domestic capabilities to come. As a creator of rather than a consumer of food, Sally occupies the role suggested on other pages of *Woman's Own*, as well as in numerous cookery books and other household manuals of the period. With the sugar ration in January of 1950 at the same level as it had been since 1948 (Great Britain, *Ministry of Food Bulletin* 1), and thus a prized commodity, Sally also displays the sacrifice called for early in the war years; she is giving over one of her more precious rations, in the forms of tarts and fudge, to please her man. Through her proper relationship to food, Sally is desexualized, despite her final giving in to Jimmy's kisses. With certain nuptials on her horizon, a few kisses surely fall within the boundaries of sexual propriety.

Postwar women's culture, such as that found within the pages of popular periodicals like *Woman's Own* and *My Home*, was a strong force in the "demobilising" (to use Sage's terminology) of women and in a pointing of female Britons back toward any domesticity they may have been abandoned for the war effort. With a large and diverse female readership, these sorts of periodicals (as well as their counterparts in other print and broadcast media) acted as forums for encouraging women to take on roles they had left behind when called to work in factories and with organizations like the WRNS and WATS. The representations of femininity displayed within their pages made these magazines some of the strongest proponents of the self-denial and domestication expected of postwar British women. Women who displayed that trusty ability to deny their own desires and appetites in the midst of austerity (an austerity that defined not only the availability of foodstuffs, but also the population of young men available as potential mates, their number having been decreased by wartime casualties) epitomized postwar expectations for a majority of British women. From the time food rationing began in early 1940, and throughout a postwar period that saw continued need for that governmental scheme, prescribed femininity included a particular relationship with food: women were to nurture and feed, to do so with thrift and scarcity always in mind, and were encouraged to do without unless it meant that their appearances would suffer. In order to transcend the trappings of her flesh (including her sexuality) and to function in an appropriate context, a woman must, like Sally, "cook like an angel and [look] like one" and must, apparently, consume like one as well. The same standards for women's household and bodily maintenance were in effect after the war as had been prior to it, and if possible, such standards were even more intertwined than they had been before as a result of the effects of rationing and the imperative of self-denial. Cultural texts such as women's periodicals increasingly reached out to a broad audience and thus for more readers combining the realms of the household and the physical body previously addressed in separate publications.

This kind of feminine self-denial and adherence to domestic perfection—or lack thereof—is at the heart of Noel Streatfeild's 1945 novel, *Saplings*, which chronicles the effects of war upon one middle-class British family. Lena Wiltshire, the woman of the household, thrives before the onset of war in a home of her distinct creation: "the last word in sophisticated living [...] . She it was who arranged the meals, and organised the house so that it appeared to run itself" (219). Her approach to homemaking, however, has far more to do with Lena's desire to command attention and affection than it does with any sense of conformity to those standards of household maintenance detailed in women's mass culture. Even as wartime changes made certain household changes necessary, Lena fights a battle to remain "the centre piece of a home," even if the "appalling war situation had swept over her" (127). For Lena, it is more about looking like the woman in the pages of *My Home* than it is about actually following the advice contained within those pages. Her ego identity is founded upon her ability to appear to be a perfect mother and, importantly, a perfect wife, but she does not seem to go the distance required by cultural mandate. Because Lena's mode of household maintenance has always leaned toward the fashionable rather than the practical, wartime shortages become difficult for her to live with. On the eve of war she heads out to secure extra food for her family, a three months' supply of what she claims to be "useful things, biscuits and sardines and things like that" (64), but the groceries come from Fortnum's, and the pragmatics of wartime are set aside as she triumphantly brings home a box of Elva plums with which to treat her children. Her "lack of maternal instinct" means that she "never even pretended the children came first" (21), and the care and feeding of her children are ornamental: she dresses them like playthings and placates her children with chocolates, and in turn they admire her in a way that she seemingly needs. Lena's indulgent nature is in direct conflict with the aesthetics—with the ascetics—of Britain during wartime, and while in any instance her behavior would likely be criticized as unfeminine or anti-maternal, during wartime her approaches to her feminine role are even more ludicrous because of the reality of scarcity that lies behind those actions. Like Mrs. Miniver, who toiled away for the sake of a nation, Lena is supposed to put first the needs of her country and to assess as a close second the needs of her family. For a woman like Lena, though, this endeavor appears to be impossible.

As the novel progresses, and Lena's husband is killed in a London bombing, Lena's inability to bounce back from her loss, to go forward stoically for her children and for Britain, becomes an obvious character flaw. As a coddled married woman, her actions seem silly and cavalier; however, as a widowed mother of four children, Lena is expected to be responsible for her family in a way that she fails to achieve. Her inability to conform to standards of femininity becomes pathological instead of defiant, and the relatively stable world that she might provide for her children crumbles as her penchant for indulgence turns inward and becomes rampant self-indulgence. While the pages of magazines such as *Woman's Own* are filled with images of women who are sending their sweets off to the front and who are existing on root vegetables, Lena dissolves into a vacuum of consumption that signifies cultural anxieties about female embodiment. Lena emerges from this nexus of consumption and sexuality. Early in the novel she is described as passionate, as the epitome of an approach to living that is "almost all body, the merest whiff of soul" (21), and indeed Lena's identification with her very sexualized body seems to be at the heart of her inability to capitulate to social and cultural prescriptions for wartime women. She is "not a family woman," but is "utterly wife" (17), and for her, air raids "produced wild excitement which needed physical expression" (134) in which her husband finds "an aftermath of exhaustion and shame" (135).

The relationship of Lena's sexuality and her consumption—both at the expense of her four "saplings"—becomes starkly evident as the war and her widowhood wear on and as she becomes susceptible both to her hypersexuality and to consumption of alcohol. Without the wartime work that other women of the novel undertake—the family governess becomes a captain in the WATS, and Lena's sister-in-law lectures to the Women's Institute—Lena in grief turns to the bottle, and her fondness for brandy is the beginning of a road that leads her to an affair with a married American and eventually to the intervention of family, who remove her children from her care. The affair with "Uncle Walter" is consummated during their first meeting, and Lena is described as a sexual depth charge in waiting; after dinner they have sex in the drawing room because Lena refuses to wait until her household staff have gone to sleep (204). Without the "temperance" of a proper affinity for feminine prescriptions, Lena is out of control. She becomes a site of overwhelming, undirected female sexuality, and without the intercession of reason or of adherence to the norms defined for women of the period, she loses her place in the social order. The result of her quest for a good time is as devastating to her small world as the Blitz is to London, and Streatfeild's portrayal of Lena as a woman who is destroyed because she cannot seem to help herself resonates with the mandates for women found in all areas of wartime popular culture.

Though an idea rampant throughout this and other periods, this notion of sexualized woman—fashioned from excess, extraneous, according to The Man-Who-Sees "a leaf lying by the roadside in the gutter"—is hardly without its avid detractors. Examples from this era of women who are represented as composites of physical and intellectual elements exist, and such examples work to problematize the notion of women as divided between these two realms, as well as the notion that women should fill a single social role. Examples from various aspects of women's and other cultures, even when not created as perfect balances of mind and body, indicate ways in which traditional methods used to delineate groups of women did not always suit, and were not always accepted by women themselves. One strong literary example of this postwar destabilization of mind/body duality can be found in Barbara Pym's 1953 novel *Jane and Prudence*. This novel emphasizes both the concept of the threatening female consumer and the ways in which such a simplistic characterization falls short of representing the complicated nature of a modern female subject. Though on one level Pym's narrative conventions seem obtuse and appear to cast her protagonists in traditionally binaried roles, closer analysis exposes characterizations that problematize the use of consumption as a trope for female transgression and sexuality, and that point to the ways in which women, once the war had shifted their social and cultural use value, could not be so easily fit into singular molds. In this novel Pym manipulates the rhetoric and imagery of women's culture, especially of women's periodicals (such as the oft-mentioned *Vogue*), in order to play upon their conventional wisdoms for postwar women, resulting in a narrative that is at once familiar but simultaneously out of synch with mass culture's glib depictions of women. In this novel Pym builds upon her characterization of Mildred Lathbury, of *Excellent Women*, whose properly (sexless) feminine life of "clergymen and jumble sales and church services and good works" (238) nevertheless deviates from cultural norms for women in its ambivalence toward those roles, even as she assumes that she desires the domestic life that mass culture offers as the norm. Written between 1950 and

1952 (Pym, *Private Eye* 337), when Britons were weary of the rationing scheme that they had by then endured for years, the narrative of *Jane and Prudence* is grounded in Pym's use of food and of consumption as modes of characterization, and this emphasis magnifies these cultural tropes, creating caricatures of Jane (the intellectualized vicar's wife) and Prudence (the worldly, single career woman). Beneath these overdrawn personae, however, lie representations of women who fit no specific roles and who defy the postwar cultural and social ideologies that attempted to narrowly define actual British women. As Deborah Donato points out, "If Pym has a 'point,' thematic or otherwise, to make by the grouping of Jane and Prudence, it emerges from the tensions that are brought to bear upon them, not by the one on the other or by men on both, but by the hurtful expectations [...] invoked by [...] romantic fictions and stereotypes" (94). Pym's playfulness illuminates the reflexive ways in which readers can be quick to assign meaning to items that ultimately defy categorization.

One initial assessment of Prudence Bates comes from Jane, a woman some years her senior who was her Oxford tutor a decade prior to the novel's initial scene. In Jane's eyes, Prudence is "like somebody in a women's magazine, carefully 'groomed,' and wearing a red dress that sets off her pale skin and dark hair" (9). Jessie Morrow (eventually Prudence's rival for the affections of widower Fabian Driver), too, imagines Prudence as someone straight from the pages of a women's periodical: "swinging her sun-glasses in her hand, like a picture in *Vogue*," with "crimson toe-nails that peeped out through the straps of her sandals" (169). This objectification of Prudence by women in the novel not only defines her as a part of the culture of women's periodicals and of their mutual agendas, but also distances Prudence from the ethos of the novel's female community, the other members of which seem much better suited in manners and in appearance to the postwar femininity expected of them. Though *Vogue* signals more haute couture than Mrs. Beeton, the slick imagery and particular prescriptions contained in high-fashion magazines are not dissimilar to those found within more quotidian publications such as *Woman's Own*. Prudence and her jaunty demeanor, her good grooming, is an example of the femininity described by Bloom and others who insisted that women's beauty be considered an important part of national prosperity and security. Associations of Prudence with a magazine such as *Vogue*, though, further distance her from those women who are more associated with the home and with the domestic occupations of cooking and wise economy. *Vogue* typically contains images that cannot be realized by most women; the photography in such a periodical captures clothing and situations that do not enter the lives of the majority. While domestic perfection is itself something that might not be reached completely (as previously outlined in Chapter 1), the setting for that type of perfection is the familiar (to most) model of a single-family household. Fashion spreads made up of impossible-to-own clothing, though, are compounded in their unreality for most readers by the rarefied settings in which they are displayed: a pristine meadow, resort beach, or weekend in the country. Fashions like the "New Look," which exemplified a movement away from the severe apparel of the wartime Utility Scheme and an ostensible surge in the availability of textiles, were for many women difficult to imagine or to achieve. Carolyn Steedman recounts her mother's dismay at not being able to own a garment constructed in this excessive style and notes that "dresses needing twenty yards for a skirt were items as expensive as children" (29). While *My Home* may have suggested domestic principles not necessarily aligned with the average British home of the postwar era, its focus upon domesticity—an encouraged national pastime for women of that era—allowed its contents a certain realism that the pages of *Vogue* cannot be afforded. Prudence is not just "like" a women's magazine: in her *Vogue*-like difference and elegance she allows for an emphasis of the social and cultural chasm between "unworldly" domestic interests and the frivolity and fantasy attached to the world beyond shortages and queues.

Anne M. Wyatt-Brown notes that *Jane and Prudence* contains an "emphasis on the austerity of the postwar economy—both the shortage of meat and the shortage of eligible men" (77–8). The loss of men during World War II adds an interesting emphasis to the place of women in this social system: they are encouraged to return to the domesticity of an earlier period, and yet for many women the war brought about a necessary independence from men, something that Pym had addressed previously in *Excellent Women*. Communities of women, which have strong historical significance, at this time carry more authority than they have during some other eras, and such social importance is evident in Pym's postwar novels. Instead of being included in this cult of femininity that is central to the English parish in which much of the novel is set, Prudence Bates is created as a romantic figure of mythological proportions. The difference that results from her *Vogue*-ish outward appearance is enhanced by the ways in which those around her (primarily other women) shroud Prudence with their own assumptions about her actions and about the significance of those actions, especially with regard to her sexual behavior. Prudence is "twenty-nine, an age that is often rather desperate for a woman who has not yet married" (7), and doesn't quite fit into the milieu suggested by her background and education. Only three women in Prudence's college class at Oxford have not married, and when it is pointed out that "Eleanor has her work at the Ministry, and Mollie the Settlement and her dogs," Jane fills in the gap in this narrative of the unmarrieds: "Prudence has her love affairs [...] for they were surely as much an occupation as anything else" (10).[3] Prudence actually has her own career as an academic editor for Dr. Grampian, an economist, although Deborah Philips and Ian Haywood believe that "she is clearly treading

---

[3]   Younger women, though, are depicted as having quite a different opinion about Prudence's love life. Two of her office colleagues "discussed Miss Bates's passion for Dr. Grampian" and "came to the conclusion that any feeling one might have for such an elderly man [of forty-eight ...] could hardly be counted as a love life" (97). Pym is careful to represent this generational difference and seems to suggest that Prudence's younger co-workers can see beyond the romantic concept that so captivates the older women and into the reality of Prudence's relatively meager social life.

water until marriage" (14). Another vicar's wife remarks that Prudence's career "must be ample compensation for not being married" (10), an opinion that might have come straight from the pages of *Woman's Own*. Likewise, a reviewer in the *Times Literary Supplement* found Prudence "sadly rootless" ("Family Failings"), ostensibly because she moves from one dating relationship to another but never settles down into marriage. Prudence's single status is not yet a popular option for a woman of the postwar era, but is viewed instead as some sad failing on her part to do her duty and either (preferably) marry or pursue a serious career. She is not willing, though, to become resigned "to being marginal in men's lives, a comforting background which men can almost forget" (Baker 49), instead opting to move "lightly from one lover to another, never allowing disappointment to sour or blight her expectation that the next time will be better" (Baker 28). With an attitude typical of the era, all of these views overlook Prudence's public status as a working woman and instead see Prudence's romantic life as primary and her persona as fully grounded in issues of embodiment, of sexuality, if only its promise. The narrative itself builds upon this feminine ideal, and Prudence is often constructed via hyperbolic rhetoric that echoes the contents of women's periodicals.

Prudence (who, like Pym herself, is no stranger to unrequited love) harbors romantic feelings for her employer, Dr. Grampian, and the explanation of how these feelings came into existence rivals the fiction found within more popular venues:

> [...] it had been one of those rare late evenings, when they had been sitting together over a manuscript, that Prudence's love for him, if that's what it was, had suddenly flared up. Perhaps 'flared' was too violent a word, but Prudence thought of it afterwards as having been like that. She remembered herself standing by the window, looking out onto an early spring evening with the sky a rather clear blue just before the darkness came [...] and then suddenly it had come to her *Oh, my love ...* rushing in like that. (37)

Here Prudence herself lends some credence to a romanticization of her character, but she also subverts the notion that she is a figure cut solely from the fantasy world of romance fiction. Her recollection of this moment in the past perfect creates an ironic distance between the actual occurrence and its turn into romantic territory. Her passion had not necessarily flared, but Prudence self-consciously admits (via the third-person narration) to having constructed that passion in such fiery terms, and the intellectual agency that is apparent here thwarts the ostensibly overt casting of Prudence in the role of woman embodied. She goes on to admit that "for want of better material, [she] had built up the negative relationship [...] with the something positive that must surely be there underneath it all" (37–8). When describing her relationship with Grampian to Jane, Prudence remarks, "It isn't so much what there *is* between us as what there *isn't* [...] it's the *negative* relationship that's so hurtful, the complete lack of *rapport* [...]"; Jane replies, "Of course a vicar's wife must have a negative relationship with a good many people, otherwise life would hardly be bearable" (14–15). The two opinions of the worth of such a "negative" relationship point to the humor with which Pym has used the term. Prudence is not necessarily comic, but neither is she meant to be viewed as a tragic heroine in a romance novel. In both passages Pym infuses a sense of irony into her portrayal of Prudence that helps to complicate this characterization.

Prudence is aware of her position with relation to the typical romance plot, and she keeps the reader aware of that position as well. Others may take the easy path and identify Prudence with the genre of romance fiction, but those who read her closely will find the gaps in Prudence as generic construct. Fabian Driver has apparently joined the parish women in romanticizing Prudence, associating her with the traditional trappings: "Wine, good food, flowers, soft lights, holding hands, sparkling eyes, kisses" (111); though he sees how evenings built upon such an ideal "have little reality," he also fails to see Prudence beyond the glamorized version of her femininity that is bolstered by popular culture. Prudence herself ingests romance fiction without any self-deception, curling up with a novel that describes "a love affair in the fullest sense of the word and sparing no detail [...]. It was difficult to imagine that her love for Arthur Grampian could ever come to anything like this, and indeed she was hardly conscious of him as she read on into the small hours of the morning to the book's inevitable but satisfying unhappy ending" (47). For Prudence, this plot is obviously as much a fantasy as her own version of a love life is, but that does not make the reading any less pleasurable. Instead, it reinforces the notion that Prudence understands her position within the fiction that she has concocted, as well as what she represents in the fictions that others have created from their knowledge of and assumptions about her. Katherine Anne Ackley suggests that, very much like Pym herself, Prudence Bates harbors a "vision of herself as acting a role" (37), and this performative aspect of Prudence as a character mocks the stereotypes with which she is connected. Her self-conscious approach to those in the parish who imagine the "worst" of her turns the tables upon the notion of the auto-objectified female subject; Prudence reconnects the embodiment that she must align with to the intellectual qualities with which she also has an intimate affiliation. In deft jabs at the ways in which women have been socialized through a binaried order, Pym mocks the very structures, such as the romance plots of popular fiction, that she has been critiqued for having relied upon.

Jane herself seems to read such scandalous publications only when she visits the dentist (78); the image she helps to construct of Prudence for Pym's readers is not only fictive, but is also created from remnants of a context quite alien to Jane's daily life. When Jane later tries to discover whether Prudence has a sexual relationship with Fabian Driver, the fact that her understanding of sexual relationships is not grounded in the real world is clear. She asks, "'[...] there's nothing *wrong* between you' [...] using an expression she had sometimes seen in the cheaper women's papers where girls asked how they should behave when their boyfriends wanted to 'do them wrong'" (123). When Prudence is unable to decipher the meaning hidden within this remark, Jane continues to imagine "full-blown Restoration comedy women or Nell Gwyn or Edwardian ladies kept in pretty little houses with wrought-iron balconies in St. John's Wood" (123). Prudence's ambiguous response to Jane's inquiry is a blithe "one just doesn't ask [...] either one is or one isn't and there's no need to ask coy questions about it" (123). Rather than confirm or deny any sexual activity, Prudence allows for the enigma created by those around her to be kept in place. Jane's blundering but coy question is met with an equally coy answer, and Prudence's sexual endeavors are abandoned as indeterminate. Because the rhetoric of women's culture relies heavily upon sexual definitions in order to classify women into social castes, Prudence's "none of your business" response does more than chastise Jane for her nosiness; rather, the fact that the question remains unanswered illuminates a critical cultural impetus to classify Prudence on the grounds of her sexuality. All who seek to "read" Prudence are foiled on this very basic level, because while Pym makes use of common tropes for female sexual transgression, the fact of any such transgression is kept a mystery. "Does Prudence go to bed with Fabian?" John Bayley baldly asks; "Jane longs to know, as any of us might like to do in real life. And yet Jane is also pleased that she will never know" (170), as is Pym's audience. Readers (of the text as well as within it) are thus led to question the existence of a lapse in Prudence's sexual morality, as well as to interrogate the significance of figurative renderings of sexuality, such as those connected with food, a central mode through which readers can understand Prudence not only as embodied, but as transgressively so, given the cultural climate for food consumption, particularly that of women. The indeterminacy of Prudence's sexual activities allows her to escape the desperate fate of Streatfeild's Lena Wiltshire, whose sexual forays become public and thus permanently brand her as a deviant woman.

Jane and Prudence is a novel of its time; the cultural climate of a Britain under its Ministry of Food is impossible to separate from the narrative that follows Prudence's quest for love and Jane's best intentions to help her along that path. Food in this novel and during this era is meted out in particular fashions with regard to practices of both governmental rationing and a more traditional, hierarchical method of dispensing edibles. The vicarage housekeeper, Mrs. Glaze, bemoans the fact that "meat has never been at such a low ebb as it is now, what with everything having to go through the Government" (18), and she offers up with a reverent tone the bit of liver put aside for Jane and Nicholas Cleveland by the town's butcher. She assures them that the butcher "shares out the offal on a fair basis [...] but everybody can't have it every time" (21); the butcher has, however, made certain that the Clevelands have meat upon their arrival into the parish. Pym has Jane muse how this gift of liver to the new vicar is like "'meat offered to idols'" (21). Its scarcity raises meat, even unrationed offal, to a sacrosanct position within postwar culture, and indeed, Jane's simile is not incongruous to the ways in which meat (and other scarce stock) is discussed during the period. Jane further extends this figurative analysis of meat's status: "'people in these days do rather tend to worship meat for its own sake'" (21). A relatively sturdy food item, meat here is metaphorically transformed into a thing of the spirit, as well as into a thing that conveys the spirit's matters.

More than a representative of the spirit, though, meat is a sharp indicator of social hierarchies. Even under rationing, an attempt to distribute food equally, meat and other items in short supply are often the domain of those with certain social importance, such as vicars and, in a text nearly as devoid of men as the butcher's case is of beef, those few men who do remain within the village. This sentiment is not a result of postwar ethos, but is a long-standing belief that appears in many ways throughout rationing codes and throughout the period of Ministry control of food. In 1940, a Mass Observer overheard a woman remark, "They ought to have more meat—men like that [laborers who load coal and cargo onto trains]. They need it. Cereals! What's the use of them to a grown man!" (MOA TC 67/2/C). Clearly any suggestion that people go without meat and other protein-laden foods, in this case as in Chatterton's cookbook, did not include the adult male population. Pym's widowed Mrs. Mayhew pronounces that "a man must have meat" (30), and Mrs. Crampton, who runs the local teashop along with her, is just as insistent that "a man needs eggs" when she serves Nicholas two eggs to Jane's lonely one (51). Mrs. Crampton suggests a meal of bacon and eggs rather than the day's menu of toad-in-the-hole or beef curry: "we can sometimes, you know, but not for everyone" (50). Some minutes later, bachelor Mr. Oliver is served "a plate laden with roast chicken" (52). Though Jane agrees with the idea that men need these foods, she also blasphemously wonders, "surely not more than women did?" (51) and concludes that such preferential treatment comes down to the idea that "the very best [...] is what man needs" (52). Jane's comment supports Annette Weld's belief that "Pym recognized that food could be an indicator of social status, with women usually shortchanged" (100). Self-denying women and others might make the most of potatoes and milk, à la Chatterton, or of "Woolton Pie," but not everyone need be content with meager meals all of the time; some rationed goods were governed by powers greater than the Ministry. The effects of postwar gender roles influenced the ways in which popular sentiment regarding food consumption was constructed and perpetuated, and cast certain foods and their consumption as distinctly masculine.

When Jane considers the spiritual implications of meat during rationing, she presents a biblical adage that will echo throughout the novel. "'You will remember that St. Paul had no objection to the faithful eating it,'" she remarks, "'but pointed out that it might prove a stumbling block to the weaker brethren'" (21). Jane is likely referring to verses from I Corinthians in which Paul asks, among other things, that Christ's new followers abstain from eating meat that has been sacrificed to idols: "Do we provoke the Lord to jealousy? are we stronger than he? All things are lawful for me, but all things are not expedient: all things are lawful for me, but all things edify not"; with respect to food, this second verse appears in *The Living Bible*, translated into modern English, as "[...] it's not against God's laws to eat such meat, but that doesn't mean you should go ahead and do it" (I Cor. 10:22–3). Paul's concern with regard to meat consumption does much to imply free will and to distance his teachings from the Levitican laws of Judaic traditions, as well as from the abject status of such consumption discussed by Julia Kristeva, but he also emphasizes the fact that temptation may as well be avoided, that for some, eating this meat will lead to former idolatric practices. Here the "dirt" is not the impurity avoided through abstinence from certain consuming practices, but is instead a pervasive moral or ethical impurity. "Ye cannot," Paul explains in a dualistic warning, "drink the cup of the Lord, and the cup of devils: ye cannot be partakers of the Lord's table, and of the table of devils" (I Cor. 10:21). Improper food consumption subjects one to temptation that under early Christian versions of dietary law threatened eternal salvation. Meat (as well as other food items elevated in importance because of their scarcity) is its own false idol in a culture governed by rationing, and covetous thoughts of meat are akin to the world of sin outlined in Paul's epistle. Rationing, too, creates a general moral climate not unlike that laid out in Paul's Christian teachings. Austerity is championed in this letter as a moral brass ring and is itself a recipe for avoiding the fall inherent in the consuming of idolized foodstuffs. "Meats for the belly, and the belly for meats," Paul preaches, "but God shall destroy both it and them" (I Cor. 6:13). "God has given us an appetite for food and stomachs to digest it," the modern version clarifies, "but that doesn't mean we should eat more than we need. Don't think of eating as important, because someday God will do away with both stomachs and food" (*Living Bible*). Food, until made unnecessary in the afterlife, is something to be taken in only as much as one *needs* to, and not as much as one would like to, never in excess. The British government's moral appeal to its citizens to conserve and to make do is parallel with the heavier layer of morality that already dominates the Anglican landscape of England and of Pym's rural vicarage.

Though some food is necessary for survival in this world, other practices are not at all tolerated within Pauline teachings. "Now the body *is* not for fornication," Paul declares on the heels of scorning pleasurable food consumption, "but for the Lord" (I Cor. 6:13). Abstinence rather than austerity is the dominant lesson of this letter, and within the same verse of this chapter Paul continues from his discussion of food consumption to a discussion of sexual sin. That one here follows directly from the other illuminates a religious foundation for cultural connections between excessive food consumption and excess sexuality (sexual activity merely for pleasure or outside the sanction of matrimony, both of which signify the body in transgression). Interestingly, in Pym's text it is the women rather than the men who read the Lessons during church services, who rely upon this Christian doctrine in order to assign meaning to the elements of the world around them. If men *need* meat, then they are certainly among the "faithful" mentioned by Jane when she alludes to St. Paul's mandates. Eating meat, for men, falls within what can be considered acceptable consumption practices, because such consumption is not excessive, but necessary. Following the logic of the parish and of collective beliefs as indicated within cultural texts, however, meat (along with those other foods equated with meat under the rationing scheme) is not a necessary food for women. Women who engage in excessive consumption of meat, eggs, or other delicacies, by extension, are implicated in the sexual transgression made complicit with excessive eating by Paul, as well as by Jane, who invokes his teachings. When the formerly adulterous and rather narcissistic Fabian Driver eats "a casserole of hearts," which leads Jane to ask herself, "Did he eat his victims, then?" (33), the obvious connections between his sexual behavior and his eating habits are made humorously explicit; however, as a man in need of meat, Driver can receive both spiritual and social atonement for any improper or excessive consumption on his part, even for figurative sexual consumption of women. The woman who dares to transgress via her palate, however, is subject to a different scrutiny.

In contrast with the deceased and therefore rather saintly Constance Driver (wife of the philandering Fabian), who "had not appreciated good food" and had been so self-effacing that she "had even invited his loves to the house for week-ends" (57), Prudence Bates, along with her glamorous appearance, possesses equally glamorous, exotic gastronomical appetites. Though she is depicted while drinking alcoholic beverages and while smoking cigarettes (both unladylike, though 1950s-glamorous, habits), those are not the actions that define her as transgressive, as excessive. Her relationships to food—to consuming food and to preparing it, as well as to her general attitude toward food—are far from those codified, justified relationships to food expected of postwar women. Prudence is no Sally Hannegan, nor is she like her precursor, Mildred Lathbury, who in *Excellent Women* makes a meal of half a tin of baked beans and eats them "in ten minutes or less, quite without dignity" (30). Alone, Prudence prepares a meal far more interesting than one might expect from a desperate spinster of twenty-nine, and certainly one far more textured than would be a meal based upon merely the basic needs of the flesh or upon the codes of British austerity: "There was a little garlic in the oily salad and the cheese was nicely ripe. The table was laid with all the proper accompaniments and the coffee which followed the meal was not made out of a tin or bottle" (47). Food considered "womanish" in this text is that which is "simple [...] the kind of thing that a person with no knowledge of cooking might heat up" (113), such as Mildred's tin of beans; for Jane, this turns out to be shepherd's pie (115). Fabian Driver can have his hearts, his steaks, his "half bottle of St. Emilion" (113), but women are relegated to simpler, less pleasurable fare. The "weaker brethren" of Jane's biblical allusion appear to be the members of the "weaker" sex who might be tempted to revert to the false idolatry of their more lenient wartime roles in society rather than accede to appropriate postwar femininity. Though they dominate the text, women cannot equally dominate the consuming practices represented by Pym.

Prudence, though, slips through this scheme, and rather than settle for her gendered allotment, she seeks out food that enhances her being and that signifies her physical presence just as much as do her red toenails or the "green-and-gold shot taffeta cocktail party dress" she dons for the parish whist drive (86). Her glamorous appearance is one straight from the pages of women's magazines, and her exotic appetites are right out of Elizabeth David, who in *A Book of Mediterranean Food*, published in 1950, rhapsodizes over

> the oil, the saffron, the garlic, the pungent local wines; the aromatic perfume of rosemary, wild marjoram and basil drying in the kitchens; the brilliance of the market stalls piled high with pimentos, aubergines, tomatoes, olives, melons, figs and limes [...] all manor of unfamiliar cheeses [...] endless varieties of currants and raisins, figs from Smyrna on long strings, dates almonds, pistachios, and pine kernel nuts [...]" (v–vi)

David's introduction of such cuisine made for a radical change in English cooking practices. Garlic, a part of Prudence's salad and something imported, Mediterranean, is distinctly separate from basic English fare, as well as from any idea of a "womanish" culinary simplicity. Janice Rossen finds Prudence's solitary feast emblematic of her "high self-esteem" (47): "the question of self-image is tied directly to what the characters eat when they are alone. [...] they place a high value on themselves because they make solitary meals an occasion" (46). Jane firmly replies to Prudence's suggestion they rub the salad bowl with a clove, "'I should have liked the kind of life where one ate food flavoured with garlic, but it was not to be'" (156). The kind of life, or lifestyle, signified by the garlic and by Prudence's affinity for the exotic is *not* the life of a vicar's wife, but instead is a life that runs against the grain of St. Paul and his admonitions to the citizens of Corinth. Interestingly, as an unmarried woman Prudence does seem to adhere to Paul's pronouncement: "I say therefore unto the unmarried and widows, It is good for them if they abide as I" (I Cor. 7:8). If Prudence does abide as Paul decrees and is a hopeful celibate, then she is merely guilty of transgressions of the palate, and not of the rest of her physical person. Gustatory transgressions, though, are more than enough to brand her in the eyes of the parish as guilty with regard to her sexual expressions because of the historical link between female consumption and sexuality.

Prudence's consuming practices are interesting for the ways in which they shift as Prudence moves from one venue to another. In *Excellent Women*, Mildred's relationship to food changes as she moves from public to private venues, but in a more guarded, more expected manner. At home and alone, Prudence presents herself with the meal described above, one enhanced by garlic and ripe cheese and freshly brewed coffee, all items relatively different from the ordinary English meal that has been defined by Ministry regulations for so many years and that is part of the makeup of prescribed postwar feminine consumption. In public, however, the food she consumes is often dependent upon both locale and companion. Consumption is a performative practice for Prudence; she can adhere to or eschew social constructs of femininity and of female sexuality, depending upon who might be watching her eat and what their interpretation of her consumption might be. When she and Jane lunch together in London, for instance, they choose to dine at a vegetarian restaurant: very unmasculine, very lacking in the meat that defines transgressive consumption for women. Carol J. Adams notes that "because meat eating is a measure of a virile culture and individual, our society equates vegetarianism with emasculation and femininity" (15), and in wartime, this equation is only underscored. The same woman seems to be dining at this restaurant on both occasions, as well, a woman who Jane imagines "looked the kind of person who might have been somebody's mistress in the nineteen-twenties" (72), but who has since been rendered safely sexless, relegated to the realm of "a raw salad [and] a hot dish of strange vegetables" (72). When eating alone, on her lunch break, Prudence reads a volume of Coventry Patmore's poems while "having to choose between the shepherd's pie and the stuffed marrow" (41). She thinks of the dining establishment as a place for "women alone," and sees it as "a small, rather grimy restaurant which did a lunch for three and sixpence, including coffee" (41). In this setting Prudence also imagines herself to be less sexually desirable than she does at other points in the text: she "became conscious of herself sitting alone at a table that could have held two. She was still young enough—and when does one become too old?" (41–2). The idea of the single, young hopeful filling her mind with Victorian verse and her body with meager fare is a far cry from the image of this same woman dangling her sunglasses or assuaging her appetite with triple-cream brie. In this public, vulnerable venue, however, Prudence simply fills the role expected of her by public mores, and shifts her consumption in order to avoid suggestions of impropriety. When she spots her colleague, Mr. Manifold, sitting across the room, she realizes that she "had never seen him eating before, and now averted her eyes quickly, for there was something indecent about it, as if a mantle had fallen and revealed more of him than she ought to see" (43). Cookery journalist Leonora Eyles, writing a quarter of a century earlier, would agree with Prudence's response: "Sharing a meal is a very intimate act [...] I think," she advises, "only people who like each other should eat together" (31). The very image of the virgin in the garden, here Miss Bates in the restaurant is shamed by the image of this man's appetite, his "'tucking into'" a steamed pudding that she herself had avoided (43). She is an unwilling viewer of an act that shocks her perhaps as much as seeing the man's genitals might have. In a deft revision of Genesis mythology, Prudence denies a connection with even original sin. Her public persona, for the most part, is impeccable.

Voracious eating is further defined as masculine through this depiction of Manifold (a definition bolstered by Prudence's prim reaction); his participation in an act of explicit dining in a public place is sharply different from Prudence's behavior in the same location. Men need meat, and they also have social license to consume it in public and in whatever fashion they might choose to without the taint of any sexual excess affecting them in the way it would a female consumer. As masculine domains, consumption and sexuality are strictly forbidden to women, and, because one signifies the other, Prudence's forays into excess with regard to food consumption imply that her sexuality should also be inspected for breeches of propriety, just as with the dirty home or the unhygienic body that is inspected for signs of sin. Prudence's consuming acts, though, are not necessarily defined as excessive by their proportions, but are very much defined by their composition, by their exotic, and therefore sexual or erotic, natures. Consumption of quality as well as of quantity is a masculinized event, and Prudence's sexuality, her tendency to overdress in adherence to fashion rather than to social situation, and the aggression lent to her by those "desperate" descriptors all add together with her consumption to cast her as inappropriately (for the era) gendered.[4] Her

---

[4]   Prudence's penchant for expensive food items is also unfeminine when compared with the watchword "economy" proposed by Chatterton. Two items she enjoys—smoked salmon and ripe cheeses such as brie, were under strict price control during rationing, but still surpassed in cost more common food items. In 1940, a working-class woman responded to a Mass Observation questionnaire about Ministry of Food suggestions for meals, "I don't know much about salmon, so much, it's too expensive [...] cheese is so dear.

penchant for Regency furniture, the style of which "was a move away from 18th-century refinement toward exoticism, greater richness, and exuberance" ("Regency furniture") and is emblematic of George IV's debauched reign as Prince Regent, is a further indication that Prudence's character must be scrutinized for evidence of transgression. Fabian Driver himself has decorated in this same manner, but in matters of furnishings, as well as in matters of consumption, masculinity has a different moral boiling point than does its feminine complement. While on her way to that grimy restaurant, Prudence passes a men's club and imagines her employer, Arthur Grampian, "shaking the red pepper on to his smoked salmon" alongside "undistinguished-looking but probably famous men [...] professors and bishops" (41); in other words, Grampian consumes exotically not only in public, but in the company of those who represent the Church and the state, as well as institutions of higher learning. His consumption is fully sanctioned, while hers is necessarily suspect and made more so by the austerity of the postwar period.

Little mentions of items such as smoked salmon resonate in this text as markers of exoticized consumption, and in this and other works of Pym's add specific effects, especially with regard to sexuality and to gender. In *A Glass of Blessings* (1958), Pym opens a later exploration of social niceties with a distinction of smoked from tinned salmon, the former definitely significant of quality tastes, as well as of evocative lifestyles. This heroine, Wilmet Forsyth, forms an opinion of "mild dumpy little Father Bode, with his round spectacled face and slightly common voice" (7) based upon the predilection that she suspects he has for tinned fish. "I was sure," she concedes, "that Father Bode was [...] worthy of eating smoked salmon and grouse or whatever luncheon the hostess might care to provide. Then it occurred to me that he might well be the kind of person who would prefer tinned salmon, though I was ashamed of the unworthy thought for I knew him to be a good man" (7). His worth, both social and cultural, is presented early in the text based upon his ability to appreciate the quality of a food item unrelated to the likes of shepherd's pie. Father Thames, who later retires to an Italian villa, has by contrast a more evolved palate than does Bode; he exclaims over the coq au vin promised to the priests by their new housekeeper (60). Though a later example of postwar Britain and relatively unconcerned with the remnants of Woolton's rationing scheme, *A Glass of Blessings* further consolidates the importance Pym places upon food consumption and gastronomical tastes in *Jane and Prudence*. Tinned salmon gets the same sort of treatment in *Jane and Prudence* when parish women discuss what Mr. Fabian Driver has been served for lunch. "'[...] Mr. Driver was to have only a light lunch—a salmon salad with cheese to follow. Not *tinned* salmon, of

---

And what you get is chalk—all crumbly" (MOA TC 67/2/C). A pound of smoked salmon, in November of 1949, was sold sliced for 16/0, and sold unsliced for 11/3. Imported cheeses were sold at 4/0 per pound during the same pricing period. By contrast, a pound of smoked bacon—both rationed and price controlled—sold for 2/4 (Great Britain, *Retail Price List*). Smoked salmon was removed from price control in April 1950 (Great Britain, *Retail Price List Supplement*); during the years when Pym drafted *Jane and Prudence*, the price of this delicacy was likely higher than it was when controlled by the Ministry of Food.

course,'" relates spinster Miss Doggett, to which Jessie Morrow wryly replies, "'No, one could hardly give a man tinned salmon'" (168). The general parish point of view concerning men's gustatorial needs is here quite precise: both quantity and quality are of the utmost importance when it comes to the food served to men. Of a meal served for a dinner party of both men and women, however, Wilmet Forsyth remarks, "[...] Sybil had chosen all my favorite dishes—smoked salmon, roast duckling and gooseberry pie with cream. The men," she continues, "would not of course have realized that [the food] had been chosen just for me, looking upon the meal as no more than what was due to them" (13). Though this might be catalogued as just one instance among many that Wyatt-Brown reads as Pym's "hostility to men" (78), in the context of examining how food and relationships to food signify various methodological elements of Pym's characterization, this small scene follows others, such as that in which Jane Cleveland muses that men need (read "expect") the best in life. Their excesses are central components of their defining masculine characteristics, while female excess is a definition of a different sort, with both explanations underlining the "isolation and hunger that twentieth-century men and women continually [faced]" (Schofield 8). The gulf between the sexes is widened by their inability to read meals, or each other, with adequate precision.

In *A Glass of Blessings*, Pym further complicates her sexed and gendered notions of consuming practices by implicating the tastes of homosexual characters, notably of the vicarage housekeeper, Mr. Bason, and of Piers Longridge's lover, Keith, whose hair "glistened like the wet fur of an animal" (192). Earlier, in *Excellent Women*, Pym's references to this overlapping of sexual and gustatory difference in gay male characters were more oblique, and Mildred remarks that William Caldicote is "not the kind of man to marry," but she "does not mind it in the least"; "His care for his food and drink, too," she assures readers, "was something I accepted and even found rather endearing" (66). This attention to food and drink is not masculine, but it is behavior that Mildred herself cannot take part in unless she is an accomplice to William's adventures in dining. In Pym's later novel, both Mr. Bason and Piers Longridge are constructed as domestic and as feminized, but their epicurean tastes exceed their gendered selves as Pym's characterizations of them emerge as far bolder than that of William Caldicote. Keith, for instance, has made a pristine "home" for Piers, who has otherwise lived in alcoholic squalor, while Bason brought civilized cooking to the parish priests used to living on British basics such as "baked beans and chips" (57). When Wilmet notes her appreciation of Lapsang Souchong, an exotic blend of tea, Bason remarks, "I feel that women don't really understand the finer points of cooking or appreciate rare things" (57). Though both Bason and Keith are explicitly defined as sexual transgressors because of their sexual orientations, neither need demur when it comes to his tastes or appetites. In the worlds Pym creates, there are ramifications of appetite and taste on levels of both sex and gender. The gay men, already considered obvious fans of excess according to dominant moral codes, need not worry about any additional scrutiny if their excess is displayed, unlike

Prudence, who must fight a more stringent set of expectations for the unmarried woman. Along with the social constructs of gendered concerns, however, Pym's worlds suggest a basic association of men (regardless of their masculinity) with the consumption of excess. While men need meat, they also "want only *one thing*" (*JP* 70, original italics), suggesting an innate animalistic element beyond gender that is injected into the way Pym's male characters are accepted by those around them; that one thing, of course, is not avaialable to women of the novel's milieu. While Pym problematizes these issues through contradiction and conflicting representations, her characters are staunch examples of postwar social and cultural expectations for individuals of all sexes, genders, and appetites.

As with her characterizations of Bason and Keith, Pym's portrayal of Prudence is one that is layered and not as easily deconstructed as those who surround her within the text may believe. As discussed briefly above, Prudence's actual sexual behavior is indeterminate: she neither confirms nor denies that her affair with Driver is a sexual one, but she admits that "he had never stayed for a night" (198), and that his good looks might have made him "no more than just another 'amusing' object" (199), like garlic, just another example of Prudence's exotic desires. Pym's emphasis, however, is less on Prudence's actual nature, and Pym places more importance upon the ways in which those around Prudence assume an understanding of that nature based upon the going ideal for women of the period. Pym herself *liked* her creation of Prudence, declaring her and Wilmet Forsyth "my own favourites" in a 1964 letter to Philip Larkin (*Private Eye* 223), and far from sketching her as a creature of deplorable or even a pathetic character, as Streatfeild did with Lena Wiltshire in *Saplings*, Pym has drawn Prudence in a way that calls attention to the dangers of jumping to conclusions. Pym's readers, as well as her created textual milieu, run the risk of misreading Prudence if the broad lines that define cultural images of women are the ones used to decipher her characterization. Though I cannot agree with Wyatt-Brown, who believes that Prudence "finds sex distasteful" (91) and assumes the same of Pym herself, nor can I with Barbara Everett, who states that Prudence's "sexual life" is "clearly nonexistent" (74), it is possible as a textual truth that Prudence Bates's sexual behavior is less than her consuming practices make them out to be. While Jessie Morrow (who wins over Fabian Driver by the novel's end) audaciously wears his dead wife's dress when she first flirts with him, is caught stealing oyster patties at the whist drive, and "'may have stooped to ways that Miss Bates wouldn't have dreamed of'" in order to gain his favor (209), Prudence operates on a more subtle plane.

A creature of women's magazines, of romance novels, of fanciful culinary excursions, Prudence is nonetheless a pragmatic character who understands the irony of her position as a woman who has been modernized beyond the roles allowed to her by a society trying hard to catch up with itself. She thinks of Fabian Driver "sensibly": "he would probably make a good husband [...] the right age, they had tastes in common [...]. And this was not unimportant, he was good-looking" (102). The unromantic way in which she conceives of Fabian is underscored when she turns from him to the menu, thinking more of the dinner to come than of her dinner companion, choosing her courses "perhaps more carefully than a woman truly in love would have done" (102). Her sexuality is not necessarily what is transgressive, but instead what defines her as such is her inability to fit into the narrowly defined definition of femininity she is asked to perform as a woman of her time. "The chicken will have that wonderful sauce with it," she dreams while "looking into Fabian's eyes" (102): her own pleasure and her own needs are, in her mind, at least equal to his, and "the pattern of her thoughts rewrites the romantic moment" (Donato 95). She has cast aside the ideology of the other women in Pym's world who posit satisfaction of the male appetite as of primary importance. The smoked salmon, brie, wine, and coffee with brandy that Prudence consumes are for her the most important part of this occasion; Driver's menu goes unnoted, and his presence is less engrossing than is the food. In this key scene, Prudence discloses that her embodied nature (which is defined via her relationships to food) does not necessarily equate with either an overt sexuality or an allegiance to the feminine codes of women's cultures of both the textual parish and the extratextual world at large. Her embodiment, instead, at this juncture provides her with agency that stems from her intellect and that transcends the strictures of the era. What Pym toys with throughout the novel—the socially driven assumptions made about women and appetite—here becomes as destabilized and as impossible to pigeonhole as Prudence's sexual actions.

Of women who, as Jane Cleveland once did, desire to pursue a life of the mind and to write books, Prudence asks Fabian Driver, "'You'd prefer them to be stupid and feminine? To think men are wonderful?'" (103). Though she is seemingly worldly, embodied, and only comes close to intellectual endeavor when "emending footnotes and putting in French accents" for Grampian (41), clearly her description of non-intellectual women is one in which she does not include herself. Prudence cannot be made to neatly fit into the mold made for the woman of excess. If her consuming practices should, by cultural definition, yield an equally excessive sexuality, then her "negative relationship" to Grampian and her disinterestedness in Driver both explode that notion. Even if Prudence's lack of sexual activity within the text is merely elliptical, a ruse to keep the reader's nose out of such business,[5] the definition of her sexuality comes, for the most part, from what is negative, from what is not there. In Prudence is evidence of the faulty qualities of the version of womanhood so prominent in women's popular cultures:

---

[5]   Though many were one-sided infatuations, through her younger years Pym did have a series of affairs, some of which were sexual in nature. Pym herself was careful with regard to disclosing the natures of her relationships with men. Pym carefully tore pages from her diary entry of 15 October 1932, for example; the lines that are left indicate, perhaps, losing her virginity: "Today I must always remember I suppose. I went to tea with Rupert [Gleadow] (and ate a pretty colossal one)—and he with all his charm, eloquence and masculine wiles, persuaded ..." (*Private Eye* 17). What followed in several pages was destroyed. Pym also burned diaries from the year during which she was in love with Gordon Glover, a man divorced from her good friend Honor Wyatt (*Private Eye* 97; cf. diary entry for 17 February 1976, p. 285).

although she is perceived to lie outside the boundaries of propriety, she most likely does not. Her explanation of a post-Fabian relationship with Geoffrey Manifold (the man of whose eating she caught that indecent glimpse) as "nothing *negative* about it. Quite the reverse!" (217) might appear to jeopardize Prudence's escape from any positive identification of her consuming self with a sexually transgressive identity. Jane, however, chimes in with lines from Marvell that allow Prudence to maintain her ambiguous subjectivity: "'Therefore the Love which us does join / But Fate so enviously debars, / Is the Conjunction of the Mind, / And opposition of the Stars'" (217). Prudence agrees with Jane's summing up through poetry her relationship with Manifold as a meeting of minds, but not necessarily of bodies. The "positivity" of this conjunction, though teasingly close to betraying a stray fact about Prudence's sexual activity, is here problematized in a way that once again disallows any easy connections between embodiment and sexual transgression. When Prudence later reappears in *A Glass of Blessings* as a dinner companion for Wilmet Forsyth's husband, Rodney (249), her sexuality once again becomes suspect according to social dogma. Her behavior, however, hardly indicates what novelist Anne Tyler calls "the whole shocking story of Prudence Bates's later life" (xvii). Tyler, it appears, has fallen prey to Pym's self-conscious use of cultural biases, emphasizing the importance of the reading lesson Pym has worked into her novel of postwar manners. Tyler misses the fact that Rodney describes Prudence as "most attractive and intelligent too" (135), a combination that in its seeming rarity is perhaps more shocking to social mores than Prudence's willingness to dine (even twice) with a married man.

Jane Cleveland, who in her disassociation from food serves as Prudence's disembodied opposite with regard to consumption, is also part of Pym's "lesson." She, like Prudence, is constructed from what on one level is a "negative" relationship to food and to her own body, but on another level has a far more complex relationship to a mind/body duality. Like Laura in Panter-Downes's *One Fine Day*, who is marked by her rich mental life but who also admits to being a "greedy woman" under the surface (35), Jane's affinity with her intellectual life does not provide her with a monochromatic characterization. Jane, too, is subject to preconceived notions that create in her a self-identification with a "negative" embodiment; in her case those assumptions are entangled with her inept domesticity and her life as a vicar's wife that cannot include such exotic items as garlic or smoked salmon. Even Prudence, who dislikes the judgments that others pass upon her unmarried status and worldly interests, unjustly sees Jane as disconnected from the "excess" that she herself admires and as a result casts Jane into a realm of unworldly blandness. When Jane invites her for a weekend at the vicarage, Prudence balks: at the Clevelands' home, the "food wasn't even particularly good; it seemed that Jane would stop to admire a smoked salmon in the window or a terrine of *fois gras*, but in the abstract" (73). Jane's relationship to food, as laid out by Pym for readers and confirmed by Prudence, characterizes her as a member of the intellectual and spiritual planes, and does not intimate a life comprising any fleshly pursuits. In fact, when Prudence forms this opinion of her friend, Jane has indeed just come from browsing in a provisions store and looking at fois gras, "feeling that she had been vouchsafed a glimpse of somebody else's life" (72). "'How can a clergyman's wife,'" she wonders, "'afford to buy *fois gras*?'" (71). Jane finds the atmosphere of the shop "almost holy" (71), but certainly the large jar of paté, at a cost of 117 shillings, is part of a mode of worship unrelated to Jane's moderate Anglican sensibilities.

Expense, however, is the least of what keeps Jane from experiencing those aspects of life so central to Prudence's existence. Even the most basic of foodstuffs seem beyond Jane's ken; she lives instead in a distracted world filled with the "vivid fancy" (17) of early Renaissance poetry and distant recollections of her days at Oxford. By her own admission she is "undomesticated," especially when compared with a woman in the Clevelands' last parish who "had one of her hints published in *Christian Home*" (68). While women such as Panter-Downes's Laura Marshall in *One Fine Day* make valiant attempts to find their way into newly minted roles as cooks and housekeepers, Jane Cleveland seems almost defiant in her ineptitude. Her lack of culinary affinity is noticed by all and is discussed like gossip by the men of the parochial church council. Jane's failings are as much up for dissection as are Prudence's perceived indiscretions. Mr. Mortlake, a member of the parish council, deplores Jane's feebleness in the kitchen as a poor reflection on her role as vicar's wife: "'They say Mrs. Cleveland hardly knows how to open a tin. It isn't fair on the vicar'" (132). Mrs. Cleveland does in fact seem able to open a tin; however, that may be the upper limit of her culinary inclination. "'We could open a tin,'" Jane suggests on their first night in the vicarage, prior to the appearance of the town butcher's tithe of liver to the new clergyman; the statement is made "as if this were a most unusual procedure, which it most certainly was not" (16). Though early in the rationing period tinned food became "one of the prizes of shopping," with "the purchase of any tin [...] looked upon by housewives as the greatest favour and privilege" (MOA TC 67/3/C), in Pym's world, the tin merely contains an unsophisticated relationship to food in its more natural, desirable states (as seen in Wilmet Forsyth's comparison of tinned and smoked salmon, and her subsequent prejudice against Father Bode). As a vicar's wife as well as a mother, Jane is transgressive by virtue of falling quite short of the imperatives contained in domestic manifestos such as Chatterton's. Far from a practitioner of Certeauian "*perruque*," when rations run short or when the food items available are incongruous, Jane suggests luncheon out rather than make do in the kitchen. "'Mrs. Glaze did say something about there being sausages at the butcher if one went *early*,'" Jane recalls, "'but I'm afraid I forgot, and now it's nearly half-past twelve'" (49). Her intellectual capacities seem to remove her from the realities of the endless queuing for food that took up much of the wartime woman's time. Lost in an aura of metaphysical poetry, Jane appears to be a complete opposite of both the properly domestic woman as well as the worldly, both of which are oddly embodied in the persona of Prudence Bates. Like Prudence, however, Jane is not a model of any one role available to women of the early 1950s.

Though her lack of concrete relationships with food causes some consternation among parish busybodies and allows for Prudence's skeptical appraisal of Jane's modest lifestyle, Jane's position vis-à-vis food actually complements her role as vicar's wife, especially during this period of austerity. The conjunction of church and state in Britain not only makes Jane, through her marriage to Nicholas, a representative of Anglicanism, but also makes her complicit in the laws of the land, including its rationing scheme. The nationalistic spin placed upon stoic adherence to Ministry mandates emphasizes the importance of self-denial for the good of the country and, in the era of reconstruction, for the ostensible good of Europe. Jane's disassociation from food increases her level of association with the statutes of the British government, as well as with its spiritual branch. Her "unworldly" ways, cast in opposition to Prudence's lavish tastes, are precisely those required of a vicar's wife. The fact that she is predisposed to think it more important to "live on Beauty than to live on Porridge" (in the words of the Man-Who-Sees), to live on poetry and abstraction rather than on the tangible dailiness of food (or even its preparation), actually defines her as a highly acceptable member of the established order. Following St. Paul's attitude toward matters of the flesh, Pym has constructed Jane in a manner that aligns her with Paul's rigid teachings and with the ideal for clergymen and their families. Jane faults her predecessor, Mrs. Pritchard, for having had a drawing room that was "a little *too* well-furnished—those excessively rich velvet curtains and all that Crown Derby in the corner cupboard" (22), preferring her own functional presentation "as long as nothing unsuitable appears among these dim bindings" on her husband's bookshelves (16). Jane's "negative" relationship to food and to excess, and thus to an explicit embodiment and any hint of impropriety, enables her to fulfill her narrative position of vicar's wife and church affiliate, regardless of any lack of domestic inclination that comes with her disembodied territory. Mr. Mortlake might find any woman lacking in domestic skills guilty of the charges he levels against Jane and her distant connection with can openers; however, as a woman defined by her public connections, her private world is second to the ways in which she displays allegiance to dominant social systems. The vicar has Mrs. Glaze to prepare his meals; his wife fulfills a different, more structural function in the narrative of the parish. Pym's characterization of Jane, which takes her out of the kitchen and away from the caretaking expected of other women, appears to strengthen Jane's position as Prudence's opposite, and in turn builds a strong foundation for the more immediately visible binary divisions of worldly and unworldly, body and soul.

Just as Prudence's positive relationship with excess masks the important fact of her negative relationships with men, though, the construct of Jane's disembodied relationship to austerity in the name of foundational British institutions helps to hide the fact that her more critical "negative" relationship is with the intellect itself, with her lost aspirations to become a literary scholar. What she terms her "stillborn 'research'" was lost in her decision to become a wife and mother, to fulfill the very roles in which she appears delinquent: "the 'influence of something upon somebody' hadn't Virginia Woolf called it?—to which her early marriage had put an end. She could hardly remember now what the subject of it was to have been—Donne, was it, and his influence on some later, obscurer poet? Or a study of her husband's namesake, the poet John Cleveland?" (11). Though her mind and her conversation are filled with the poems she studied and loved while at Oxford, that verse has developed into little but matter that blocks her ability to approach life head-on. Jane is prone to filtering the world around her through verse, but her poetic utterances are only fragments of the life work of others. Jane's "consumption" appears to be accomplished via reading the written word, but the basis for Jane's subjectivity, for Pym's characterization of her, is not at all central to who Jane has become as a midcentury woman: vicar's wife, Flora's mother, Prudence's good friend. Her abilities to be any of these are compromised by her intellectual attributes, though that intellectualism was long ago thwarted by expectations for feminine conformity. When she attempts to rediscover her lost scholarship, years later, she finds only relics of her "early promise" (11):

> She sharpened pencils and filled her fountain-pen, then opened the books, looking forward with pleasurable anticipation to reading her notes. But when she began to read she saw that the ink had faded to a dull brownish colour. How long had it been since she had added anything to them? [...] Then she remembered that her copy of the *Poems on Several Occasions* was upstairs and it seemed too much of an effort to go up and get it [...] She sat for a long time among the faded ink of her notebook, brooding, until Nicholas came in with their Ovaltine on a tray and it was time to go to bed. (131)

What Prudence calls Jane's "'great gifts'" (103) are about as useful to her as would be a book by Elizabeth David. Her association with the life of the mind is undermined by the fact that for Jane, that life ended upon her marriage and entry into a world dominated by standards for women embodied in social institutions and by cultural ideology so central to constructions of femininity during the mid-twentieth century.

Though presented as one half of a mind/body schema, Jane, like Prudence, does not fit neatly into her assigned slot. This unworldly vicar's wife with her heady thoughts and her lack of contact with the tangible world of food and embodiment is not, under closer inspection, the representative of the intellectual realm that she appears to be when viewed through a lens of cultural expectations for women such as those presented in numerous examples of women's culture of the time. Once Jane's position is exposed as more complicated than might initially be perceived, her character can be interpreted as a complex example of women during this period who, although adequately adhering to dominant social codes, cannot fully comply with the going cultural notions. Niamh Baker explains that through Jane, "Pym's treatment of marriage is critical and ironic, but not tragic" (48). Jane muses over the idea that men need meat (or eggs, or smoked salmon) and asks herself whether they need life's best more so than do women (even during food scarcity and culturally mandated self-denial), and she expresses her opinion that Milton's "'treatment of women was not all that it should have been'" (30). Her approach is one of cautious criticism rather than of patent acceptance. If such ideas come from a disembodied woman seen as complicit with the staunch ideologies of Britain, then they can easily be forgotten as non sequiturs in the same way that her random quotations from Donne and Marvell can be. Once these same beliefs become part of a female subjectivity that cannot be defined in the ways often used to categorize women who resemble Jane, however, her atypical philosophies indeed do follow from an identity that on an integral level refuses an allegiance to the system. Jane is another example of the ways in which modernity and forward motion, both prior to and during the years given over to World War II, have redrawn indelibly the ways in which women will fit—and not—into the postwar world.

Though the Man-Who-Sees suggests this mingling of the physical and intellectual components of human beings, his own rhetoric stops short of the sort of problematized notion of subjectivity proposed by Barbara Pym in *Jane and Prudence*. "You can't keep the soul alive in this world," he claims, "without the help of your body" (26), and, regardless of whether his treatment of mind/body duality in the pages of *My Home* reaches its attempted mark, his premise presages Pym's vision of the aftermath of World War II and the ways in which women might be able to proceed in a changed Britain. Ultimately, neither Jane nor Prudence is a character composed of qualities found on only one side of a binaried representation of women. Instead, Pym's rhetorical stance, as evidenced in her characterizations of these two women, suggests the spectrum and necessary commingling of elements present within both corporeality and intellectual identity. The changes in women's public roles made necessary by war, combined with the relentless effects of twentieth-century modernization, provide implicit examples of women that cannot be founded upon older, more tested methods. Jane and Prudence are not, however, represented as the shape of things to come, but signify the very indeterminacy of women's place in a changing social order. While the novel seems to belong to Jane when it opens upon her arrival in the parish and appears to become the tale of a woman (Prudence) who has cast aside traditional definitions of femininity in order to brave an unmarried path and the consequences of sexual excess (whether actual or imagined), Prudence herself is seen as a "'cast off'" (191) by young Flora, Jane's daughter. Flora, who studies English literature at Oxford like Jane did, who is "domestically and socially competent and clever with her dress" (Dunlap 184), and who imagines herself on the cusp of a life that will include love affairs and exotic interests, may provide more promise than either of Pym's protagonists. Flora Cleveland is a young woman whose life will include little from the era that has passed as a result of the second war. As she comes of age at the end of European reconstruction and with the dissolution of the scarcity that works to create feminine caricatures of the women of her mother's and Prudence's generations, excess will no longer pose the threat that it does in Pym's novel, and Flora, perhaps, will become a still finer merging of the mind and the body.

Chapter 3
Body as Text, Body in Text:
Reader Response and the
Consuming Body

Daily, our bodies are "read." We read the bodies of each other as we pass in streets or come together in offices and classrooms. Reading the body as text is one of the most fundamental literacies in which we engage. Reading the body as object— its size, shape, the cultural significance of the body as a *thing*—is an automatic response, but it is also naturally a very subjectively determined evaluation. As symbols, as purely "intelligible" bodies, objectified (and auto-objectified) bodies convey only the meaning bestowed upon them, much like texts taken to be readily transparent, fully accessible in at least similar ways to a variety of readers. Because interpersonal relations are part of the goal of communication, the body must surpass an object-status in order to convey not only meaning derived through cultural assumptions on the part of the reader, but also meaning that stems from the resistance of a textualized body. Texts—both the written, printed texts and those textualized bodies that I implicate here—are always both intelligible and resistant; like the always resistant body discussed in Chapter 1, the textual body, with its echo of actual flesh, poses some of the same resistant qualities. Though the static, material text (the "book") may not change except as pages weather and print fades, the meaning of that text can shift with each reading experience, from reader to reader and from reading event to reading event. Some meaning will appear as hardly arguable, such as actions and empirical effects: here is a book, here are its pages, here is my body. Questions of desire, impulse, or motive, though—amorphous aspects of texts and of bodies—are not always easy to discern. Furthermore, such questions can most often only be answered through a complicity of both the text and the reader. Nonverbal communication such as posture or facial expression offers readers both the casual meaning of, say, a frown that denotes sadness and at the same time presents a series of questions: Why is she sad? How can that emotion be changed or rectified? Am I only reading sadness where there is really none at all?

Beyond the "face value" of the body's communications, beyond the international symbols of frowns, happy faces, and the like, a literacy of embodiment depends upon a physical empathy or understanding between reader and body/text as well as an emotional or intellectual interpretation. To watch someone rush across a room, and to begin to understand the activity, one must not only understand the pace of the actions and the movements of that body. One must also be willing to interpret how it feels to be rushed, how such strides feel in muscles, and how the material body moves through space. In short, one's own body image (to return to the theories of Paul Schilder discussed in the introductory chapter) comes into play when one reads the textual body of another. A psychical understanding of one's own physicality is what allows one to negotiate his or her own actions and motility, and that knowledge of the "self" (a physical and mental conglomerate) allows for responses to the nuances of physicality in general. The body image interprets what it means to move through space, to extend one's arms and legs, and to insinuate through expression that one is in a hurry, please step aside. This image, as well, is the empathic device that lies between one body and another, between the reader of a body and the textuality of the body undergoing interpretation.

As with the material body—which is textual but also certainly exists for purposes other than interpretation—the represented body *within* a text, that which we might more easily understand as a "textual" body, can be understood via the body of a reader. The extension of a reader's own body image is a large part of what enables that reader to comprehend a represented body within a text. Trained to appropriate our own physicalities as material objects and to "read" our own bodies as we (auto-)objectify them, we naturally read the bodies of others in social and literary contexts as we do our own, a result of the codification of the body within a given cultural ethos. As a mixture of mind and body, the body image is analogous to that meeting point between text (printed material) and reader, between an amorphous "meaning" of language and the experiential existence of the lived body. If a body represented within a text is to be considered as something other than pure object, if it is to be understood as representative of the human model that I have discussed in the introductory chapter to this study as a gestalt of mind and body, then the body of a reader, that reader's body/image, is a necessary element of the reading experience because that projection of the self is the aspect of the reading "self" that will comprehend the validity of embodied intellectual processes. The body's basic epistemology is critical to the integration of information, of knowledge, to the epistemology of the reading subject.

A primary goal of this project has been to examine ways in which the mind and body can and do come together, rather than to argue for the insistence of one over the other. Polarized discourse, though, is by no means limited to theories of the body. As the impact of social and cultural orders upon human psyches and upon the products of human labor has become an important part of contemporary theoretical discourse, those very attempts to consider beyond dualities the relationships between an individual and his or her surrounding environs have created quite problematic theoretical contexts through which to examine society and culture. Results of cultural production—art, literature, music, media—can no longer be thought of as discrete objects, but rather should be viewed as part of a larger milieu of interconnected thoughts and practices. Literary interpretation, while benefiting from ever-broadening terrains of inquiry, has also become a part of the conundrum of recent theoretical trends. Whether the reader and text create each other has become a moot point in many ways; instead, theoretical discourse of interpretation has become caught up in the same sort of chicken-or-egg scenario as have theories of embodiment. Just as the body and the mind cannot be separated but instead necessarily work together, the reader and the text—one hardly meaningful without the other—have often been posited as oppositional quantities, while both actually serve to constitute a mutually defined system. Some theories of textual analysis have done much to free the idea of the text from any definitive method of interpretation, but in the process, notions of "reader" and "text" are often segregated in ways that limit critical assessment of the reading event. While, for Roland Barthes, the "more plural the text, the less it is written before I read it," Barthes also suggests that "*I* is not an innocent subject, anterior to the text" (10), and in this circular commentary accedes to the importance of balancing the malleable text with the active, working reader, what Jane Tompkins outlines as occurring when "[r]eading and writing join hands, change places, and finally become distinguishable only as two names for the same activity" (x). Such balance, though, is precarious if only because of a naturalized desire within contemporary culture to posit the relevance or importance of one (reader, text; mind, body) above the other. The idea of a preeminent text or reader, rather than of their unique combinations, is a threat to the ways in which we read and interpret texts of all kinds, including the text of the human body. What must become important, if anything beyond a radical relativism is to be considered in any dialogue, is how parts work together to become whole experiences, even if those experiences are idiosyncratic and transient.

In order to examine how readers and texts work together and in various combinations, this chapter examines how the interaction between the two in turn mirrors interactions of minds with bodies. Both dyads are caught up in a theoretical struggle between discourse and materiality, and to examine the two pairs together, to consider the ways in which each binary construct sheds light on the other, can help to assert how it has become more important to look at the mechanics of contemporary thought rather than at its mechanisms, to understand the ways in which our theories work rather than stagnate in a circuitous search for a definitive model for anything. Further, in the novels that I examine in this chapter—Helen Dunmore's *Talking to the Dead* and Angela Carter's *The Magic Toyshop*—represented bodies within the texts are necessary catalysts for readers' interpretations of those texts beyond their obvious surface narratives. Both novels rely upon familiar, generic conventions in order to mask embedded, more difficult narratives of incest and murder, and considerations of the represented physical, consuming (female) bodies within these texts allow for the ways in which the two narratives within each novel are interdependent to be clearly discerned. By presenting the body as a conduit for reader response, the narratives themselves play out the inseparable natures of reader and text, of mind and body.

Represented eating is pure (if merely represented) activity and provides one basis for an emergence of the body from within a text. When characterization occurs through represented acts of eating, and thus through representations of the physical body, it can, as I have explained, indicate anxiety linked to various aspects of consumption, such as class and sexuality. As Louise Rosenblatt asserts, "any reading act is the result of a complex social nexus" (20), and as such reading acts carry the weight of cultural assumptions, including those about the body and its activities. Through cultural associations of eating with such anxieties and assumptions, though, characterization based upon consumption can also provide a simplistic way of reading based upon cultural assumptions and attitudes about the consuming body, especially when that body is female, as seen in the previous chapter's examination of Barbara Pym's play with social expectations for consuming female bodies. In Dunmore's and Carter's novels, this "narrative of the flesh" is easily understood by readers who are well versed in general cultural attitudes toward eating and who accept, even if only unconsciously, the idea that taking extreme pleasure in eating is abhorrent, sinful, suspect. Other, more problematic narratives, when they are less familiar to readers and especially when they are removed from the reader's body (the vehicle of response) and bodily experiences, are subjugated to the story of the body and of its actions: "given any two phenomena, the one that is more visible will receive more attention" (Scarry, *Body* 12). More complex narratives, especially the narratives of discomfort that appear in these two novels, are clouded by the idea of the body, by the sharable nature of the body that, present within the text, communicates with the reader's body without. Textual bodies that take pleasure in the world of the flesh—in this case in worlds in which consumption is slated as primary to female characterization— draw the attention of readers whose own bodies interact with narrative bodies in a call and response that is underexamined as a method of reader response.

In Helen Dunmore's *Talking to the Dead*, two sisters, Nina and Isabel, are characterized through their relationships with food perhaps more than any of the female characters discussed in this project. The two are opposite in other ways: Nina is an urban Londoner, and Isabel lives in rural Sussex; Isabel is maternal, while the younger Nina creates instead through artistry. Their most prominent opposition, though, is constructed through food. Nina's character is founded upon her relationships to food, both its cooking and eating. Isabel's character is not simply absent any represented activity of eating; this characterization is based upon a lack of food and a lack of the multiplicity of desires made explicit in Nina. "There was a time," Nina recalls, "when Isabel used to be able to eat in front of me, as if I were part of herself" (80). The time when Nina and Isabel were thus united, though, has passed and, in the present time of the novel, the two are far removed from each other. The embodied Nina has been cleaved from Isabel through their divergent relationships to the process and the sharing of eating. This dualistic characterization sets mind and body at odds on the surface of the narrative action, and Nina and Isabel quickly become known to readers by their relationships to food and subsequently to their own bodies.

The novel's prologue indicates that the narrative to follow is Nina's: Isabel is dead, and the tale to come will be explanatory and will lead readers to an understanding of the inevitable event. Nina's narration begins on a note that makes the idea of food, of eating, central, and her emphasis on the importance of food creates a schism early on between her own value system and that of her deceased sister. "After a funeral you have to eat, to prove you're still alive," Nina muses. "There are foods that are suitable [...] ham, or cold chicken. Quiche is very popular, and Australian wines [...] . Someone was asking me if I would like fresh pineapple to garnish the ham, or tinned" (3–4). Food here is equated with life, with a life force, and is both something for the living and something that resonates with life; it reminds us that we are alive, embodied. The choice of foods and of preparations stems from an agency that is complicit with the act of living. Isabel, though later revealed to be a disorderly eater who may not make such choices at all, at the inception of the text's prologue certainly cannot make any choice regarding food, because she is no longer alive to eat it. Nina belongs not only to the realm of the living, but to its auxiliary spheres of choice and of agency, and through her immediate association with food and with life, she takes on a role of solidity, of the flesh. In addition, food here is not just for the practical task of feeding mourners at a wake, but is also a matter of style. Nina is not simply a living and eating entity, but is also a discerning consumer whose tastes elevate her beyond her intrinsic position as Isabel's survivor. At the center of a complex network of meaning suggested through food, Nina emerges early as synonymous with activity and agency, and with the potentially positive qualities associated with the active role of protagonist.

As the novel proper opens and shifts into the past in order to lead readers to Isabel's death, Nina is more specifically viewed in an act of eating in such a way as to further align her with matters of consumption and of the body. Nina recalls the event that has brought her from London to Sussex, Isabel's home and the setting for the novel. Isabel has just given birth, but because of complications also has undergone a hysterectomy. Her illness establishes a need for Nina to visit in order to help Richard, Isabel's husband, with the day-to-day running of their home. When Nina hears from Richard about Isabel's emergency surgery and weakened condition, she becomes frightened and concerned: "[m]y hands shook [...] I had a pain in my throat" (12). Her next action, really the first action of Nina's beyond the dialogue with Richard, is to eat. "[...] I went straight into the kitchen," Nina recalls, "cut a thick crust of a fresh white loaf, smeared it with butter and then with apricot jam, and ate it fast, cramming it into my mouth. There was sweat on my forehead, so I wiped it off and kept on eating. I was not going to think of the things Richard had just said [...]" (12–13). In order to block out the psychical aspects of her subjectivity, Nina resorts to an act of eating that is charged with both desperation and energy. The verbs used here to express her actions—"smeared," "cramming"—indicate forceful action as well as an action that can help to mediate between thought and flesh. As a receptor of images related to Isabel's ruptured uterus and "brown summer belly, her deep navel" (12), Nina can partially imagine through her own body image the acute reality of Isabel's experience. She must remind herself of the differences between their bodies: "I touched my skin and ran my hand across it to feel that it was unscarred" (12). This initial scene brings in an idea of the ways in which bodies can understand each other, a concept that will become critical as the novel progresses and its narratives divide. Nina's passion for food in this scene is evident. Her act of eating bread and jam, an act that could be treated as negligible, is fraught with information about

Nina that will soon be necessary in order to understand her further acts of passion and self-indulgence. The act of eating helps to define Nina as impulsive and rash, but also as a creature of comfort. Eating in this scene carries with it the notion of food's healing properties, and, again through Nina, the understanding of food's life-giving and -sustaining powers are reinforced.

Nina's relationship with food does not come simply through the act of eating, however. Her character is founded on multiple associations with food, and, in addition to her enjoyment of the consumption of food, Nina also enjoys food preparation, and a love of good cookery is another central part of her characterization. Her presence in Isabel's home ensures a certain bounty, and Dunmore's poetic voice in this novel works in no other passages as well as in those that express Nina's culinary visions. For Nina, food is not only something to take pleasure in, but also—perhaps even more so—a medium through which she can offer pleasure to others. Just as her freelance photography and its "splinters of light, splinters of sound" (90) allow Nina a way to express outwardly what she experiences inside, careful construction and composition of a meal, with each course complementary of the others and each guest taken into consideration, gives rise to Nina's creative prowess. Her narrations of food and of her plans for each ingredient are meditative, and the final products are combinations of parts, whole expressions of the palate available to her: "Today I'm going to cook. [...] I'm going to bake the salmon, very slowly, with dill and juniper berries. I'll serve it just warm, with hollandaise sauce, with new potatoes, French beans, a big ripe cucumber that tastes of fruit, not water, and plum tomatoes [...] then an apple tart, and a gooseberry fool" (66). Like Pym's Prudence Bates, who exhibits exotic influences of Mediterranean food culture, Nina is a product of a new age of foodism, and her culinary creations are carefully considered masterpieces that go beyond the typical English meal. As she imagines each component of the meal, their shapes take on new meanings. Her voice orchestrates her vision of the meal just as her camera would capture the Irish gypsies or Romanian orphans whom she exposes onto film. The verbal creation is synesthetic; the warm flesh of the salmon against the crisp, full feel of the cucumber is hard to discern from the gin-spice of juniper. Nina's description of the apple tart she will bake explains her theories: "When you close your eyes and bite you must taste caramel, sharp apple, juice, and the short, sandy texture of sweet pastry all at once. No one taste should be stronger than another" (68). This precise imagery is one way that the narration calls for a visceral response from the reader. Who but the recently fed or those allergic to salmon would not read this description and begin imagining the feel of food's textures, the flavors making their ways across the tongue? Without asking, Nina draws those who listen to her recipes to respond to them, to invest not only in the creation of the meal, but also in its outcome.

This call to the palate is instructive as well as inviting. As I address throughout this chapter, Nina, as narrator, offers continual clues as to how a passage or a representation should be read and decoded, and through her culinary discourse she also hooks readers into accepting her narration as a reliable source of information. Simple exegesis of the meal at hand would not have the same impact as this deliberate, sensual description of Nina's feast. There is a precise, authoritative quality to the way in which she expresses her plans for the fish and its accompaniments; this is no novice expressing doubt in her own ability, but a sure hand, a ready professional. Though Richard calls Nina a "food snob" (158), her attitude toward food and the generosity with which she presents her products express a different motive. In Nina, there is a deep appreciation of the craft of the kitchen, and her day job as a photographer, her connection to high art, lends extra credibility to her domestic expertise. There is room for experimentation, but none for error; Nina assures readers of that:

> The tart will take the longest. I've bought white Normandy butter, pastry flour, three pounds of sharp, sweet, Jonagold apples. They are not the right apples, but I won't get better in the tail end of the season [...]. They must be cut evenly, in fine crescents of equal thickness, which will lap around in ring after ring, hooping inward, glazed with apricot jam. The tart must cook until the tips of the apple rings are almost black but the fruit itself is still plump and moist. (68)

The interest she takes in providing just the right ingredients, and in creating a desired effect both visually and gustatorially, surpasses snobbery and indicates a certain care for quality and for the experience that others will take in her cooking. For this meal, her attention to the simple, seasonal fare advocated by many chefs of contemporary cuisine only adds to her "lady bountiful" pose and undermines any distrust one might have for the food dilettante who only dabbles in what's fashionable. Right down to the brown sugar Nina will sprinkle on vine-ripe tomatoes, her knowledge is exact, secure. Early in the novel, at the time of this first feast, any doubt of Nina's integrity resulting from her passion for eating is tempered by her prolific culinary nature. Her care with the hollandaise, which "swallows" twelve lumps of butter, "fattening on what I've given it" (69), and with buttering her hands before lifting the salmon so as not to mar the perfection of its scales, reinforces the nurturing, durable nature of food and of Nina, and emphasizes her ability to provide as well as to consume.

In stark contrast to Nina, Isabel's character is removed from food on all levels. Without Nina, her kitchen is sorely lacking: cupboards contain "[i]nstant coffee, two packets of Weetabix, cheap jelly marmalade," and a freezer is "full of white bread and beef sausages" (156), a woeful catalogue of what to some might be considered typical English fare. Husband Richard, a financial consultant, is away on business often, and Isabel adamantly avoids food. She "can't eat round a table with other people" (79) and is somehow able not to participate in Nina's grand meal, instead watching, a passive onlooker distanced from the activity of eating. Her substitution for eating, as it is for many others, is smoking: "the cigarette makes a barrier between her and the plate" (181). But Isabel is not simply an overly motivated dieter or a picky eater. Her ability to eat in front of others, perhaps to eat at all except for a meager sustenance, has been limited for twenty-five years, since the sudden death of Colin, the brother of Nina and Isabel, who ostensibly succumbed to cot-death (SIDS) while an infant. Nina wonders whether, in fact, Isabel has ever eaten for enjoyment, the way that she does: "Was there a time once [...] that we could stand in front of the baker's shop together and point at cream slices and Eccles cakes and eclairs? [...] when we'd both watch jealously as the tinned pineapple was divided [...]? (184). Even though she is a new mother and is nursing baby Antony, Isabel refrains from too much food and indicates to a concerned Nina that she exists on "'oatcakes and dried apricots,'" justifying this diet by adding that "'they're full of iron'" (79). Isabel is weakened by the birth and by her recent surgery, but her invalid status seems to have much deeper roots. She appears to be emotionally tough, but her frailty and her fondness for close quarters, construed by Richard as even potentially agoraphobic (a psychological effect linked by Susan Bordo to anorexia), all add together to discount any vitality of Isabel's near to that of her sister. The one thing she seems most emphatic about is her lack of desire for food, which she equates with her distaste for sex: "'You soon get used to not having it. I remember thinking the same about food. All those people thinking they had to have food all the time or they'd die [...] and yet it wasn't really necessary at all'" (185). This knowledge is a sort of secret for Isabel, who flits at the edge of its annihilating boundaries. Regardless of her attempts to assuage Nina's worries with her drawer filled with healthy snacks, later and closer examination shows the apricots at Isabel's bedside, which "should be plump and moist," to be dried out: "the packet's been open too long" (289). Isabel seems to exist on nothing.

Though through characterizations dependent upon their relationships to food Nina and Isabel are obvious concoctions of the body and of the mind, they are never completely or easily relegated to their respective realms. The typical division of women via the body and its sexuality—that old madonna/whore division—of course becomes important here, but again, as in Pym's text, that separation does not happen in any neat fashion. Dunmore's division of female characters is rife with the tensions of auto-objectification, tensions engendered by the impossibility of removing subjectivity from the physical body. Dunmore has complicated the division between flesh and psyche in several ways, and at base she plays with the opposition of the two most obvious methods of representing female embodiment: the sexual and the maternal. Food, however, problematizes this division for Dunmore's purposes, but in a wider sense also helps to illuminate the basic problematic of the division itself. The idea of the nurturing mother joins together femininity and feeding (a most basic nurturing) as almost synonymous aspects of caretaking, with "the giving away of food [...] announcing connection, goodwill, love" (Sceats 11). In *Talking to the Dead*, the two are woven together in ways that both work with and tear through traditional schemes that suggest motherhood is a natural mode for women and part of the same domestic arrangement as are food and food preparation. The already introduced stress in the novel on the connection between nurturing and food skews the traditional division, though, because the main representation of nurturing is the childless Nina, and not Isabel. Isabel, though disembodied—nearly literally—through her lack of connection to food and eating, nonetheless does produce food in the form of the milk she produces for her child, Antony. In the scenes where her role as food provider in this sense is illustrated, though, Isabel's breasts seem removed from her body because her nurturing is forced, her body otherwise inactive. When Nina first arrives, Isabel is weak, thinner, but "her breasts are round and hard as stones beneath the thin lawn of her nightdress" (29). Under her clothes, Isabel's breasts are as like the rest of her body as stones are, and just as remote. The next day, Nina notices that Isabel's "wrists are oblong, showing their bones. Only her breasts are heavy" (56). As Isabel evaporates, her motility dries up, her body and body image become reduced. Her potential for agency, therefore, becomes limited almost to the point of extinction. As a provider of breast milk, Isabel is like a machine; she has no desire to feed Antony, and in no other way does she pursue an active, culturally acceptable mode of motherhood. The only "active" elements of Isabel's body, her breasts, which might in another case signify maternity and maternal nurturing, here only emphasize her lack of connection to the body in spite of her inability to become completely disconnected from it.

As might be expected, the passionate, sensual, and consuming Nina, by contrast, is not only sexual, but transgressively so. "As they say in the north of England, anybody can fook, but not many people can cook" (Barr and Levy 20); Nina, apparently, not only can do both but thoroughly enjoys one as much as she does the other. Nina is the sort of woman fondly referred to by culinary writer Erin Pizzey as a "slut": "seldom very good at anything in particular except sensual pleasure. Food, therefore, comes high on her list" (10). "Both in her kitchen and in her bedroom," Pizzey smiles, the slut is slave to nothing except for her "innate creativity" (9). In *The Slut's Cookbook* (1981) Pizzey writes amusingly of a new breed of woman for whom pleasure is primary, and she does so from a modern vantage point less complicated by the sorts of prescriptions for women's food relationships outlined in previous chapters. Nonetheless, in Dunmore's novel, Nina's sexual transgression represents abhorrently gendered behavior, just as it does for other female characters examined in this study who relate improperly to food. Nina's masculinized persona, while at odds with her roles of nurturer and cook, is created through her affiliations with food, but with her consumption rather than with her cooking. This adds yet another complication to the ways in which one might read images of nurturing, mothering, and sexuality in Dunmore's text. Not only does Nina control the pace and disclosure of the narrative, but she also directs the domestic and social patterns of her sister's home from its helm, the kitchen, and thus the level of social discourse within the text. Nina's position within the text, with respect to gender, does surpass binaried divisions, even if her physicality attaches her to another dualism. As a photographer, too, Nina is placed in the subject position: both her voice and her focalization control the novel's structural development, most importantly its division into two narratives. While such a position of power and control might seem desirable, it eventually calls into question Nina's behavior, which is often found far from the normative mark, particularly with regard to her femininity. "It took me years," Nina thinks, "to realize that it might be easier to do things like shave my legs or make an appointment at a good hairdresser's than not to do them. [...] I'd like to believe those things were a part of me [...]. Maybe that's why it suits me to take pictures. No one looks at the person behind the camera" (20–21). Nina herself directly relates her bogus femininity with her desire to be behind the scenes, subject rather than object. Her subjectivity, like her sexuality and her consuming practices, emerges as masculine and complicates her more appropriately gendered duties in the kitchen.

Though her cooking is active and feminine simultaneously, her eating is what ultimately pushes Nina into this realm of gender transgression. Eating not only signifies sexuality in her case, but also further works to masculinize Nina and her behavior. Just after arriving in Sussex, Nina eats alongside Isabel's husband. She cuts a slice of pie for Richard, initially a "feminine" task of feeding the man of the house. Responding to her own hunger, though, she proceeds to slice another piece for herself, and then douses them both with heavy cream, "thick and yellow" (38). "I've always liked eating with Richard," Nina notes, "because he is greedy, as I am. [...] He leaves the plumpest gooseberry until last [...]" (39). This equality through consumption destabilizes the gender codes of the novel. Nina becomes a troublesome figure who demands sympathy and yet who also defiantly mocks the ground upon which sympathy for a protagonist is generally founded. Her consumption, forceful in the bread-and-jam scene, is reinforced here as "greedy," and greed is not a desirable trait, particularly in women. Gluttony and lust are equally mortal sins, and Nina embodies both.

Nina's greed, and not Richard's, seems to parallel the greed of Isabel's friend Edward, another visitor in the house who is homosexual.[1] Though nothing in the text indicts his sexual orientation, he is set up as a foil for Nina's transgression. Both Edward and Nina thwart the propriety of the heterosexual and domestic scheme of Isabel and Richard's home. Edward, too, is greedy. He is also furtive about his consumption, both a silent admission of guilt and an acknowledgment of the nature of greed as sinful within the boundaries of social norms. When Nina cuts the pie for herself and Richard, she notices that "Edward has been at it since lunch, digging out the fruit, which he prefers to the crust" (38). Not only does Edward eat between his meals, but he eats in such a way that destroys food for others. By leaving the crust and not its contents, Edward displays a lack of respect for the next person who might want some pie, not to mention a lack of manners as

---

[1]   The addition of Edward to the group collected at Isabel's creates a cast of characters much like those assembled in Virginia Woolf's *Between the Acts*, discussed in the introduction as a forerunner of the novels examined in this study. In a related conference paper, "Consumption Asunder: Woolf, Dunmore, and the Mind/Body Split" (delivered at the Eleventh Annual Virginia Woolf Conference, University of Wales at Bangor, June 2001, and forthcoming in the published proceedings of that conference), I explore the possibility of Dunmore's novel as a revision of Woolf's. Dunmore has acknowledged (in an e-mail to the author) that Isabel's Sussex garden is modeled after that at Charleston Farmhouse, which was the home of Vanessa Bell, Woolf's sister. Dunmore has also explained that the relationship between Virginia and Vanessa, in part, forms the basis for that of Isabel and Nina.

regards the going social mores. At other points in the novel, he also has left only one slice of almond cake in its tin (110) and devours gooseberry fool—uneaten during the salmon dinner discussed above—straight from its bowl (81). Edward's greedy eating constructs him as both unlikeable and untrustworthy, and thus complicates the notion of greed, of consumption and its relationship to Nina's character traits. While Nina's greed places her on par with Richard and seems to free her from gender constraints, Edward's greed calls for a reevaluation of Nina's consumption practices. As a potentially questionable member of the house party, Edward reflects back upon Nina what she hopes, through her disparaging comments, will stick only to Edward and leave her own persona free from the taint of transgressive consumption.

A character such as Edward, who casts doubt upon Nina's role and in turn upon her narrative authority, is important if Nina's sexual narrative is to receive the attention that it must in order to mask the hidden narrative of Colin's death and of who may have been responsible for it. Although Nina initially emerges as a sympathetic and reliable narrator-protagonist, her relationship to food and to her body—to sex—calls this first impression into question. If Nina were simply sexualized, then her role would not be so muddled; it would be easier to discount her place in the text. Her complicated characterization, though, is integral to the novel's divided narration and to an unraveling of the text as a whole. In order for Nina to become suspect, readers must identify her body as transgressive and must share in the identification of certain actions and decisions as beyond the range of acceptability. Nina's body, as well as its actions and motility, are the focal point of this readerly response, and her eating habits, from early on in the novel, are what signify her physicality. By the time Nina herself equates her appetite for food with her sexual desire, it is almost already a given because of the long social and cultural associations of female consumption with unfeminine sexuality and because of Nina's strong affinities with both. "I like food, and I like fucking," (94), she tells Richard, and this comes as no surprise for several reasons. The most obvious, maybe, stems from Nina's deep sensuality, her bodily reactions to things as unsexy as Isabel's kitchen, which "calls out in me that small almost sexual shiver I can't fake" (17). Nina's responses to cuisine are akin to the sensual rhetoric of Nigella Lawson, who prefaces her cookbook *How to Eat* with reminders that "[...] in cooking, as in eating, you just have to let your real likes and desires guide you" (6), emphasizing the connections between proper (culinary) and suspect (sexual) responses that underscore Nina's sexual expressions. A less acute, but more important, reason for Nina's sexuality to emerge as an issue from early in the text results from her characterization as an eater, as someone who embraces the idea of greed and who has no qualms about her own body and its actions and responses.

Cultural and social codes regarding food neatly identify Nina as likely to transgress in additional ways beyond those of the palate (as seen in Prudence Bates and to some degree in Carter's Melanie of *The Magic Toyshop*). Readers who share in (whether consciously or unconsciously) these ubiquitous, culturally constructed attitudes toward female consumption will likely make such a leap of definition through their own bodies and attitudes toward embodiment while negotiating Nina's corporeal infractions through their reading. Like Richard, who carries "some pattern in his head" (108) of Nina's body, readers of the text will necessarily form an image of Nina within their own psyches, one based upon their own body/images. Partially made up of psychical elements, that image will be infused with the codes that help to fashion our social behaviors and responses. Because there are relatively strict cultural norms for women's eating practices, what diet-skeptic Mary Evans Young calls "other people's rules" (178), such expectations will become part of the individual body image. Direct, unabashed eating like Nina's, then, directly at odds with acceptable eating standards for women, will skew the level of comfort available to the reader from within the projected image of a body such as Nina's. The push-and-pull of these elements of her characterization present Nina as at once sympathetic and offensive to readers on both the cognitive and visceral levels that together make up an epistemological model of the body/image. By the time Nina begins an affair with her brother-in-law, the act is hardly shocking, because Nina has long been coded as transgressive by Dunmore's use of food-related activities and imagery. This understanding does not negate Nina's more positive qualities, however. Rather, Nina is created from the tension that flows between the psychical realm and the physical, and unraveling her story is nearly as difficult as would be a true division of the mind from the body.

Isabel, as indicated earlier, relates to her own sexuality in the same manner as she does to the act of eating: she doesn't. She explains this to Nina, noting that pregnancy and hormones have had little to do with the absence of any physical desire on her part for Richard. "No, it was never much good," she recalls, "[...] now I can't bear it. I can't have him near me" (183). Like food, sex is something in which Isabel finds no desire and little necessity. "She'd got it worked out so it only took one go," Richard confirms in a discussion of Antony's conception (179). Aside from that unique procreative moment, sex for Isabel has no meaning, does not signify. Her own body, too, once stripped of any desires for food or for sex, appears as beside the point, an afterthought. Without any culturally identifiable measure of embodiment, Isabel retreats into an ephemeral state. She is "mother" and "wife," but simultaneously lacks most of the mechanisms necessary to adequately perform such roles. She is void the "vivacity" suggested by Elaine Scarry as necessary for mimesis (a subject that I will soon return to), and as such it becomes difficult to mold Isabel into a viable image of embodiment. The reader has little, if any, access to "knowing" Isabel because one primary route to comprehension of her character, her body, has been removed. By negating her own embodiment, she denies others—but primarily denies Nina—access to her histories, her motivations. While one might assume that her lack of connection to food and to her sexuality makes Isabel a "positive" character, just as Nina is sullied by her own eating and sexual activities, this is far from the case. Isabel herself is more complicated than such an assumption would allow and serves as more than merely an opposite against which Nina can be defined. Isabel's lack of corporeal accessibility to readers is perverse in its own way. Through a denial of the body within the text, the reader is asked to deny his or her own physical existence, and, because of the actual embodiment of the reader and the embodied nature of the act of reading, this cannot quite ever be done. It is one thing to suspend disbelief while reading in order to envision new worlds or to accept bizarre coincidence; it is a far different thing to extend belief beyond the edges of one's own body. Apart from the body/image, there is no way to know the world or to fully accept the existence of another individual. So, while Isabel's gustatory prudence and chaste ways coincide with a century's cultural expectations for the feminine woman, her own nullification of her body offers little but discomfort for readers whose bodies are hardwired to comprehend the textual bodies that they encounter. In different but equally compelling ways, Isabel and Nina simultaneously subvert and adhere to feminine norms, thus making it difficult for readers to accept either woman's version of events past. Both evoke some level of accord from readers, but neither is to be completely trusted.

Like Dunmore, Angela Carter, in *The Magic Toyshop*, uses the trope of consumption—or, in Carter's case, the lack of consumption—as a way to obfuscate the narrative that runs counter to that which rides the surface of her novel. Carter's oppositional characterizations, though, are more complicated than Dunmore's, because in her novel opposition constructed via food and eating is itself hidden through the figure of a third, mediating female. The appearance of two mind/body oppositions in Carter's novel—one providing a narrative effect that veils another, more damaging dualism—allows for the novel's two narrative strands to remain separate until the secret of incest is uncovered. Melanie, the ostensible protagonist of the novel, is showcased in a manner that confuses the incest narrative that ultimately trumps the novel's tale of embodiment. Though she initially figures as the character cast against her thin and spectral Aunt Margaret (134), Melanie proves to be little more than a ruse who is cast from idioms of the flesh in order to complicate the two strands of narrative progression. She is a proverbial wrench thrown into the workings of Carter's novel. Five-year-old Victoria, Melanie's sister, is actually the character who figures as the novel's voracious female consumer, but Melanie must stand between Victoria and "Our Lady of Famine," Aunt Margaret (113). If Margaret is to keep secret her sexual relationship with her brother, Francie Jowles, then her body and its potential for (sexual) agency must be minimized. Instead of emphasizing Margaret's ephemerality (as embodied females have been shown to do), Victoria suggests the underside of Margaret's history, her errant sexuality and self-satisfaction at the expense of cultural propriety, and Melanie's narrative must interfere with readers' connections of Victoria with Margaret. Margaret is a woman of the flesh who cannot risk readers' identification of her embodiment and its transgressive actions. In each of the novels I have examined thus far, the pairs of female characters who are created from images of consumption and its lack are relative peers and can provide adequate contrast for each other. At five years of age, though, Victoria is hardly visible as a narrative component of Margaret's physicality. She instead provides a provocative balance for Carter's characterization of Margaret and is as much a necessary part of Margaret as she is an individual character. Without Melanie to provide a division between this constructed mind/body pairing, Victoria's presence would jeopardize Margaret's secret through suggesting Margaret's decadent self. To this end, then, Melanie is foregrounded in a gothic-style narrative of her own, and she diverts readers' attention away from the incest narrative that Margaret must conceal.

Melanie initially appears as an embodied character and functions as the narrative's primary, obvious opposition to Margaret. The novel's opening line presents Melanie as "of the body": "The summer she was fifteen, Melanie discovered she was made of flesh and blood" (1). Her adolescent quest to discover this new-found body leads her to what is nearly an obsession with that body and its appearance, with the ways in which it can be manipulated and dressed (enactments of auto-objectification) in order to maximize the effects of a burgeoning sexuality. Her embodiment becomes particularly important to the narrative once Melanie and her siblings are orphaned and subsequently sent to live with Margaret and her husband, Philip, maker of toys and sadistic patriarch, in a south London squalor significant of the transgression that historically has been affiliated with dirt and shabbiness. Melanie's body must be conjured up in order to suggest her role as a gothic heroine prior to her entering the bizarre world of her uncle's home. Her role as such a heroine necessitates a fear of sexual peril, and in order for this peril to become a real possibility to the reader, Melanie's body, young and lissome and vulnerable, must show itself. At times Carter does undermine this presentation of Melanie as embodied, but Melanie's position in a narrative that feels familiar because of its gothic cast pulls readers through such moments too quickly for them to make much difference. Melanie is noted as "skinny" (15) and described in relation to the human skeleton: "She felt [...] as if she had taken even her own skin off and now stood clothed in nothing, nude in the ultimate nudity of the skeleton. [...] her very hands might have been discarded like gloves, leaving only the bones" (21). Regardless of Carter's attempts to provide readers with signals that point to Melanie's doubled, liminal role in the text, the initial emergence of an embodied and sexualized young woman is the representation that lingers.

Of course, body size should not necessarily be considered a primary marker of physicality, but the imagined evaporation of Melanie's body here signifies its tangential status in the narrative. Without her parents, and placed in a role dictated by Margaret's secret narrative, Melanie becomes "an amputee" (31); part of her becomes like the phantom limb examined by Schilder and considered by him to be a critical example of the workings of the body image, a "reactivation of a given perceptive pattern by emotional forces" (67). She has lost "a tender, budding part" of herself (Carter 31). If what is lost (or "amputated") is replaced by phantom physical extensions, then Melanie, from this early point in the novel, is herself mostly phantom and will experience her own corporeality as an afterthought rather than as a vehicle for agency. As with Margaret, whose embodiment is masked by a constructed psychical characterization, with Melanie, Carter performs a parallel (if reversed) bait and switch of the mental and the physical components of her narrative makeup. Constructed as an embodied woman, Melanie finally exists only as a construct that will disallow identification of Margaret with her body and its potential for agency.

Though Melanie is not the novel's primary consuming female, she is the second, and most visible, polarized "body" to Margaret's represented ephemeral status. Uncle Philip grumbles of Melanie, "God knows she eats enough" (133), and, along with Melanie's initially embodied characterization, his opinion strengthens Melanie's apparent opposition to Margaret. After the death of Melanie's parents, she "could not eat for the weight of guilt and shame which seemed to have settled on her stomach" (23), much like the aversion of Dunmore's Isabel to eating after the death of brother Colin. Melanie's fear—that she herself is somehow to blame for the death of her parents in an airplane disaster—accompanies her shift away from a central position in a narrative that initially appears as if it might become a Bildungsroman and toward a more peripheral, contingent position vis-à-vis the story of Margaret and her secret existence. Caught between the surface, gothic narrative of her own romance plot and the submerged narrative of Margaret's incestual love for Francie, Melanie occupies a difficult position that is difficult to assess. She is a complementary body to Margaret's disembodied state, but appears less solid than the young Victoria, who is all impulse, all id. Melanie ponders that "a cool nothing [...] was her own climate. No extremes [...] She was in limbo and would be for the rest of her life" (76). She occupies middle ground rather than any definitive oppositional extreme. As a mediator between Margaret and Victoria, as well as between the novel's two narrative strands, Melanie is placed in the position of "ego," navigating the way between Victoria's raw desire for creature comforts and Margaret's mute performance of duty, and between a fanciful gothic romance and a love affair that breaks social and cultural taboo. Viewed in this way, the shifts in Melanie's characterization can be understood as mechanisms of narrative mediation rather than as problematic representational effects. The important represented qualities of consumption and of the body are components of Carter's characterizations of Margaret and Victoria, and the narrative functions of eating provide some of the few clues to their interdependence and to the submerged incest narrative.

In the midst of the chaos of *The Magic Toyshop*, Victoria can almost escape the casual reader. Her extreme youth relegates her to that less important, seemingly simplistic world of childhood, and her appearance is often more comic relief than serious suggestion of either the depravity of the Flower household or of anyone living within. Victoria is a consumer *par excellence*: she does not stop to consider her actions and, at five years old, cares nothing about any of the consequences of unbridled eating that an older female might consider. As opposed to her sister, who "was afraid that if she ate too much [...] she would grow fat and nobody would ever love her and she would die a virgin" (3), Victoria "had no sense of guilt. She had no sense at all. She was a round, golden pigeon who cooed" (5). When Melanie cannot face food after the death of their parents, Victoria "demands," "'Can I have Melanie's nice bacon?'" (23) and focuses only on her own immediate gratification. Melanie is introduced as a body ripe for objectification à la Toulouse Lautrec or D. H. Lawrence (1–2), which Patricia Juliana Smith sees as Carter's "sardonic exploration of the artifice-laden foundations of modern-day sexual fantasies" (338) and thus as insubstantial; Victoria, by contrast, first appears "beating her spoon upon the table," awaiting bread pudding (3). A "'fine, plump little girl'" (48), Victoria is a solid, material contrast to the Melanie who is embodied only to the extent that her body allows for her sexual fantasies and suggests the sexual danger that she must be ushered into as her gothic narrative progresses. Victoria, on the other hand, does little but consume food, which anchors her most firmly in the realm of the body. Considerations of the two sisters together can belie the fragility of Melanie's embodied construct, but because of Victoria's marginal role in either of the novel's narratives, such considerations are not those that are most readily presented to readers. Victoria's childhood innocence allows for her associations with Margaret's embodiment to escape notice.

The language used to position Victoria in the realm of the body is curious; her entire characterization depends upon the rhetoric of food. She is shown to be eating nearly every time she appears in the text and sometimes eats inappropriate foodstuffs, such as "the fringes off the hassocks" in church (9). Consumption is not simply sustenance for Victoria, and it goes beyond indulgence, as well. Her eating borders on the compulsive and carries with it an implied pathology that reflects Margaret's hidden activities. Her eating is reckless, and, like Nina in *Talking to the Dead*, Victoria comes to food through forceful, willful verbs that indicate an uninhibited desire. At various points in the text Victoria accesses her food through the use of verbs such as "demand" and "clamour" (5, 27), and shouts "'I want my pudding NOW!'" when crisis detains her dessert (27). Carter's descriptions of Victoria also borrow from the vocabulary of consumption: Victoria has "lollipop paws" (6), a "melon-wedge grin" (42), and speaks "with fat satisfaction" (183), emphasizing not only her relationship to food, but also an unselfconscious ease with regard to eating. Though as a child Victoria might arguably be exempt from the cultural anxieties about eating and "fat," when compared with the eating distress of Dunmore's Isabel at age seven (or even to the self-conscious eating that Nina performs while a child), Victoria's attitude is strikingly different in its single-mindedness.

Victoria's connection to food occurs very much at the sensory, rather than at the intellectual, level, and with Victoria, Carter's method of representation is an effective one for engaging readers via the body. Because she is a child, Victoria escapes sexualization through her relationship to food and eating in the way that Prudence Bates and Dunmore's Nina are both depicted as sexual with regard to consumption, but her eating does not escape a direct connection to the idea of passion, of complete abandonment to the act itself.[2] Carter underscores this

---

[2]   In an interesting aside, Melanie likens Victoria to Bertha Mason of Charlotte Brontë's *Jane Eyre* and imagines her "like Mrs. Rochester, a dreadful secret in the back bedroom" (7). While this reference supports Melanie's self-identification with Jane Eyre, and works to create the gothic context for Melanie's narrative, the allusion suggests something sinister and perhaps sexual *in potentia* about Victoria's consuming practices. Bertha Mason is "intemperate and unchaste" (302), both of which "prematurely developed the germs of insanity" (302). The wild nature of Rochester's wife, when invoked in

immersion in food by literally immersing Victoria in food: more often than not, Victoria is wearing her food as well as eating it. In episodes that intensify over the course of the novel, Victoria not only takes food into her body, but also wears it upon the surface of her body. In this way, food becomes a method of inscription that remarks upon the interconnectedness of the material and the discursive: food signifies, culturally, but at the same time is a physical marker. For Victoria, food is the language of representation as well as the ink with which that language is written. With "cream and jam smeared on her cheek" (41), Victoria's sloppiness at first appears whimsical; kids always get a little something on them during the course of a meal. Later, though, the food-turned-body-art accelerates, and the hedonistic streak in Victoria's eating becomes apparent:

> With a spoon, she scoured the crumbs from a used jar of raspberry jam [...] Her hair was stuck in spikes with jam. An angry rash of jam surrounded her mouth and her dress was smeared and sticky. She was content. She had grown fatter than ever. She was always clutching a fistful of sweets or biting into a between-meals snack of bread and condensed milk or scraping out bowls [...]. (88)

Her passion, though contradicted by her contentment, is obvious, and here even a bit unnerving. By age five, children are expected to have become somewhat socialized and to have accepted a more rigid mode of behavior than that exhibited by Victoria. For Victoria, food as "matter out of place" is simply a matter of course; her consuming practices betray social codes and mores. Her voracity is not the greed that can be seen in Nina or in Edward, because her consumption is the result of gifts freely given and does not rob someone else of sustenance or enjoyment. Victoria, defined through the act of eating and through almost becoming the food that she consumes, is the embodiment of consumption as a pure act. Unlike Melanie, whose body is contingent upon another's desire (whether real or imaginary) as well as upon narrative function, Victoria is constructed as wholly embodied in a primal sort of way. Her connection to consumption, and to orality in general, bestows Victoria with the missing bodily qualities of the ghost-like Margaret.

Victoria's orality extends beyond acts of consumption to include the practice of speech as a way to emphasize the confounding link between Margaret's lack of consumption with her muteness. The vehicle for Margaret's embodiment, Victoria has the ability to speak freely (if in a way limited by her age and relative vocabulary) in a way that the mute Margaret does not. As noted above, Victoria demands her food and other creature comforts; she asks without hesitation for the things she desires. She also can point out Philip's undesirable nature: "''E's 'orrible!'" Victoria pronounces soon after the children are sent to live in the Flower household (75). She is the only female in the household who dares to speak her

---

relationship to Victoria, adds a depth to the passion of her consumption that creates an idea of sexuality where there would otherwise be none. Though, at five, she lacks the biological and psychological wherewithal to be a sexual creature in the manner of the other female consumers examined within this project, Victoria, it is implied, certainly will grow to fill a role similar to those of the other consuming women examined here.

mind against the head of this motley clan. While Francie and Finn, Margaret's youngest brother, make known their attitudes toward Philip and his tirades, neither Melanie nor Margaret expresses herself on the subject. Margaret, of course, cannot (in most respects) because of her muteness; her lack of speech, especially viewed against Victoria's childish boldness of speech and of consumption, underscores the negation of her orality, of her agency and her perceived ability to desire. Her muteness, too, when compared with the stony silence of her husband, which "had bulk, a height and weight [...] could crush you to nothing" (168), emphasizes her disembodiment and her vulnerability, though in a questionable manner. On one hand, Margaret's loss of speech "on her wedding day, like a curse" (37) easily signifies the loss of power and agency that has occurred as a result of her marriage to the oppressive Philip. Margaret's muteness, however, is more problematic than such a reading calls attention to.

Margaret must remain mute in order to avoid a rashness such as Victoria's, yes. She must also avoid the "unspeakable" subject of incest, must not dare speak of her taboo love for Francie. Most importantly, however, Margaret must be presented in such a way that any reference to her as desiring, as libidinal, is erased. The site of primary consumption—the mouth—must be rendered virtually unnecessary in order to construct a screen that keeps her "real" story hidden from view. Her aphasia, a result of psychological rather than of biological determinants, is at once her "curse," as Francie suggests, and her option. Margaret's lack of speech helps to present her as "passive, and compliant [...] the perfect 'castrated woman'" (Wyatt 565), and thus to conceal her actual agency, phallic or otherwise. But it is also most duplicitous in that the very muteness is itself an act of social agency. Her code of silence is broken at the novel's end because her ties to Philip have been severed and because her secret has been discovered: "Catastrophe had freed her tongue" (197). Once she has no need for muteness, she discards it as suddenly as she came by it. Her muteness, too, renders invalid Margaret's adopted psychical, discursive construct. Those "true" natives of the intellect (such as Pym's Jane Cleveland) are inextricably connected to language and to the ephemerality of discourse. Margaret, an actual natural citizen of the physical world, has no such allegiance to the sphere of language, and her muteness is a negative factor of her hidden embodiment.

In addition to her speech disorder, Margaret is denied access to the desire signified by orality through a distancing of her character from the consumption of food. She is not totally distanced from food itself, though; her role as oppressed domestic caregiver is strengthened through Margaret's perpetual occupation of the kitchen. As the sole source of sustenance for her family, Margaret is a fixture in the family kitchen, which is the domestic and social center of the Flower home. "'She's a gran' cook [...] Such pastry!'" Finn proclaims as an introduction of Margaret to the children when they arrive in London (38). Throughout the novel, Margaret resides almost exclusively within the kitchen and at the center of the household routine, and food or the suggestion of food shapes both the progression of the narrative(s) and of Carter's characterization of the mute, disembodied Irishwoman. Whether the meal consists of simple fare, such as morning porridge, or the more extravagant meals served on her Irish china each Sunday, Margaret is the one who undertakes its preparation, who presides over the consumption of others. Her kitchen produces food that is aligned more with the domestic prescriptions of Mrs. Beeton, though, and that is more staunchly English than any food produced in Nina's sultry, sensual world. Sarah Sceats notes, "What it means to feel at home in a culinary tradition—where the practices are understood and some of the meanings attached to foods are familiar—is important to many women writers," and continues, "Angela Carter often deliberately locates her fictional characters in relation to archetypal English food" (127). Margaret's ostensible submission to patriarchy and to Phillip is underscored by her subscription to traditional foodways. In Phillip Flower's home, Sunday tea is "shrimps, bread and butter, a bowl of mustard and cress and a rich, light, golden sponge-cake baked that morning in the oven with the Sunday joint" (113). A roast goose appears for Christmas dinner, much to the chagrin of Philip, who forbids the celebration of holidays. Margaret's culinary repertoire is vast and exhibits expertise not commonly associated with slums or with the poverty otherwise rampant throughout the rest of the home, and this emphasizes the performative femininity that masks her sexual transgressions.

Her transgression through the preparation of a Christmas goose, though, is her only subversive attempt to utilize food as a weapon or as a method of power. Carter uses the kitchen and cooking in this novel to signify traditional roles for women (such as those outlined in earlier chapters), which in turn are linked to the severe oppression that Margaret endures as Philip's wife. Margaret's culinary endeavors appear as hardly more than her domestic duty. Unlike Nina in Dunmore's novel, who takes sensual pleasure in cooking and in the feeding of others (and whose relationship to food via cooking is sexualized), Margaret cooks because of the duties associated with her gender. A reason for this differing use of cooking activities might well be the sexual and culinary revolutions that took place between 1967, when *The Magic Toyshop* was published, and 1996, when *Talking to the Dead* first appeared. Not only have women's social and cultural roles shifted away from those largely associated with domestic duties, but the role of the cook (as well as that of the heretofore male chef, whose place in the public kitchen has been successfully encroached upon in recent years by numerous women chefs) in society has changed dramatically over the last few decades of the twentieth century. At the end of the twentieth and into the twenty-first century, culinary skills are sought after, are big business; depending upon the bill of fare, eating can now, more than it has been in recent history, be an activity significant of cultural capital and of pleasurable excess. "Behind all this," writes Brian Harrison, "lies a revolution in food retailing [...] Sainsbury's tandoori chicken and Marks and Spencer's avocado pears from Israel and plums from Chile promoted new tastes and defied the tyranny of the seasons" (146). In Dunmore's world, take-away and exotic food items are plentiful, and one can imagine Nina, when in London, riding home on the underground during rush hour, an M&S bag between her ankles. In the world developed by Carter for Margaret, however, neither sexual nor culinary revolution has taken place; this kitchen is one built upon a quest for British normativity after the end of World War II. The homely Sunday joint, when compared with Nina's buttery salmon and fresh cucumbers, provides a contrast between tradition and experimentation, between the old ways and those new methods of cooking that have more recently crossed over from the sanctity of the chef's kitchen into the average British domestic sphere. Nina's cooking borrows from the authority of the chef, while Margaret's cuisine, though good, still represents the traditions of home cooking and of feminine duty to her family's basic needs. "She must [...] be nice if she cooks so well," Melanie thinks (47), connecting the stereotypical dots of maternal/feminine domesticities and sympathies, and underscoring the quite traditional context in which to view Margaret.

An even more overt representation of Margaret's oppressed (feminine) positions of housekeeper and caregiving wife occurs via the only piece of jewelry she owns and that she wears each Sunday. This necklace is made "of dull silver, two hinged silver pieces knobbed with moonstones which snapped into place around her lean neck and rose up almost to her chin so that she could hardly move her head" (112). In keeping with the special Sunday use of fine china and with the extraordinary tea that Margaret prepares each week, Margaret's sabbath appearance is more spectacularly fashioned on that day than on others. The collar of silver (made by Philip as a wedding gift for his mute bride) is *de rigueur* for Sunday dinner, as are styled hair and Margaret's one good dress. The neck gear is an obvious symbol of Margaret's status as chattel: it is a collar or yoke, and it impedes her ability to function as she would normally. We know from Finn that "'they make love on Sunday nights, [Philip] and Margaret'" (114), and so the connection between her oppressed position and her sexual relationship with her husband is far from subtle. Margaret is not a willing partner in any facet of this relationship except for the most basic: she remains in Philip's household, "chooses" not to remove herself in order to pursue a better existence for herself and for her two brothers. This "choice," however, is in keeping with the extremely limited amount of actual choice to which women such as Margaret—indeed, even women much less restrained than is Margaret—have historically had access. In the context of the novel's more obvious of its two narrative trajectories, the amount of agency Margaret has within the confines of her marriage to Philip Flower is nil. The silver collar—"sinisterly exotic and bizarre" (112)—represents the lack of freedom that Margaret has within this relationship, and because of its obvious nature is one of the novel's most clumsy signifiers.

This collar, though, allows for a comparison of the two instances of Margaret's food consumption within the novel. Margaret's first meal with the children and Philip together presents her as equally without agency and appetite:

> Aunt Margaret, frail as a pressed flower, seemed too cowed by [Philip's] presence even to look at him. She had only the tiniest portion of porridge, a Baby Bear portion, but she took the longest to eat it, nibbling in tiny crumbs from the edge of the spoon. She had not finished it when Uncle Philip crashed down his own spoon on an empty bowl. (73)

Her relationship to the meal at hand illustrates, as well as her silver collar or aphasic symptoms do, the lack of visible drive with which Margaret is endowed. Her portion is that of "Baby Bear," but regardless of any "just right" quality, Margaret is unable to eat more than a fraction of what her husband and the others present at the meal can consume. Presumably, if one is aware that one's meal will end when the plate at the head of the table is empty (the etiquette of 1928's *Etiquette for Women* still in place at Philip's table), then one would learn to eat at a pace rapid enough to allow for the consumption one wishes to undertake. Margaret's inertia at the breakfast table, while yet another representation of her plight under Philip's rule, is also a misleading (lack of) action. Through Margaret's relationships to food and to eating, Carter has characterized her in terms of old-fashioned subjugation and submission, and has woven her from common perceptions of women living with domestic violence. In addition to emphasizing the charged nature of the household, her apparent lack of agency disguises Margaret's actual transgressive sexual behavior and is a divisive technique used by Carter to maintain two separate narratives within the single text.

The second passage in which Margaret is depicted while eating occurs during Sunday tea. While Philip eats "a battalion of shrimps [...] a loaf of bread spread with half a pound of butter" and "the lion's share of the cake," all Margaret can do is to "sip painfully at a meagre cup of tea and toy with a few shoots of mustard and cress" (113). Her consumption here is presented as different from the eating she does so little of in the previous scene by virtue of the moonstone-encrusted collar: "When she wore the collar, she ate with only the utmost difficulty" (113). This difficulty actually varies little from the truncated meal of porridge earlier in the text, but is still emphasized here through the significance of the collar and its relationship to Margaret's purported total-victim status. Both scenes draw heavily on the ways in which oppressed women commonly have been depicted. Carter has capitalized on the understanding that many readers would bring to the tale of Margaret's life with Philip—that her diminished physical and emotional capacities indicate a lack of ability to shake the shackles of his control—in order to draw attention away from the fact that as her brother's lover, Margaret is actually making choices laden with more social and cultural significance than any decision to remove herself from marriage would approach. As with the breakfast scene, the passage that introduces the collar uses food and eating imagery as a way to bluff readers. While the collar can certainly (how can it not be?) be a symbol of restrictive traditions and gender mandates, it is "hinged" and can be removed from the throat that will not swallow, will not speak. On each day aside from Sunday, Margaret is free of this neck-piece and all it signifies; the rest of the week is void of Philip's sexual demands and of the prescribed feminine apparel he insists that Margaret wear. The collar, which surrounds a neck that otherwise is the predominant site of Margaret's symptomatic muteness (and which is also the gateway to her thin, disembodied physicality), illuminates how beneath the artifice lies a different truth. Free of the bonds represented by the collar, Margaret finds ways to access the agency signified by her voice (hidden but available to her eventually) and the body so closely identified with the pleasures of eating.

Both Helen Dunmore and Angela Carter in these novels use cultural assumptions about the consuming female in order to direct readers' attention toward narratives that veil each novel's ultimate truth. Though each author uses such imagery differently, both play upon widely accepted stereotypes and anxieties associated with various social and cultural roles for women: voracious consumer, sexual siren, nurturing caretaker, oppressed victim. While some women certainly do fulfill these roles, in these works of fiction the images of women that are evoked—especially within the surface narratives of each text—exist primarily as catalysts for reader response. By evoking the body through represented acts of eating and consumption, Dunmore and Carter both call forth the reader's body/image as a site of that response. With the entrance of the physical body into the act of reading, reader attention can be effectively directed away from the narratives of discomfort that become apparent at each novel's end.

Louise Rosenblatt's early work in reader-response theory, in particular in the theory dubbed "transactional" response theory, provides a useful foundation for an understanding of reading events that are dependent upon readers' embodiment. Within transactional reader response, reading is a nonlinear relationship between readers and texts that manifests as "a situation, an event at a particular time and place in which each element conditions the other" (Rosenblatt 16). Neither text nor reader can claim *a priori* status within a given reading act, and depending upon context and upon situational aspects of each reading act, a third entity— "meaning"—is created when each factor is "conditioned by and conditioning the other" (17). The lack of primacy granted to either text or reader within this analysis of reading events is synonymous with the interactivity that I have proposed for that other binary created from the mind and the body, and just as I have shown through my examinations of that dualism, in the reader/text dyad there is a necessary interaction, transaction, between the mutual components of the grammatical "whole." Elizabeth Flynn notes the potential for feminist reading strategies that lies within Rosenblatt's theories, particularly for cultural-feminist perspectives (112). If the attitudes of a time and place that a reader has internalized become part and parcel of a reading act, then those cultural attitudes about women, female embodiment, and female consumption all infuse the reading of any text with both consciously and unconsciously understood (and resisted) biases resulting from acculturation. Readers bring to texts a wealth of cultural knowledge, and popular culture and activities such as household and bodily maintenance, as well as auto-objectification, that result from cultural ideas become hinged to the act of reading and interpreting texts. In order to untangle the dual narratives of Carter's and Dunmore's texts, I wish to propose a theory of reader response that is transactional in nature and in which the body is complicit, in which the body/image of the reader acts as a central catalyst for a comprehension of the bodies within texts. Both Carter and Dunmore rely upon female consumption in order to create and maintain clear character sympathies and reader responses, and the consuming bodies in both texts help to signify "appropriate" ways to read the surface narratives of each text. For Barthes, the human body is the "single object from which the [symbolic field] derives its unity" (214), and as such the represented body within the field of a text commands a certain amount of notice: it makes sense of a variety of symbols that otherwise may have little meaning for the reader. If the body (or signifiers of the body, such as food consumption) is absent from the textual field, then it can become difficult for readers to understand the text in any way beyond the purely intellectual. Because readers are creatures of both intellect and materiality, those readers make sense best from information that appeals to the gestalt of their individual experiences, from information that passes through the body image of each reader. The various bodies present in Dunmore's *Talking to the Dead* and Carter's *The Magic Toyshop* assist readers in their reading experiences and simultaneously illuminate and obfuscate the narratives contained within each text.

As I have discussed in earlier chapters, connections between the female body and the activity of consumption invoke a general cultural anxiety of woman as licentious, sexual, and transgressive. As transgressive, female consumption displays a means of resistance to the social order, but also indicates for the reader the fact that a network of codes, such as those found within the volumes that outline proper bodily maintenance, exists against which to transgress. Through a retrieval of social codes from the reader's unconscious and recall of these codes by the reader, the act of reading becomes a self-conscious one. Consumption within the text signifies consumption from without, and the lessons that can be extracted from the narratives of bodies such as Nina's or Melanie's are indeed the lessons of readers' bodies. In his understanding of reading as "only one aspect of consumption, but a fundamental one," Michel de Certeau helps to shed light on the connections between the consumption of food and the idea of reading as consumption (167). There is a basic error in the assumption "that the public is modeled by the products imposed upon it," states Certeau. Reading, as active, interpretive, and for Certeau a potentially resistant activity, helps to explain how all forms of consumption can be viewed as modes of agency. Too often, consumers are viewed as passive receptacles of commerce, of food, of information. "To assume that," according to Certeau, "is to misunderstand the act of 'consumption.'" This misunderstanding assumes that 'assimilating' necessarily means 'becoming similar to' what one absorbs, and not 'making something similar' to what one is, making it one's own, appropriating or reappropriating it" (166).

Reading is not necessarily an act of control, one in which the text predictably plays upon the reader (although that certainly can be one function of the text). Reading is an act of play, as well: the reader "insinuates into another person's text the ruses of pleasure and appropriation: he poaches on it, is transported into it, pluralizes himself in it like the internal rumblings of one's body" (Certeau xxi). The pleasure derived from this form of consumption, from reading as an appropriation of the texts of others, is at once intellectual and physical. As a source of pleasure, reading can act upon the body in similar ways as do other sentient experiences. Molly Travis defines the pleasure within Certeau's theory to be specifically sexual, and redefines it as "jouissance" (8), but to locate such pleasure only in the realm of the sexual is to remove from it the very plurality Certeau emphasizes in his discussion of reading as an everyday and resistant act. The body's pleasure can take many forms, can "rumble" through the body in diffuse ways, but it will always resemble the locus of its pleasure, will always recall through a psychical experience of pleasure the physical sensation from which it has been engendered. Though Certeau insists that in the act of reading the "autonomy of the eye suspends the body's complicities with the text" (176), the represented body within the text recalls for a reader that reader's own body. The reader's body is inherently complicit with the text; therefore, one pleasure of reading lies, in part, within pleasurable experiences chronicled within the text.

For most readers, acts of reading require imagination and revelry. Imagination, in turn, requires a referent, something that stands in psychically for the material, physical entity created through the power of recall. Hardly separate from the thing that is imagined, the act itself—the intellectual act of inventing, imagining—is dependent upon the object at its base: "the object tends to be coterminous with and only knowable through that object" imagined (Scarry, *Body* 164). When that object is the human form represented within a text, that body/object is understood through the reader's own embodiment, with the reader's body/image providing a map for understanding the actions and sensations of the textual body. "I cannot understand the function of the living body," writes Merleau-Ponty, "except by enacting it myself, and except in so far as I am a body which rises toward the world" (75). Our bodies "rise toward the world" through their textuality; they rise as bodies within written texts rise toward their readers' own bodies and toward transaction and communication. As the nexus of solid flesh and the mind's emphemerality, the body image is the conduit for interplay between the reader and the text, between the physical experience of reading and the discourse laid bare on the page. This is not to say that the act of reading equates the experience stored within the reader's memory and the experience recounted by an author within a text, but rather that the two interact through the mediation of the gestalt of the body. Between the experience of physical practices and any recording of them into language, "the image, the phantom of the expert but mute body, preserves the difference" (Certeau 42) and at the same time mediates the exchange.

The human body writ large, recreated through the text and through the (textual) image of itself, is fundamentally a site of a production of knowledge, knowledge of our own bodies and of the bodies of others. The body image, both physical and mental, indicates the lexical nature of the body: as communicable, the body envelops a system of language and of communication through one body image and to another. In language as well as in relation to external objects, the human body is "transformed to be communicable and endlessly sharable" (Scarry, *Body* 255). "The mute facts of sentience" can only be, according to Elaine Scarry, shared within a "culture of language" (*Body* 256), and I agree, but with the understanding of the body itself as linguistic, as the origin of a certain form of communication transmitted by the psychical extension of one's own body. Spoken or written "language" does not bind the body's meaning; the body shares itself through its self-image. The body image is the way in which one body "perceives the body of another, and discovers in that other body [...] a familiar way of dealing with the world" (Merleau-Ponty 354). Reading the body of another, whether within a text or within the world, involves a fundamental relating of experience, of both sentient and intellectual encounters. The "whole" of the body, when met with some other whole, morphs into a new version of each body/image, each body becoming an extension of the other and at the same time forming a new, larger unit made cohesive by the interaction of both body images. One gestalt considers another: "as the parts of my body together [comprise] a system, so my body and the other's are one whole, two sides of one and the same phenomenon" (Merleau-Ponty 354).[3]

Schilder's work on the subject of the body image strengthens this idea of the body as "sharable," as a way to gain understanding of the realm of the body.[4] "Experience of our body-image and experience of the bodies of others are closely interwoven with each other" (16), he explains, in a way that makes the body inherently social through the body image concept. Some of Schilder's cases involved patients whose inability to locate sites of sensation on their own bodies or to point out their own body parts (agnosia) was linked to their abilities to make the same identifications on the bodies of others. From this discovery, he believes that "where we are not able to come to a true perception of our own bodies, we are also unable to perceive the bodies of others" (44). It is possible, then, to reformulate this to state that we can only "know" the bodies of others in as much as we know our own physicalities. Where there is a limited ability to function or a lack of experience, the body as a receptor of information is self-limiting. One might be able to imagine climbing Half Dome or running a marathon even when one has not, but only in a much different way than can one who has shared a similar experience. Without certain commonalty of sentient experience, one can only imagine via analogy: how like that experience is this one that I have had? Running a shorter race might enable one to explore some of the physical sensations of marathon running, but running through a grocery store in order to purchase a missing ingredient for dinner is an experience that limits the analogy and thus one's ability to adequately imagine all physical experiences of another. The body image is a critical part of motility and of perception, both sensual and psychological. The boundaries of one body image in part define the ability to comprehend other corporeal experience, including experience represented in discourse. Regardless of this limitation, however, the body image is central to our ability to understand,

---

3   The original (*Phénoménologie de la Perception*; Gallimard, 1945) reads: "désormais, commes les parties de mon corps *forment ensemble* un système, le corps d'autrui et le mien sont un seul tout, l'envers et l'endroit d'un seul phénonème, et l'existence anonyme dont mon corps et à chaque moment la trace habit désormais ces deux corps à la fois" (40, emphasis added). I have changed the word "compromise," which appears in the Routledge Smith translation, to "comprise" in this sentence.

4   A related study investigates links between "awareness of body topology and auditory comprehension of body part names" and discusses patients' difficulty in naming body parts on charts when given a linguistic referent. See Maria-Jesus Benedet and Harold Goodglass, "Body Image and Comprehension of Body Part Names," *Journal of Psycholinguistic Research* 18.5: 485–96.

to "read," the experiences of another. Without the fundamental knowledge of our own states of embodiment, there would be no foundation for any creation of connection and analogy as we work toward comprehension of others.

The confines of our own body images and experiences perhaps lead to what seems to be an often exorbitant, sometimes prurient interest in the most common of human experiences. Not all of us have run a marathon, but there are some activities shared by most, if not all, individuals. These "everyday" practices allow for a network of experience that creates commonalty where there might otherwise be none. As such an everyday practice, food consumption works in this way and creates the potential for an understanding of the scope of another's motility and impulse. As a phenomenon with a distinctly psychological dimension, the body image contains within it the cultural codes absorbed by the psyche, and so the relation between one body/image and another is more than the interconnectedness of physical beings and experience. There are also connections between what is represented by the body image and its experience, by what becomes "intelligible" through socialization and through the sociability of the body image. Eating is a standard practice, and it is an activity that must be carried out in order for existence to be sustained. Eating can thus be understood as an action based in need and that most often brings with it a certain satisfaction, whether that of simple sustenance or of pleasure derived from grander fare. As a social and cultural practice, though, eating is also fraught with messages about the body: its maintenance, class, sexuality. The body's psychological responses to food, too, play a part in the reaction of one body image to another. Depending upon the cultural messages incorporated into one's psyche, for example, the feeling of satiety may engender a response of pleasure or one of abhorrence (or in the cases of some bodies, such as those of bulimics, a combination of such responses can occur). The body image carries with it these by-products of culture, and this can add a layer of further connection and understanding for those who share cultural practices and information. The level of one body's comprehension of another will depend upon how these two registers of knowledge occur together and upon whether they occur together at all. But even when cultural assumptions about bodily practices are quite different, the sharable body image is a prevalent part of human experience and allows for an essential understanding of other bodies, whether those bodies are actual or representational.

There is certainly an advantage to reading the textuality of "real" bodies in the immediate world, but the body image also works as a site of mediation during the reading of represented bodies within written texts. One basis of knowing the bodies of others in our surroundings is vision, and vision is perhaps the main sense evoked during the act of reading. Not only is written information taken in through the visual apparatus, but the information processed during the act of reading is often of a visual quality: sights and scenes are large parts of our literary landscape, and the world of objects is more easily transcribed than are those of taste or smell. The secondary senses can only be approximated in language through metaphor and simile or with the use of adjectives, and the margin for interpretive error with such figurative language is much greater than with language used to explain the phenomena of visual objects. A sense of sight is, next to the kinesthetic sense, the primary way in which sighted people understand the world. There is, therefore, more precise and more sharable language to define and describe the physical world. The body image exists without sight, but it has a definite, important "optic" quality that lends itself to reading representational bodies. Bodies represented in language are created from language that relates directly to our sense of the visual, and a reader's comprehension of represented bodies can be understood as originating from sensory impulses similar to those that create our actual visual impressions.

In some of Schilder's cases, patients with certain brain abnormalities could begin a motion only if they were looking at the limb in question (22). The embodied self that we visualize psychically is an important part of the mechanism of the body image in that it allows for motion and sentience without making necessary the sense of actual sight. Even when "the majority of the optic images of normal persons never come into the full light of consciousness" (Schilder 22), the optic impressions made by the body image upon individual consciousness are a necessary component of body comprehension. Unconscious knowledge of our own bodies (and of their extensions within the body image) creates strong sensory impressions within the psyche: the visual quality of the optic image is the forerunner of all other sensory data. In order for one to register where the body is touched, what it is touching, or how it will move toward obtaining something it desires, the optical, projected version of the body must mediate the sensory experience. The body must "read" itself in order to process motor impulses and sensory information. Importantly, too, the "optic impressions concerning our own body [...] are in no way different from the optic impressions we have concerning the bodies of others" (Schilder 234–5), including those bodies rendered from language. External stimuli such as verbal instructions can alter the optic image and create derivative optic perceptions, such as when "the subject is asked to imagine his hands three times their normal size, [and feels] his imagined giant hands heavier" than they actually are (Schilder 115). Schilder points out that this shift from optic image to optic perception takes place through a "clouding of the consciousness" (115) and does not cause a permanent adjustment in the body image, simply a situational change sympathetic to the stimulus from which it derives. This clouding of the consciousness can also, in some cases, be called the "imagination," and the imagination is the primary clearinghouse for the information and ideas taken in during the act of reading.

Imagination, typically understood as a flight of fancy or as "the ghostly enfeeblement of images in daydreaming" (Scarry, *Dreaming* 40), is redefined by Elaine Scarry, in *Dreaming by the Book*, as an act that can supply vivacity to its perceived objects, especially such imagination as that required in the reading process. More so than in other media, she theorizes, "in the verbal arts [...] images somehow *do* acquire the vivacity of perceptual objects" (5). Whereas in painting there can be actual texture and color that will be absent from a written text, painting as a method of communication has "elaborate commitments" to its "*immediate sensory content*," while verbal arts are completely lacking in sensory stimuli and only present "*mimetic content*" (6–7, original italics). The difference in the perception necessary to read a painting and to read a written text is the act of perception itself: "the verbal arts enlist our imaginations in mental actions that in their vivacity more closely resemble sensing than daydreaming" (16). The content of these "verbal arts" is altogether hidden within the imagination of the reader, while different levels of sensory and other "content" are provided for the viewer/listener/consumer in music, visual art, and theater. Imagining the visual qualities of the written text demands the full participation of the reader. The act of "mimesis," Scarry writes, "is perhaps less in [the objects represented in a text] than in our seeing of them" (6). Language is not the sole source of mimesis, but reading is also mimetic action; mimesis is performance. As a mode of reading, mimesis is also an act of consumption: "imagining the flowers is also a way of ingesting or at least interiorizing them" (Scarry, *Dreaming* 66), and here Scarry echoes Certeau's suggestion of how the assimilation of language surpasses the act of inscription. In order for the mind to make meaning from not only the words on the page but from the objects that they represent, the vehicle of the material body must process language into something like life. The vivacity that goes missing from the imagination without the verbal instruction of the text—the "enfeeblement" evoked by Scarry's theories—is restored to the act of reading by virtue of the embodied action and motility with which reading is invested. "Perceptions are only formed on the basis of their motility," Schilder notes, so that "[...] changes in the motility in its broadest sense will be of determining influence on the structure of the body image" (15). Each image within a text will thus interact with and change the body image itself, if only for the moment of reading, the way a verbal cue can result in a perceived "growth" of the image of one's own hands. The connection of the physical and mental aspects of our beings are quite evident in the acts of reading and perception, for without an idea of how we move through time and space, the spatiality and vivacity of represented images within a text would have no method by which to present themselves; the reader would have no way to make meaning from actions represented by the printed word. According to Schilder, "imaginations [...] change under the influence of motor impulses and motor imaginations" (115), under the influence of the body and its self-made image.

Scarry's work on imagination in *Dreaming by the Book* extends from her earlier work on embodiment and from the ways in which she herself has tried to posit the sensory experiences of the body as "knowable." The vast divide between discourse and the body that hinders (one could say "enfeebles") Western thought, though, also limits Scarry's exploration of *The Body in Pain*. The body is part—a necessary part—of the sense-making processes of the mind and its perception. The body is always complicit in and part of language, not simply derived from it or marked by it, as some theorists seem to suggest. For Scarry in her earlier work, "the sentient fact of the person's suffering"—and I'll extend the issue of pain outward to include all of the body's sensory experiences—"will become knowable to a second person" only "through one means of verbal objectification or another" (13).

While Scarry reaches toward this more complex nexus of mind and body, materiality and discourse, when she states that "the advantage of the sign is its proximity to the body," she never moves beyond this nearness and into a full transaction of the mind and the body. In the second half of this sentence she discounts her first assertion: "its disadvantage is the ease with which it can then be spatially separated from the body" (17). The sign or referent, however, must not necessarily *be* the body in order for the body to be implicated in the act of reading. When the body is that which is imagined through reading, its representation has extra significance due to the embodied nature of the act of reading. Though Scarry's later work moves theoretically beyond such a sharp divide between mind and body, the act of imagining remains a circuitous route from object through psyche and back again. That sense of reading as play, as pleasurable and unpredictable, is missing from her later ideas. The interplay of mind and body, their always interdependent state, is needed in order to invigorate and expand upon her imaginings.

As with Scarry, for whom the response of the imagination depends upon the "vivacity" of the image at hand, for Marie-Laure Ryan, "immersion" in a text "depends on the vividness of the display" and, like perspective in a work of visual art, such a vividness integrates the reader into the text ("Immersion" par. 5).[5] The primary element for response to a text is the quality of its image and of the ability of the image to evoke mimesis. Daniel Punday contextualizes this with regard to bodies within texts: "The degree of embodiment within narrative character is in many ways corollary to" what he denotes as character "individuation." "The potential distance," he continues, "between body and character is an element of interpretation of a narrative" (66). This degree of embodiment will affect the degree of mimesis available from a textual body, and the more clearly readers can "see" that body, the more physical the interactivity of reading becomes as bodies on either side of the reading experience interact, and the more the lived experiences of readers' bodies will become parts of the total reading event. As an act of the gestalt of the body and the mind, mimesis—perceptive reading and image-making within the imagination—enables the act of reading to move beyond the sphere of immersion, which implies a one-way activity of reader onto or into text. For Ryan, immersion allows for the imagination to take over the reader, and "the medium must become transparent for the represented world to emerge as real" ("Immersion" par. 8). In this way, the verbal medium must transcend the materiality of printed pages and book boards, the chair beneath the reader, as well as the rest of his or her environment. As with Scarry's proposals, which fail through their inability to integrate the body with the mind, Ryan falls short of this same integration through her separation of immersion from interactivity, which she defines through an examination of virtual reality (VR) and related

---

[5]   During the writing of this book, Ryan released a full-length study of the relationship between interactivity and narrative. Later in this chapter, I use that full-length work to refer to theories she began in the original article, from which I quote here in the chapter and elsewhere.

technologies. Interactivity, she explains, "requires a dynamic simulation" of the external world, and certainly virtual reality provides a high level of that type of interaction ("Immersion" par. 25). Dynamic exchange, however, is not limited to VR's altered ontology.

Ryan does allow for a relation between reading and interactivity, but does so only through a discussion of postmodern texts and metafiction:

> The most efficient strategy for promoting an awareness of the mechanisms of fictionality is [...] to engage the reader in a game of in and out: now the text captures the reader in the narrative suspense; now it bares the artificiality of plots; now the text builds up the illusion of an extratextual referent; now it claims "this world is mere fiction." Shuttled back and forth between ontological levels, the reader comes to appreciate the layered structure of fictional communication. ("Immersion" par. 28)

This "in and out" of interactivity is precisely the way in which the extratextual body and the body within the text relate: each reflects the textuality of the other; each creates, through the mediating body image, itself in the other's likeness. The narrative need not be fragmented; it need not be self-referential in order for "interactive" reading to take place. Represented embodiment within the text is itself a referent for the body of the reader. Through the activity of the imagination in its perceptions and mimetics, the body within the text is "ingested" by the body of the reader looking in. When Schilder's idea of the unconscious optic image of the body (22) is revisited, we can understand that these responses need not, in fact are not likely to, be visible or understood on the conscious level: they occur simply because the mind and the body work together in the act of reading as they do in all other activities, because "in some way there may be a continuous interplay between the body-images of ourselves and the persons around us" (Schilder 235). The merging, through the body/image, of the text and the reader may just be the "complete agreement" that Wayne Booth believes can exist between an author and a reader, agreement that enables the "most successful reading" of a text (138).

Ryan imagines an eventual dissolution of the tension between immersion and interactivity by way of turning "language into a dramatic performance, into the expression of a bodily mode of being in the world" ("Immersion" par. 39). This very tension, though, is what defines her idea of interactive reading; tension is necessary for the dynamic interplay of reader and text, of bodies, that will enable a text to be imagined differently than it can be if the realms of the mind and body are left intact and separate. A false distinction, it is a split that nevertheless has saturated the way in which we think about language, about bodies, about being at all, whether in the world or in the text. The amount of new life, of unexplored levels of narrative that can be explored once the mind is theoretically harnessed to the body, will be an amazing quantity. Perhaps especially for women writers, who have so obviously worked with this tension as their attempts to move between mind and body—and to negotiate any resulting auto-objectivity—have led them in new and interesting directions, this way to imagine reading through and of the body will prove a fruitful tool. The realism of the everyday, of the domestic, of the small objects and resistant qualities that make up a life provides the means for readerly immersion in familiar perspective, long-trod ground. The vehicle of the body, however, is what will carry readers across that ground as they travel unique journeys through the text and among the bodies that populate it. In the next section I will explain how these theories of reading and embodied interactivity, signified by the representations of eating so central to both Carter and Dunmore's texts, directly affect the ways in which readers can understand the progressions of the separate narrative strands in each text, and will show how the cultural effects of represented eating within these texts implicate the body image of the reader and allow for the respective secrets of each text to be withheld until its final moments.

Both Dunmore and Carter have created novels fraught with the tensions inherent between the culturally divided spheres of mind and body, and each works with this tension in a slightly different manner in order to provide the same narrative protection for her text's ultimate revelation. These divided narratives, along with their divided female protagonists, both imitate and exacerbate the problematic effects of wrenching the materiality of the body away—even if only figuratively—from its necessary psychical counterpart. The novels' structural bifurcations are disruptive: the textual representations of consuming female bodies are skewed and result in two distinct narrative "realities." The texts suffer from the same sort of distorted (re)presentation as does a typical anorectic who sees reflected back in the mirror not the "real" body and its true dimensions, but instead an alternative image of her own creation, an image based upon social and cultural assumptions that have become internalized and eventually inscribed upon not the physical body itself, but upon the body's own perception of itself (body image) and of its place in the world at large. Body image disturbance common to anorexic disorders is a result of a disassociation of mind from body, of what I have called "auto-objectification," and, though the textual body is not a direct corollary for the real flesh and blood of real women's bodies, the metaphor is apropos of the sort of distortion that occurs within these texts when the mental and the physical are forced into separate and unnatural realms. In both the Carter and Dunmore texts, one narrative is inscribed upon the other in a way that results in the masking of the actual "reality" of the text. Like the real proportions of the anorexic body, however, the underlying, uncomfortable narratives at the bases of these two novels are hidden from view by accumulations of culture that mirror those prescriptions found in beauty and other maintenance books, by networks of social significance related to the consuming female body.

At the risk of overextending a metaphor, consider the two narratives in each text as "big" and "small," "fat" and "thin" paths of progression through the novels.[6] As with the anorectic's narration of a self-image much different from her actual thin body, the "large" narratives in these texts are not the expressions of the "real"

---

[6]   I owe a debt of thanks to Michelle Massé for her suggestion that I consider using such a metaphor in my investigation of differing narrative trajectories.

facts of murder or of incest, but instead are narratives of consumption and of its attendant cultural baggage. These "large" narratives are in no way in excess of their thin counterparts simply by virtue of their relationships to food consumption, but instead because of the nature of their construction. The surface narratives— those that direct readers to experience the texts through a shallow lens of cultural association—are composed from little-challenged analogies made between strong appetites of all types, and such construction has little basis in the ultimate reality of either text. The "thin" but very real narrative that hides behind the façade of consumption in each text is the narrative of real female agency and very real, if socially deviant, female activity. The actions associated with the submerged narratives of both Isabel's and Margaret's transgressions must be denied by the text, as well as by the reader, in keeping with the denial perpetuated by each character through her disassociation from food consumption and, by extension, from her own body and its errant potential. The more benign bodies of Nina, Victoria, and Melanie are invested with negative social and cultural messages attached to food consumption, resulting in "inflated" narratives that enable the narratives of discomfort to remain hidden until the final pages of both novels.

One way to express how readers might navigate the divided naratives of these novels is through Rosenblatt's notion of "aesthetic" and "efferent" reading as discussed in *The Reader, the Text, the Poem.* Her sense of transactions in reading extends beyond the reader/text binary to include a spectrum of ways in which readers might read that ranges from pure fact-gathering on one end ("efference") to immersive reading, labeled "aesthetic," in which "the reader's primary concern is with what happens *during* the actual reading event [...] *the reader's attention is centered directly on what he is living through during his relationship with that particular text* (24–5, original italics). While Rosenblatt is careful to maintain that texts might be read in both manners, that narrative can and does appeal to both sentience and intellect, her focus in this study is the transactional "aesthetic" reading act and its impact upon readers: "Sensing, feeling, imagining, thinking under the stimulus of the words, the reader who adopts the aesthetic attitude feels no compulsion other than to apprehend what goes on during this process, to concentrate on the complex structure of experience that he is shaping and that becomes for him the poem, the story, the play symbolized by the text" (26). Rosenblatt's ideas here parallel those of Barthes, for whom "readerly" texts are "what can be read but not written" (4) and are results of transactional reading events. Given the sensory qualities with which Rosenblatt's aesthetic reading acts are imbued, the mediator of the senses—the physical body—must be a component of such reading experiences. The immersion suggested by Ryan here under Rosenblatt's rubric for reading necessitates a complicity of the body not merely as a sensory vehicle— corpus containing hands to turn pages, retinas with which to see—but as a critical aspect of comprehension. The surface narratives of Carter's and Dunmore's novels promote aesthetic reading experiences by virtue of their appeal to the senses. These narratives are rife with food, with sexuality, with violence, all trappings of the body and significant of life in a material, physical world.

Carter and Dunmore both rely upon more than codes related to food and food consumption in order to "flesh out" the surface narratives of their novels. Both also rely upon certain generic constructs of fiction as a way to create with the broadest of strokes a familiar and captivating narrative, the progressions of which readers can identify and likely will not interrogate. If readers were not granted the familiar signage of genre fiction, then the narratives below the surfaces of these novels might very well trigger that more distanced "efferent" reading discussed by Rosenblatt in which "the reader disengages his attention as much as possible from the personal and qualitative elements in his response to the verbal symbols; he concentrates on [...] the information, the concepts [...] that will be left with him when the reading is over" (27). Guided by the multiple components of the surface narratives, reader responses based upon the consumption of food and, in turn, upon the body/images presented in the text, join with responses to the trappings of, specifically, mystery and gothic genres. Pierre Macherey explains that in the genres of the gothic and of mystery, the "depths are less fascinating than [the] frail and deceptive surface," and Carter's and Dunmore's respective utilization of these generic conventions, as Macherey continues, indeed "lasts for as long as it can cling to appearances" (29). Such novels are the products "of two different movements" that are not "successive [...] but are inextricably simultaneous" (Macherey 34). Once reader attention is shifted to more obvious and more comfortable (or traditional) narrative developments, the thinner lines of the novels' transgressive underpinnings can exist without detection by the reader, and such a narrative strategy allows for appearances to be clung to and for narrative tension to become well established before it is reconciled via the production of narrative closure. The tension produced by such narrative divisions, though, and by the narratives of discomfort present (if relatively invisible) creates the suggestion of difficulty in both *Talking to the Dead* and *The Magic Toyshop*. Because of the interconnectedness of the material and psychical components of human experience, there is an inherent discomfort in separations of mind from body, whether social or textual, real or represented. The divisions within these novels result in ambivalence both within the text and within the experiences of reading the texts and of making sense of their narrative structures. To escape this uncomfortable reading experience, readers gravitate toward the conventions that they can best make sense of: culturally defined gender and sexual codes—genres in and of themselves—and the codes of generic plot development. The broad, obtuse narrative achieves primacy when readers resist the uneasy rumblings of the submerged alternatives.

Along with the narrative conventions relied upon by both Dunmore and Carter, the actual narrations of these novels are integral to their complexities. While Carter places her narratives under the care of a disinterested third-person narrator, Dunmore metes out information through the voice of Nina herself. This difference is important to consider in a discussion of the ways in which the novels' submerged narratives reveal themselves: the secret narrative of Colin's death at the hands of his sister in *Talking to the Dead* appears to readers in bursts that are often connected to Nina's acts of consumption and of bodily awareness; Margaret's incestuous relationship with her brother is announced quickly and brutally, and provides final punctuation for the novel itself. A less than scrupulous close reading of Carter's text reveals nothing of this relationship, and even reading with the intention of discovering the clues to the incest discloses few fissures in the surface narrative that might allow for the thinner, darker narrative to emerge. Margaret's muteness extends to her ability—perhaps to her refusal—to dictate the details of her own plot. Any references to the transgressive connection between Margaret and Francie come from Francie himself. "'It is right,'" he tells Melanie at their first meeting, "'for brothers and sisters to be close'" (37–8), and his "strange grace" at the dinner table, "'Flesh to flesh. Amen'" (46), implies some moral, if not legal, validity to their physical union. Rather than prayer for delivery from the "sin" of sexual transgression, Francie inverts the traditional morality that governs such behaviors, as well as those domestic arrangements that signify a socially codified morality. Margaret's inability to speak allows her to divest herself of any narrative accountability or agency and places the decision to express or to suppress the truth squarely within the domain of her male counterparts. "'There is no law, that I know of,'" Finn reports, "'to prevent'" the Jowles from being Irish (35), but Finn's reference here to the law underscores the patriarchal duty of the brothers both to common law and to their own familial law. Finn's wry observation about law and ethnicity implies that there are other laws that dictate a proper understanding of bloodlines and of shared heritage. As the bystander who holds the knowledge of incest but who does not participate in breaking the laws of the land, Finn actually emerges as the novel's gatekeeper. The level of omniscience granted to the narrator of Carter's text is limited to an excruciating degree, and Finn holds the key to the novel's silence on the matter of incest. Like Margaret, whose lips clamped shut on her wedding day, the narrator, ostensibly in control of the progression of the narrative, is actually in the grasp of the unsayable beneath the novel's gothic plot structure and of Finn, its antihero.

In Dunmore's text, Nina's narrative authority is key to a reader's making sense of the novel's intertwined narratives. Although Nina provides a relatively stable commentary on daily events throughout the novel, her role as adulterous sister calls into question her point of view and her motives. Nina is what Susan Lanser calls a "female personal narrator," one who "tells the story [and] is also the story's protagonist" (19). As such a narrator, Nina "risks the reader's resistance if the act of telling, the story she tells, or the self she constructs through telling it transgresses the limits of the acceptably feminine" (Lanser 19). As a first-person narrator, Nina also runs the risk of the narrative unreliability that accompanies such a narration, since hers is "a narration that cannot be verified" because "when a story is told in the first person, narrator is equal to any other character belonging to the realm of ordinary mortals and, therefore, fallible" (Glowinski 104). Nina's frank sexuality and close association with her physical body are flaunted through her narration, and her delight in the physical world of food and of the senses in general is perhaps more an affront to any "acceptable" femininity than are her sexual transgressions with Richard. Though Nina is the "true" narrator, her reliability is precarious throughout the bulk of the novel and is jeopardized by Isabel's version of the same histories that Nina relates. Isabel, who conforms to traditional and acceptable modes of the feminine, subtly co-opts Nina's memories, and thus her narration of the past, and this act helps to ensure the reader's resistance to Nina's rendition, thus protecting her own role in Colin's death. As mentioned above, though, Isabel's disassociation from her own body and from her psychical/intellectual self indicates that her point of view might not be much more believable than is Nina's. As the younger sibling, Nina's sensibility includes her deference to Isabel and to Isabel's authority as suggested by chronology: when it comes to stories, Nina is "in the habit of believing Isabel's version" (19), and in order for the mystery surrounding Colin's death to remain submerged, the reader must also accept, to some degree, Isabel's differing narration.

As Nina's older sister, Isabel has certain privileges with regard to reconstructing their mutual childhoods. Nina, although the de facto narrator of Dunmore's novel, does not actively own her narrative purpose, but instead discounts her own recollections as they surface, acquiescing to her sister's familial authority. Nina's transgressive behavior already calls into question her license to speak, and responses to Nina from Edward and from Margery Wilkinson (Isabel's neighbor and the mother of Susan, her nanny) based upon the more typical suspicions of embodied women (such as those levied against Pym's Prudence Bates), assist with a destabilization of her narrative authority. Margery, a "carefully dieted woman" (104) who sports "expensive blondness" and "lot of gold jewelry" (103), exhibits success in the arenas of socioeconomics and femininity, and for Nina she is a watchful someone "you have to look out for" (108). By contrast and through her distrust of Nina, this visitor adds an additional layer of suspicion to that which has already settled over Nina's narration. Regardless of her unstable, suspect narrative authority, however, Nina's memories slowly come to the surface of her narration, beginning with more benign moments of sibling difficulty and eventually coalescing into her version of the events leading up to baby Colin's death. "She was the big one," Nina recalls of Isabel, "the sensible one, and I was the toddler who could scream and bite" (43). Isabel was the narrator of Nina's childhood, though she sometimes delivered a version of questionable validity. Nina comments, "Isabel was so sure of things that sometimes I thought it was her certainty that made them happen. [...] She even knew when I was going to cry" (44). But those childhood stories told by Isabel do not always measure up to the facts lodged in Nina's psyche. Nina recalls how once Isabel had played at drowning her doll during a game of "baptism" and then had attempted to explain to their mother Nina's hysterical tears upon having been told that her "baby" was "dead": "'Nina's crying because Mandy fell into the water and she thinks she's dead. I keep telling her that she isn't, but she won't listen'" (101). Isabel fails to mention the fact that she had held the doll beneath the water, watching as her sister's reaction became increasingly desperate and emotional. This foreshadowing of Isabel's own death by drowning here also casts as circumspect the authority Nina has constructed for her sister.

Dunmore's dueling narratives are thus further problematized by a seeming lack of any reliable source for "truth" in the novel. Each sister's relationship to mind/body duality provides the total narrative with social and cultural instability, and the discrepancies between their individual authorities further complicate readerly abilities to decipher any hidden verity within the sisters' conflicting histories.

Eventually, Nina defines Isabel's authority differently than she has in preceding pages: "She's so persuasive that it doesn't seem like persuasion, but like the truth" (130). Once Isabel's version of the past is acknowledged as a rhetorical situation, rather than as an absolute version to be accepted and disseminated via her sister's narration, Nina becomes free to adjust her memory to include events that she has previously either suppressed or neglected. Their vastly different versions of Colin's death become the defining conflict between the two sisters and their respective narratives and, along with the food narrative, drive apart two women who at one time seemed inseparable. The neutral story of a brother who died of cot-death becomes a struggle for each sister's reclamation of innocence and of denial over having taken an active role in Colin's early passing. When Nina recalls the day of their brother's death, she begins to imagine a distressing alteration to what had beforehand served as her memory of the event:

> [...] Isabel is braced, on tiptoe, leaning over the baby. [...] She is pressing down on the baby's back, pressing and pressing, pushing him into the mattress. I can see his weak purple legs thrashing, but there's no sound. His face is hidden in a muslin cloth. [...] Her face is cold and hard, like a snake's face, but her face is soft as a whisper. "He was crying. I'm getting him to sleep. Go back to our room." (142–3)

If Isabel could serve as a stable point of reference for the truth, then this memory might pass as a flight of childhood fancy revisited by Nina as she watches Isabel tend to her new child. Nina, however, has already established Isabel's situational indifference to the truth in her flashback to the baby-doll baptismal enacted by Isabel and her in their youth (as well as in other like recollections). But while Nina's narrative authority and her sister's questionable narratorial status combine to drive doubt into the long-believed medical cause of Colin's death, Nina's sensual connections to the world of food and her sexual behavior have long since derailed her ability to command any solid control of her own narration. The "bulk of Isabel's truth, advancing like an iceberg" (145) enters to contradict Nina's own: "'I went in and I found what you'd done. The pillow was still over his head,'" states the elder sister (146). Already at odds vis-à-vis their relationships to food and to eating, as well as to any embodiment signified by those relationships, the sisters here verbalize the significant differences between them, before made implicit only through characterization and represented effects of the body. The conflict between Nina and Isabel, and their attempts to superimpose subjective or constructed truths over objective fact, strengthens the division that Dunmore has initiated through her use of mind/body duality as a method of character construction.

What ultimately allows for Nina's narration to emerge as more believable than her transgressions might allow, however, is the very fact of her body, regardless of the ambivalent status of that body as it relates to her sexual expression. Though her embodiment creates a problematic for the way in which Nina is characterized, the interrelatedness of textual bodies and the bodies of readers—as understood through those social qualities of the body image explained by Schilder—allows for comprehensions of and sympathies with Nina's experiences that Isabel's relative lexical disembodiment denies readers, even if the elder sister's domestic and maternal qualities allow her to appear as the more socially acceptable character and voice. The qualities of unreliability inherent within her first-person narration are, for Nina, recovered through the presence of her body and its role as a catalyst for reader response. The "immersion" of a reader within a text, as discussed by Ryan, suggests that for the duration of a reading experience, a reader is "inside" the world invoked by mimetic narration, and such proximity of the body image of the reader with the represented body/image within the text complements and strengthens immersive experiences. Ryan presents a caveat for understanding first-person, present-tense narrations such as Nina's, but the addition of an embodiment that foregrounds the sensual responses of the reader helps to ensure that this narration of events—but namely of the events surrounding Colin's death—destabilizes the "truth" of the narrative whole.

Ryan writes that the "immersive edge" of the present tense "becomes considerably duller when the present invades the whole text," and that "[c]ontinuous presence becomes habit, habit leads to invisibility, and invisibility is as good as absence. For immersion to retain its intensity, it needs a contrast of narrative modes, a constantly renegotiated distance from the narrative scene, a profile made of peaks and valleys" (*Narrative* 137). The lack of shift from one narrative mode to another, the reliance of Nina's narration (and of Dunmore's novel) upon realistic mimesis, is balanced by the very "real" presence of Nina's body as a carrier of narrative experience. The narrative structure of *Talking to the Dead* may not invite readerly attentions to the narrative act, and indeed may not in itself provide the immediacy or "presence" necessary for immersion in the narrative, but the narrative as defined by Nina's embodiment is hardly a narrative of invisibility. If the full circumstances of Colin's death are to be withheld from the reader in the generic manner of the mystery novel, then the presence of Nina's body is key to the success of the narrative structure as a whole. While Nina's flaunting of sexual and gustatorial proprieties destabilizes her narrative authority, her embodiment also provides the key to immersion as the object that the reader-as-focalizer (a full participant in the narrative system of the novel) must follow as the narrative progresses. The contradictory explanations provided by each sister cannot be reconciled if narrative tension is to be maintained and if the secret of the novel's submerged narrative is to remain hidden until its final instance.

While critics such as Peter Brooks have considered the role of desire in narrative and the role of the (female) body in the construction of narrative fiction, I would like to move beyond an examination of Nina as a desiring or desired body, and even beyond the role of desire in potential reader responses to the display of her body and its sexual exploits. While immersion in a scene of sexual interaction can certainly result in the sexual arousal of a reader, the narrative function of

Nina's physical display and overt sexuality does not constitute disclosure or an invasion of privacy devoted to "consciousness of a reserved space of intimacy" that "strangely, perhaps pathetically, depends on relentless intrusion into it" (Brooks 257). Nina's physicality is a formal mechanism necessary for the stasis of secrecy that defines the novel as a whole as well as the mystery genre upon which it is modeled. So, while reader response to scenes of sexual intercourse or of other erotically charged moments may encompass certain aspects of desire, such response is not of primary importance to the totality of the narrative structure. Passages such as those that detail Nina's sexual encounters with Richard, for example, as well as her sensuality in the kitchen, serve not simply to open doors closed upon transgressions (or their signifiers), but also to occlude the passage of information from one level of narrative to another, from the submerged level of narrative accessible only through Nina's memory and into the larger plot structure. Identification of readers with Nina's material presence, with her visible and textually tangible presence in the text, maintains reader response to the familiar narrative bound together by conventions of gender and of genre and limits reader ability to become immersed in the taboo subject of fratricide that lies beneath. The social qualities of the body image allow for "an interplay of parts or of wholes" (Schilder 235) of one body/image with another, both in actuality and, through the dimensions of imaginative play (such as outlined by Scarry and discussed above) and mimetic construction, during the act of reading a text. Because, as Schilder states, it "might almost be said that the erogenic zones of the various body-images are closer to each other than the other parts of the body" (236), represented sexual encounters can induce strong relationships between readers and texts, perhaps some of the strongest degrees of textual immersion via the body.

Nina's sexuality, then, both obscures her authority as a narrator (and thus her version of events) and draws readerly attentions to her body as the bodies of readers comprehend her physicality through their own. When Nina narrates a sexual experience with Richard, it can appear to be a gratuitously explicit scene in a novel otherwise given over to psychological effects:

> The grass is short, crisp, and prickling with drought. I get down on hands and knees, then let the weight of my body fall onto my forearms. There is a marigold at eye level, so close I smell its peppery smell. The dry grass under me, the grainy heart of the marigold, the long, still exposure, are all one. I get into position, raising myself, and Richard's finger slides, parting the lips of my wet vulva. [...] My body stretches, every membrane willing to let him in. (96)

The sensory qualities of this passage, however, and its emphasis upon Nina's movement, her motility, as well as the ensuing act of intercourse, all invite the reader—a voyeur now and not simply a sleuth working with clues to the truth of the narrative—along the journey Nina takes as she sinks to the ground, positions herself for sex, and actively engages in sexual performance. Nina's deliberate explanation of her movement onto her forearms and into a sexual position draws readers along that path with her via the social qualities of readers' body/images.

The sensations narrated by Nina can be synthesized only as far as a reader can conceive of the feel of the grass, the weight of her body, and the sexual anticipation running throughout her body but narratively located in her genitalia. The weight of Nina's body mass shifts as her physical positions shift, as does the reader's experience of her body through his or her own. The sexual nature of the passage (as well as others like it) does not necessarily create a ruse that turns a reader's attention from other aspects of the narrative, but rather aligns a reader with Nina through her, and his or her own, body/image. More than a prurient interest, readers' involvement with Nina and Richard's afternoon dalliance occurs by virtue of their sharable body images, because those whose physical bodies have engaged in similar activities will have the ability to comprehend the scene through their body-based knowledge. Isabel, lacking in the qualities of textual embodiment granted to her sister, cannot command the same reader identification. Although her word and Nina's are at odds and occasionally Isabel even appears to have a firmer grasp of the truth than does Nina, textual embodiment in its active, subjective form controls the ways in which readers can immerse themselves in this particular textual world. In Nina, discourse and materiality together provide her with an edge that Isabel, whom readers can know only through that more intangible sphere of language, cannot access.

An interesting problematic of Nina's physicality as it relates to concentrated reader response (and to the maintenance of narrative duality), however, is that while her sentient presence helps to guide readers' attentions toward the gendered narrative of sexual transgression and betrayal, her unfolding comprehension of childhood experiences is nearly always simultaneous with her most embodied experiences. While readers experience Nina's body as a catalyst for response to the surface narrative, Nina herself experiences her own bodily epistemology in ways that force the submerged narrative to engage with that other, broader narrative above. While Isabel began to deny her body through a denial of food soon after Colin's death, and thus to suppress her role in that death, Nina continuously calls forth that other version of the "truth" each time she indulges in physical excesses of both sex and food consumption. Her embodied characterization, as it maintains reader focalization during instances of such excess, ensures that readers are thus present (to varying degrees of physical identification) with Nina each time she revisits events that call into question Isabel's version. Nina's body as both a barrier to and a key to the submerged narrative controls the pace of access to the hidden aspects of the novel.

When she recalls Colin's funeral, as well as the eating distress that overcame Isabel at that time, Nina is lying beside Richard after one of their garden encounters. She watches her sleeping brother-in-law, thinking he "looks content, fucked out," and then immediately her thoughts turn to Colin: "I can remember Colin's funeral. His coffin was so small that my father carried it down the aisle of the white church as if it was a baby" (113). She also remembers imagining, at that earlier time, "me and Isabel without bodies, but [...] couldn't" (113). The connection of sexual transgression with her recollection here is the first of several such narrative conjunctions of Nina's embodied agency with her memory of losing her younger sibling through questionable circumstances. Her vision of Isabel's smothering their brother directly follows from a later tryst with Richard, and that emotional, condemning encounter with Isabel prompts a dream in which Nina conjures up the voice of a woman telling the girls' mother that Isabel had turned "'her back to [Colin's] pram, though she'd gone and left it right on the edge of the pier with the brake off'" (152). Nina wakes from that dream "hungry" (155) and heads to the bakery to buy "cheese bread and a wheel of fresh pizza in a white cardboard box, two French sticks and a sticky dark loaf with sunflower seeds in it. [...] a box of homemade shortbread, and five cream-filled doughnuts" (156). Back in Isabel's kitchen, Richard feeds a croissant to Nina in a scene that clearly evokes fellatio: "I eat it with my eyes shut: the jam, the cold, salty butter, the warm, dissolving layers of pastry. He feeds it into my mouth inch by inch, and I eat it down to the crisp, burnt point" (162–3). The back-and-forth between sensual gratification and Nina's recollections infuses readerly experiences of one with the other, and although the force of her embodiment drives the narrative most visible to readers, the connection of that embodiment with the novel's primary point of contention also enables a slow but steady unfolding for readers of matters that lie beneath Nina's plot of excess.

Unlike Dunmore's novel, in which the submerged narrative unfolds slowly and is both obscured and illuminated by Nina's body, Carter's *The Magic Toyshop* depends exclusively upon the reversal of the roles of mind and of body in order for Melanie's constructed embodiment to emerge as a device that conceals Margaret's actual alignment with the body and with a sexual agency that transgresses social norms. As previously mentioned, Melanie's embodiment is concocted; she is presented as "body" in order to reposition Margaret into the sphere of the mind and away from an embodiment that would betray her relationship with her brother. Melanie's narrative—the "fat," surface narrative that almost completely hides Margaret's tale—is one of gothic chaos, and within this generic construct Melanie is the heroine who must both attract threat and escape from it. Her state of chronic peril consistently raises her body into view as the object of sexual and other threats, and the danger presented to Melanie is simultaneously presented to the reader and to the reader's body image. The same social qualities of body images that allow for reader identification with Nina's body in Dunmore's novel also allow for perceptions of danger to be filtered through the bodies of Carter's readers.

Schilder explains connections of body image to human perceptions of pain and of danger, and finds it "more than probable that the child's conception of pain is prior to its conception of danger, and that danger means for a child something which will sooner or later inflict pain and disrupt in this way the unity of the organism and its image" (103). For Schilder, then, pain is a basic, primary theme of human orientation to the body. As Scarry elaborates in *The Body in Pain*, that sensation is important to the ways in which the body's epistemology has been socially and culturally defined, as well, and thus when pain or its perceived precursor, danger, is presented within a text, readers are invited to respond to that commonality between the external and textual worlds. Pain invites immersion into a text in similar ways as do sexual stimuli, and danger of disruption of the body, of its image, or of the ontological gestalt of mind and body calls forth the possibility of pain, and thus also invites the interactivity of readerly and textual bodies. Melanie's perpetual danger, even when it is cast as the result of an overactive adolescent imagination, functions to maintain a heightened awareness of her embodiment and therefore controls reader attentions through the submission of Melanie's young body to the necessary dangers of the gothic genre. With all eyes upon Melanie, Margaret can slip beneath to the narrative below, a level of narrative that is nearly imperceptible as a result of the casting of Melanie in her role as embodied young woman in distress.

Because of this correlation between perceived danger and the body image, the most immediate dangers connected with Melanie are more likely to result in reader response than is any assumed distress on the part of Margaret. While the idea of the older woman's weekly sexual duties to her brutish husband might be cause for disgust, Melanie occupies a more precarious position because of her age, her lack of parental protection, and her generic status as gothic heroine. Sexual threats to Melanie can be directly associated with her represented physical body, whereas Margaret, whose body is narratively suppressed, cannot call forth as visceral a response from readers as can the younger woman. Melanie's vulnerability, too, allows for scenes that only border on the dangerous to blossom into threats with greater resonance than they might exhibit in other contexts, or if related to other of the novel's characters. The specter of Bluebeard (who survives in legend as a man who kills women by dismembering them) is invoked throughout in the novel, for example, an allusion that both underscores the gothic vein of Carter's text and strengthens the aura of physical and sexual precariousness that surrounds Melanie, even when the related event is actually her hallucination and not a real physical or sexual threat.[7] One afternoon in the kitchen, Melanie opens a "dresser drawer to put away the knives and spoons" and in it "was a freshly severed hand, all bloody at the roots" (118). The passage continues,

> It was a soft-looking, plump little hand with pretty, tapering fingers the nails of which were tinted with a faint, pearly lacquer. There was a thin silver ring of the type small girls wear on the fourth finger. It was the hand of a child who goes to dancing class and wears frilled petticoats with knickers to match. From the raggedness of the flesh at the wrist, it appeared that the hand had been hewn from its arm with a knife or axe that was very blunt. Melanie heard blood fall plop in the drawer. "I am going out of my mind," she said aloud. "Bluebeard was here." (118)

---

7   Heta Pyrhönen discusses Carter's Bluebeard allusions at length, particularly as they relate to her adaptation of Sade's erotic ethos in certain works. See "Imagining the Impossible: The Erotic Poetics of Angela Carter's 'Bluebeard' Stories," *Textual Practice* 21.1: 93–111.

Although Melanie has only imagined this severed limb, the fear factor of the scene, and the implied threat to Melanie's physical well-being, all add up so that readers can perceive of dangers to come for this young protagonist. While Melanie's narrative—even hallucinated trajectories of that narrative—maintain readers' suspense and focus, Margaret's narrative continues, almost without notice.

A good juxtaposition of these narratives, and of their quite different appearances in the text, is presented over the course of the novel's two presentations of Uncle Philip's creepy puppet shows. The puppeteer is an overbearing perfectionist who insists that all members of the household turn out to view his craft and to be entertained by the twisted scripts meant to deride certain members of the audience. The first show obviously implicates Philip's wife, Margaret, and her brother/lover, Francie. In retrospect, the scene is a nod to their sexual connection, perhaps even an indication that Philip suspects the incestual relationship that takes place under his own roof. Without the benefit of such hindsight, however, and buried in the midst of Melanie's larger narrative, this puppet show can easily be overlooked as readers focus upon Melanie and in turn upon Finn, Melanie's erstwhile protector, who is pushed from the rafters by Philip at the show's finale for having botched the performance. The puppets, which represent Mary, Queen of Scots, and her lover, Bothwell, are described as representations of Margaret and Francie: the Queen "wore a collar like Aunt Margaret's" (129), and Bothwell "walked with Francie's toppling fall" (130). This clue to the existence of the submerged narrative, available to readers only after the disclosure of the incestuous relationship, at this point in the overall narrative has little significance. In addition, because Margaret is only represented by the wooden puppet, and because any physical presence on her part is completely removed from the event, any sense of danger to her physical person is nullified. Margaret, therefore, is unable to invoke the bodily response of a reader in the same way that Melanie can. The scene does more to underscore Philip's zest for mocking and abusing his mongrel household than it does to suggest his knowledge of secret events or any anger that might exist as a result, and because of this there is no perceived danger to Margaret's physical being (though perhaps to the emotional and mental components of her being). Ostensibly "castrated" and without her body there to serve as a catalyst for reader response, Margaret's secret remains safe, even if it glimmers at the center of this particular passage.

The later show, a Boxing Day event that does not limit itself to wooden creatures, but also includes Melanie in its cast of characters, is the *raison d'être* for a scene that not only strengthens Melanie's identification with the body, but also provides one of the most important moments for the type of embodied reader response theorized in this chapter. The holiday performance takes mythology, rather than history, as its theme, and Melanie is cast as Leda to Uncle Philip's handcrafted swan. This passage provides a pinnacle to the dangers encountered by Melanie, and, unlike the scene of the imagined hand in the kitchen drawer, this narrative event is played out at the site of Melanie's body in a simulated rape by a beast controlled by Philip. Though the rape is an act of performance, and not what might typically be thought of as a "real" sexual violation, the narrative threat to

Melanie at this point reaches its height and seemingly solidifies her alignment with the physical world. Such violent physical threat calls to the bodies of readers, who can react as they might to physical threat to their own bodies and thus identify with Melanie and her plight. Melanie follows her uncle's bidding as he directs from above. "'Leda attempts to flee her heavenly visitant but his beauty and majesty bear her to the ground'" (166), and Philip manipulates both wooden and fleshly participant as the swan "settled on her loins" and "mounted her," with "its head [...] nestled in her neck" and "gilded beak dug deeply into the soft flesh" (167). In a white chiffon tunic and with flowers in her hair, Melanie's Leda is the picture of innocence, and of innocence defiled once "the passionate swan had dragged her dress half off" (167) and completes the figurative rape.

The contrast of this puppet show with the earlier performance that implicated Margaret with the body is drastic. There is no equating the suggestion of sexuality through wooden puppets with the actual use of Melanie's physical presence, a presence that by this point in the novel has become fully established. The danger to Melanie in this scene is both real and perceived, and the pain (as well as other sensations) that results from the simulation adds with that perceived through imaginative elision of the performance-rape with the actual violence that this act signifies. Like the earlier puppet show, which helped to guarantee Margaret's secrecy through a denial of her body, this show functions to contain the novel's thin, submerged narrative by foregrounding Melanie's embodiment, thus reinforcing reader responses to that embodiment and to the larger narrative trajectory. This narrative distancing is jeopardized, however, by the inherent "castration" of Melanie by the mock rape. Jean Wyatt argues that the novel "presents a careful, if parodic, inventory of the practices, cultural and familial, that rob a young girl of agency—indeed, of subjectivity—reducing her to the position of feminine object" (555); the Leda scene locates Carter's use of "rape as a metaphor for the psychic 'dismemberment' of a young girl" (556). As Melanie's perceived agency is diminished through not only a psychic castration, but also a loss of her embodied subjectivity, her ability to maintain narrative prominence vanishes. The disclosure of Margaret's truth becomes imminent.

As with Dunmore's Nina, Melanie is exalted by a narrative of the flesh that commands primary attention from readers as it works to erase the narrative of discomfort contained within *The Magic Toyshop*. Ultimately, though, both Melanie and Nina are destabilized as designated textual bodies when the embodiment, and embodied agencies, of Margaret and Isabel are brought to light. When Philip returns home to find his wife and her brother engaged in sexual congress, the delicate balance of the Flower household, and of the novel's narrative structure, is irrevocably upset. With no additional need for her affected aphasia/castration, Margaret regains her ability to speak and escapes with Francie and Victoria from a toyshop set ablaze by Philip in his wrath. Thus reunited with her "other half," with the child who has all along signified her actual allegiance to her own body, Margaret takes her "true" position in the narrative. Margaret, and not Melanie, becomes the protagonist who earns the right to escape from the gothic context of Phillip's toyshop. As the two strands of the novel become one, so do the two components of Margaret's characterization. The novel's ending, devoted to this disclosure and to a subsequent re-embodiment of Margaret through the addition of Victoria to her composite, turns from that which might be expected from a gothic tale. Melanie, through this narrative turn, is disenfranchised. Her constructed embodiment, only necessary while Margaret and Francie's relationship remains hidden, no longer has a place in the function of the novel's narrative projection beyond its final pages. Wyatt sees this effacement of Melanie as a result of the rape scene: "Rather than being split into an object which is seen and a subject who sees, Melanie is split into an object—viewed from a male perspective external to her—and, perceived from within, a nothing" (557). Neither subject nor object, mind nor body, she is the true orphan of the family, abandoned as her narrative goes up in flames.

As the text closes upon Melanie and Finn, who "faced each other in a wild surmise" (200), their world is an apocryphal one promised by the generic codes of the surface narrative that has now become a part of Margaret's, and not of Melanie's, future. Without her narrative, and without the structure of the genre to carry Melanie forward, Melanie's story has come to a close. She and Finn stand as last man and woman left to reconstruct, perhaps to repopulate the world to which they have been abandoned, a sure recall of the novel's earlier suggestion that Finn and Melanie will not find their happiness in any fruitful, life-sustaining relationship. When he kisses her first in the "'graveyard of a pleasure ground'" (101), their relationship begins on a bleak impulse, the same bleakness with which it narratively closes. This "graveyard" is the park at Crystal Palace, the location to which Prince Albert's Great Exhibition of 1851 was moved after its first run in central London. The monument to the innovation of the Empire later burned to the ground, leaving little but the stone statues that stand alongside Carter's would-be lovers. A significant starting point for British domestic and cultural order and maintenance, as well as for the machinery that drives cultural modernization, this site—now the end of the line for several south London bus routes—ironically serves as a strong allusion to the doomed, antimodern world left to this young couple.

Smith points out that through Carter's allusions to and eschewing of high Modernist works such as D. H. Lawrence's *Lady Chatterley's Lover*, "Melanie does meet her working-class hero, but he is [not] Mellors, the idealized sexual Übermensch of Lawrence's self-mythology" (349); Finn is not recognizable as one of the heroes that she imagined at the cusp of her sexual awakening. The life that Melanie imagines that she will have with Finn, one of "pervasive squalor and dirt and mess and shabbiness" (177), indicates the end of the modern cycle, a retreat back into the world preceding order and cleanliness and domestic tranquility. Though Melanie reaches the end of the novel with Finn by her side, as could be expected from the gothic romance plot contained within Carter's larger project, she also observes, from that moment when the toyshop "burnt like a giant chrysanthemum" and she and Finn stand in a "neglected garden [...] full of discarded tins, jam jars, rubbish thrown over the wall" (199), the end of her narrative self. Cast out from the sphere of embodiment as Margaret reclaims her natural place in that land, Melanie remains only as a ghost of her former self, and stands in the midst of a garden gone to rubbish, a plot of former natural order in which the idea of organic life has become extinct. The life force commonly found at the end of romance plots has been extracted from Melanie's, and the young woman who was figuratively compared to an amputee after her parents' death becomes narratively disembodied through the role reversal of mind and body, of herself and Margaret.

As in Carter's text, in Dunmore's, the revelation of the buried narrative comes at its final moment, and that revelation is cause for a reassessment of the ways in which Isabel and Nina have been relegated exclusively to realms of mind and body in order to maintain narrative tension and obstruction of the actual circumstances of baby Colin's death. The fact that Isabel was the sister who actually smothered the baby, however, is not the last detail on the subject to be disclosed. In fact, only Isabel's suicide by drowning, expressed as a reflection of her guilt, is there to mark the fact of her physical, embodied role in the death of her brother. No admission of guilt or material fact bears absolute witness to her true place in the narrative. Unlike Margaret, though, who emerges as an embodied character at the end of *The Magic Toyshop*, Isabel rejects her embodiment through this extreme act of self-abnegation. For Isabel, motherhood has opened a door to her own body that she cannot not pass through without acknowledging her role in her own brother's death and in "what Colin's death had done": an eradication of "Love and hope. Those things my mother had felt," says Nina, "when Colin was born" (293). For Isabel, coming to terms with her embodiment means accepting her act and its results and risking the same deep despair that she faces as a mother of a child who might at any time be taken from her. For Isabel, whose embodied agency has led to painful and lasting experiences, permanent disavowal of the body through death is preferable to embodiment.

For Nina, however, the death of her sister does not put to rest the question at the heart of this "moral whodunit" (Kino). In a *New York Times* review of *Talking to the Dead*, Carol Kino asks, "Does guilt lie in desire or action?" and ultimately *this* is Dunmore's central question. Regardless of Isabel's guilt-in-action and her actual embodied status, Nina's complicity in the act becomes apparent and inverts much of what has been understood of Nina over the course of the novel. At last, as she recalls her sister, as a child, telling her, "'I'd do anything for you'" (299), Nina recalls the rest of the story:

> The baby is everywhere. The baby has opened the door to my mother's room and then closed it again behind the two of them, leaving me outside. The baby fills my ears and my mouth until I can't think of anything else. My lips move, and Isabel bends to hear me. I speak.
> "Will you really do what I want?"
> "You know I will," she answers. "I'll do anything you want." (299)

As the novel closes upon Nina and Isabel, in recollection, heading "up the endless staircase, hand in hand" (300), Nina's selfish desire and her role as the impetus of a death that has plagued both sisters ever since becomes clear to her and to readers at the same moment, as does the power of Nina's language, even at the age of four, when she asked her sister to perform for her a most horrific favor. Though infused with elements of the physical world, Nina's characterization is ultimately clarified by a reassociation of her character with the field of language and with an active, forceful life of the mind. She is not disembodied or disenfranchised in the way Melanie is, but the destabilization of Nina's character is the last and lingering effect of the narrative. A return to the preface, narrated by a Nina who is fully aware of her own role in an action that fractured the life of each member of her family, finds Nina thinking to her sister, "I am on your grave, the warm mound of it shaped to me like a body" (6). Newly defined as an inhabitant of the intellectual, discursive world, Nina seeks out her sister's embodiment, though she can find only a poor substitution, a simile that cannot measure up to the actual embodiment that she needs in order to appear as an accurate representation of a mind/body totality. She imagines that "[n]othing can separate" her from Isabel (6), but the embodiment that expired with Isabel off the coast of Sussex escapes her needy reach.

The dual narratives that interact in *Talking to the Dead* and in *The Magic Toyshop* cannot sustain themselves beyond the reconciliation of body with body, and of mind with mind. Both novels, finally integrated into one narrative strand at their respective ends, become "whole" tales of complex interactions that belie any surface representations or novelistic reliances on the cultural assumptions attached to female consumption and to female sexuality. Interestingly, each text mimics in its own duality the mind/body divide so central to their constructions. The mirroring of form and content suggests a more ready convergence of "fat" and "thin" ways of seeing and of reading, however, than is generally possible for those whose body image dysphoria pervades each encounter with her reflection. My use of this metaphor might not hold up if considered in that manner, but instead I imagine the ways in which both texts discussed in this chapter, and the multiple ways in which they can be read and responded to because of the interactivity of bodies and of body images, suggest the many and varied ways in which women see both themselves and others, and the ways in which we both concede to and resist cultural attitudes that shape our experiences. Though neither Carter nor Dunmore is able to solidly reconcile mind with body in any one female protagonist, both emphasize the interconnectedness of the two components and explore through formal, narrative expressions of auto-objectification a suggestion of such wholeness and its possibility for future women, for future readers.

Chapter 4
Whole Numbers, Strange Remainders

Perhaps to read experiences of embodiment that extend beyond the mind/body duality so embedded in Western culture is also to imagine, to change our own bodily epistemologies. Encounters—in the text, in the world—with new combinations of the physical and the psychical can perhaps allow contemporary women to integrate the sorts of embodiment denied to them through numerous aspects of culture and by many social prescriptions. Though many women, including the authors whose works have been examined in previous pages, have understood—if perhaps only unconsciously—that the division of mind from body in actuality belies the lived experiences of women, we all are trapped to some degree within a duality that presupposes a primacy of the intellect. Embodiment, even when perceived as a positive vehicle for female agency (as seen to degrees in Pym's Prudence and in Dunmore's Nina), is still anchored fast to the cultural baggage of female sexuality, a problematic that thrives within contemporary times even as women have made great strides toward owning their own sexual expressions. Discourses across academic disciplines have asserted the importance of embodiment for decades, and yet our language, our primary frameworks for conceiving of our own bodies, leave us with limited scope through which to acknowledge the very real world of the human body. Where, then, can we look for representations of female experiences that repair this division that has become seemingly irreconcilable?

In 1886, Anna Kingsford suggested that the stress of city life, of "modern" life, was a cause for physical malaise: "it is extremely difficult, in the era and centre of perpetual motion and constant excitement," she so wisely explains in *Health, Beauty and the Toilet*:

> [...] in the country, hours are more regular, letters, telegrams, and similar worries less frequent, sleep more undisturbed and prolonged, and the general current of existence smoother and more peaceful in its flow than is possible elsewhere. [...] an animal of fidgety temper never fattens well, nor do nervous and anxious persons ever 'put on flesh' to the same extent as those of an even and placid disposition. (9)

Though Kingsford here prescribes a placid country life for those who wish to gain weight, her words work well within a metaphoric conception of modernity and of the increasing privileging under a modern aegis of an intellectualized self at the expense of a figurative embodiment that has all but evaporated within discourses of subjectivity. Of course, each epoch will have its detractors, and perhaps Kingsford's glance behind her toward a "simpler" time is the same glance cast backward by some of every generation that has grappled with change and with shifting value systems. Regardless of Kingsford's place in a long line of nostalgics who refuse to see the future in all its potential, she was on to something; she only presented an idea, already established by the late nineteenth century, that has since followed generations of women. Modernity has brought with it many beneficial advances and advantages, but at the heart of its mechanisms lies a fundamental problem for the human subject, and particularly for the female subject. The idea of "country life" or of some idyllic past is not in itself the cure for modern restlessness and discontent, but instead these anti-modern concepts act as metaphors for moments in cultural history when the human (female) subject was not as subject to the insidious workings of a quest for perfection, for the negation of the body in order to assert the primacy of rational thought and its dominance over each individual's docile flesh. Over time, the project that has driven subjects to participate in their own auto-objectification and subsequent self-effacement has only grown as the pace of progress has quickened, carrying the necessity of embodiment along in its swift-running currents like so much cultural detritus. Ironically, Kingsford seems to yearn for a time that existed prior to the period that embraced volume upon volume of prescriptions like her own that only furthered the division of the body and its subtle intelligence from the modern jostle made possible by the elevation of a higher mind.

For Virginia Woolf, the historical Ellen Terry provided a model of a woman who had somehow reconciled her contradictory natures. Rather than look forward, as she does in her 1940 essay "The Leaning Tower," in her essay "Ellen Terry" (written in January 1941) Woolf glances backward, away from the modern moment and toward an unstable future. Early twentieth-century beauty writer Helena Gent, too, saw Terry as an ideal woman, "remarkably attractive and magnetic" (31). What might it have been about Terry that captivated women who searched for successful blends of psyche and soma? For Woolf, Terry was a "mutable woman, all instinct, sympathy, and sensation" (71), a changeling who emerged equally as "mother, wife, cook, critic, actress" (71) and who defied the laws of a culture that perhaps would rather have affixed to her only one or another of those labels. Woolf's fascination with Terry, as well as her growing comprehension of the actress as a full complement of mental and physical, of public and private spheres, is evident in typescripts of the piece, worked out during the last months of her life. While Woolf worked to revise *Between the Acts*, in which she struggled to explain a woman such as the fleshly, sexual Mrs. Manresa, she also worked to imagine how a woman such as Ellen Terry could hold both sides of a crippling binary system in each of her two hands.

Woolf was moved by the discrepancy between the actress who was physically trained for her craft as a child—"her ears were boxed, her muscles suppled" (68)—but who, once upon the stage, became bodiless: "Her body lost its weight" (67). Though the body of the actress must be in top form in order to convincingly portray the lived experiences of another, the actress-body must also be able to recede, to become with each performance merely an iterative image of a single vision. Terry, however, defied such a will to disappear each night; her physicality and her ingenuity merged in a way that Woolf was drawn to. In a fragment of writing deleted from the finished essay, Woolf explains of Terry that her "expression [...] was spoilt by a look of extreme vivacity. For the beauty of a woman's countena[nce] consists, it has been said, in a still repose, as of a sheet" (MHP/B4 16). Unlike a smooth, inanimate length of linen, and unlike women such as Woolf's own mother, Julia Stephen, whose portraits stare without emotion from within their frames, Terry, for Woolf, exuded life through her physical being as well as through the inner Ellen projected through craft that each night was "rubbed out," leaving "only a wavering, insubstantial phantom" (67). "But," Woolf points out, "she is quick to tell Mr. Shaw that she does not work with her brain only" (71). The body was a part of the persona of Ellen Terry with which Woolf seems to have been amazed. In the figure of Ellen Terry, Woolf finds together those components that she had divided in *Between the Acts* among two women, but she still muses over how Terry had managed to encompass both sides of the binary: "Was she a great actress, or was [...] the gift of acting merely one of her gifts?—& was she at heart, a mother [...]" (MHP/B5a 3). In the final version, Woolf simplifies this query to imagine "the two Ellen Terrys—Ellen the mother, and Ellen the actress" (70); however, the ampersand with which Woolf joins these two sides of Terry in her earlier typescript is both semantic conjunction and figurative slippage. Woolf, who perhaps might have written "but" rather than join these two Ellens, does in her typescript what she remains skeptical of in the questioning polished prose of the final draft.

The Terry to whom Woolf is drawn is at once complicated and simple. Terry's autobiography, *A Story of My Life* (first published in 1908), provided the basis for Woolf's contemplation of a woman whom she had all but spoofed a few years earlier in *Freshwater*. Woolf is drawn to the type of domesticity, detailed by Terry, that is reminiscent of that which she knew in her youth. In a deletion, Woolf notes, "She read Mrs. Beeton, not Shakes[pea]re" (MHP/B5a 35), and the analogous passage in Terry's life writing confirms this: "I studied cookery-books instead of parts. Mrs. Beeton instead of Shakespeare" (Terry 67). Terry's few years in the country, away from the London footlights, rivet Woolf, who later expanded the passage from its previous mere echo: "[...] in the heart of domesticity. She is up at six. She scrubs, she cooks, she sews. She teaches the children. She harnesses the pony. She fetches the milk. And again she is perfectly happy" (69). And Terry's domesticity, though constructed by a woman who for much of her life had little appreciation for convention, conformed to social standards to such a degree that "when a doll dressed in a violent pink was given to Edy [Craig, her daughter], she said it was 'vulgar'!" (Terry 67). Woolf initially saw these two Ellens—she who commanded the stage as Desdemona and she who maintained a country cottage— as "incompatible" (MHP/B5a 44). By the time she had completed the essay, however, Woolf changed the adjective to "contradictory" (69) and had begun to imagine how to "put the scattered sketches together" in order to form a complete picture of the famous actress who was also a mother, the sexualized woman for whom "the main-spring of her art is imagination" (71).

Woolf ends her essay with an assertion that Terry was one of a kind, a new type of woman: "now and again Nature creates a new part, an original part.

The actors who act that part always defy our attempts to name them" (72). In her assessment of Ellen Terry, Woolf is sensitive to the limitations of language in describing such in-between beings. In the past, and not in the mechanized future, Woolf found an ideal of the embodied mind in Ellen Terry. "So though she read the book," Woolf wrote, "she read it with her body; she read with the whole of her" (MHP/B5a 60); here a phenomenological Woolf is able to accede to the idea of a comprehensive subjectivity. While for Isa Oliver of *Between the Acts*, reading is metaphoric consumption that serves to stave off "mind hunger" (15), and thus is only linguistically and intellectually tied to acts of embodiment, in "Ellen Terry" Woolf bursts through the limitations of semantics and finds the syncopation of a mind embodied.

Though Woolf came to find such combinations possible, as the twentieth century wore on and drew to the millennial close that brought with it new technologies and new ways of communication, women writers who attempted to craft contemporary archetypes of their own that would blend the two sides of mind/body duality have not always found models for such a being. The authors whose fiction I have discussed in earlier chapters have been able to confront such a duality, and to suggest the importance of bringing together the material and the intangible worlds, but are ultimately unable to do so themselves. Contemporary culture gives a mighty lip service to the idea that the mind and body (and, occasionally, the spirit that moves the binary to an equally troubled trinity) are mutually important, but the increasing and increasingly invasive methods for controlling the auto-objectified subject abound and override whatever discourse is available for a reconception of a mind/body totality. When she does appear—the woman who, like Woolf's version of Ellen Terry, is able to somehow reconcile the ostensibly mutually exclusive parts of her whole being—she is often a creature of discomfort, a woman who is difficult to recognize within normative cultural frameworks and who is difficult to describe with language built of faulty dualities.

Even in the final decade of the twentieth century, as the need for a composite female "self" became more than apparent in certain theoretical circles, it became equally fought against via the insidious avenues of women's mass culture. Just as with the books and periodicals of earlier eras, the 1990s beauty, health, and domestic tracts fueled an understanding of divided experience even as debate questioned the validity of such divisions. Those books that call into question the rituals of dress and diet cannot move beyond our limited linguistic framework for the mind and the body. Kay Cooke, in *Real Gorgeous: The Truth about Body and Beauty* (1994), assures women that one must "make friends with your body, live in it and trust it" (48), which is a positive message and seemingly inverts the historical message that women have received to auto-objectify their flesh. Cooke conceives of the body, however, as an "other" that must be negotiated nonetheless, even if in friendship and not as an unwitting foe. Similarly, in *Diet Breaking: Having It All Without Having to Diet* (1995), Mary Evans Young writes, "Our body is our home, where we live" (117). Not only does she reinforce the notion of the physical body as a shell for some transcendent self, but she conflates female embodiment semantically into *one* body, underscoring the normativity present in issues related to maintaining one's self to code. The female subject is a wandering thing within such an ontological model, and the flesh provides a home that is lived in but that is not a direct aspect of life itself. Though the ostensible message of some of these books can appear to be potentially radical when considered within a century's production of similar texts, the rhetoric of these works remains stuck in the same place as it has been since the late nineteenth century, when such volumes began to proliferate.

Contemporary volumes that provide mandates for female beauty and success have begun to echo philosophical and theoretical approaches to mind/body duality, but they have not been able to move beyond the fear of transgression that has been instilled in generations of individuals who seek the narrow middle path between extremes. Like Michelle Leigh's notion of "Zen beauty" discussed in Chapter 1, new ways to achieve our ideals do exist; however, they seek only to change the route toward the same old end. Just as the "Man-Who-Sees" wrote in the 1940s about women divided into mental and physical capacities, Leslie Kenton, in a more than six-hundred-page volume titled *The New Joy of Beauty,* explains, "Each woman is in reality two women. [...] the *outer* woman [...] can come in many different forms. [...] For each outer woman there is also an inner counterpart, an individual Self that is utterly unique. [...] The outer woman is the vehicle for what the self creates" (3). Even in 1995, the concept of a spectrum of female experience made of the intellectual *and* physical components is underwritten by those old ideals: a self that is strong enough to manipulate the object of the body into becoming what it "should" be. The outer component, the "vehicle" for a self that is somehow always superior to what appears to the external world, is in this and countless other volumes on the subject simply something to be guided and manipulated, so that women can become, in Kenton's words, "*authentic*, not something imitated or artificially imposed" (4). Ironically, the authentic self is one that must be engineered rather than a self that is an already present part of the human subject. Her techniques for bringing the two selves together, however, promote results that are far removed from what is likely to be "authentic" for most women. During meditation, she suggests that one "substitute the word 'slim,' 'lean,' 'trim,' or 'health' [...] for your ordinary mantra" (300), hardly a move toward adapting the beauty project to reflect a "whole" individual, but rather a co-optation of Eastern philosophy along the path toward auto-objectification. In the world of the beauty manual, even one that surpasses six hundred pages, language limits our abilities to conceive of the range of experience encompassed by women's lives. In this context, the body remains a site of potential transgression, the only hope for which is a proper female subject that will agree to remedy the defects of the flesh on an ongoing and spirit-consuming basis.

One example of a woman who attempts, through the medium of food, to reunite mind and body in a way that challenges auto-objectifying practices is Britain's Nigella Lawson, whose television series *Nigella Bites* and *Forever Summer*, and whose cookery books, which include *How to Eat* and *How to be a Domestic*

Goddess, have turned her into a sensation not only because of her cooking techniques, but also because of the sensual pleasure that she takes in cooking and in eating. Nicola Humble remarks that Lawson's "performance was hypnotic, though one didn't look much at the food" (241). *Nigella Bites* was hailed as "gastroporn" due to Lawson's inability to keep separate her sexualized embodiment and her intellectualized role of food expert, a challenge to the notion that food writer Anne Mendelson christens "a smirky pretense that there's something morally wrong about either the food or the enjoyment." If, as Mendelson argues, the rhetoric of foodism has become infused with the rhetoric of sin, then it seems as if this might be a result of mass culture's revulsion for those who publicly enjoy their appetites, as seen in the complex characterization of Nina in Dunmore's *Talking to the Dead*. Just as dirt and other household excess fell prey in the early part of the twentieth century to the same moral codes as do sexual expressions, an appetite for food—good, appealing, indulgent food—has come under the same rhetorical fire at the close of the century and into the new millennium. Lawson flaunts her ability to be both a member of the intellectual and cultural elite *and* a sensual, fully embodied female. She has been called the United Kingdom's most beautiful woman, and her high profile as the daughter of Margaret Thatcher's Chancellor of the Exchequer has allowed her to cross those lines that prevail between luminaries of one class and another. She writes, "in cooking, as in eating, you just have to let your real likes and desires guide you" (6), and her sensual persona is parallel with this attitude. Humble points out that in *How to Eat*, Lawson shows "little concern about fat or other dietary hang-ups of the moment," which plays to Lawson's decadent persona, but adds in a parenthetical aside, "there is a chapter on dieting in which she usefully introduces the notion of Temple food—as in 'my body is a'" (246). Even the more hedonistic of cookery books cannot escape the full impact of modern body-consciousness.

Lawson's mixture of blatant embodiment with a dash of Mrs. Beeton provides considerable contemporary fodder for thinking through the ways in which as a culture we seemingly want balance within ourselves as subjects but simultaneously are not yet comfortable with exhibitions of the entire spectrum of female subjectivity. She self-consciously speaks of such a subject as "[...] a fond, if ironic, dream: the unexpressed 'I' that is a cross between Sophia Loren and Debbie Reynolds in pink cashmere cardigan and fetching gingham pinny [...]" (*Domestic Goddess* vii). Imelda Whelehan notes that Lawson's "fulsome sensuous descriptions of the process of cooking and eating all of her recipes evoke nostalgia as the key inspiration" (*Feminist* 186), and in this way the simplicity of another time (even of a time only a few decades prior) undercuts the transgressive qualities of contemporary sexual expression. The "basic" cuisine that she promotes and her domestic-goddess agenda are simultaneously incongruous and appealing: why not be both an advocate for simplicity and a gourmet who advises that a cook should simply "relax and do what tastes best to you" (86)? It seems, though, that Lawson has been a better object of ridicule than a model for some millennial woman. She makes permeable the boundary that has divided women into subjects who through acculturation processes have become more comfortable with considering their bodies and their sexualities as *things* to be controlled and maintained. When Lawson stands before the camera, as have Julia Child and Delia Smith before her, and then licks her fingers and indulges in the sensuality inherent in her native sentience, we balk. The kitchen is the domain of that omnipresent figure in countless midcentury cookbooks: pinned-up hair, New Look skirt, tray of inviting snacks on hand for others to consume. Lawson has invaded this femininity, and we are fascinated by her prowess, but particularly in the United States, where her series (much like pornography) can be viewed only via particular cable and satellite television arrangements, Lawson remains a bit of a freak show to be hidden away and brought out at odd hours to be marveled at. Even in Britain, where mass culture tends more toward the bawdy than it can in the United States, her series have been available to all who desire to watch her, and yet her reputation as a novel thing in the kitchen and as a sexed-up version of the more typical domestic matron has surpassed any other aspect of her programming or food writing. We have demanded new ways to conceive of being female, and yet we cannot quite fathom the results of our requests.

What ties Lawson interestingly to the other authors whom I have discussed in this chapter, though, is her will away from the bustle of modern life. Perhaps in order to become a domestic goddess, or any version of a redesigned female subject that includes mental and physical components of being, the constructions of modernity must be themselves reconsidered. Lawson explains:

> That's why I love this sort of cooking; the rhythms are so reassuring. I no longer feel I'm snatching at food, at life. It's not exactly that I'm constructing a domestic idyll, but as I work in the kitchen at night, or on the weekend, filling the house with the smells of baking and roasting and filling the fridge with good things to eat, it feels, corny as it sounds, as if I'm making a home. (77)

Her domestic patter and promotion of eating well combine throughout *How to Eat* in ways that recall those cookery books of earlier times and that echo the thoughts of cookery guru Delia Smith, who muses, "Traditionally cooking has been a skill handed down within families [...] . When Britain ceased, in the wake of the industrial revolution, to be a predominately rural nation, families lost their links to the country (which is where the roots of good cooking lie)" (8). The notions of food as central to family and of the slow-paced country life are at the hearts of many cooking guides, including Lawson's. Her books, though, are quite different in that Lawson blurs traditional domestic activities with a sensuality that defies some strongholds of femininity. Women such as Lawson may pave the way for hybrid constructions of the feminine that include the body, that make a bit more acceptable female consumption and excessive revelry in the senses, and that clearly indicate the need for a voice of one's own that is grounded in everyday life. Though Lawson is still a bit of an oddity, as are other women who exemplify that attempt to unify what has been divided, as more examples of such variants on the age-old theme of duality are presented to readers and to viewers, then perhaps slowly, definitions of female subjectivity will move beyond the limitations of modernity and will resist its rigid restrictions. Until that change comes, though, such representations can appear to be merely caricatures of real women, roadside attractions that lie beyond the equation of normativizing cultural practices.

Helen Fielding's popular novel, *Bridget Jones's Diary*, provides a good example of such a strange remainder in the eponymous Bridget, who, though a product of the British university system and a working, self-sufficient woman, cannot seem to reconcile her sense of embodiment with her female subjectivity. If not the sort of perfect blend that Woolf presents in Ellen Terry, Bridget is a fine example of the sort of auto-objectification faced by women in a culture that demands perfection from both their careers and their figures. The project of modernity, with its insistence upon increasingly rigid prescriptions for its citizens, is central to Bridget's dilemmas and is what illuminates her seeming shortcomings. The landscape of Bridget's London is riddled with popular cultural references that "remind us that we are in a world in which the mixing of the high- and low-brow has to some extent been achieved [...] and that popular culture has become the lingua franca of a whole generation" (Whelehan, *Feminist* 184). Although women such as Bridget actually exhibit the full spectrum between and including intellect and embodiment, the effects of a culture that continues to define female subjectivity as an auto-objectifying process demand that Bridget and others like her partition off the components of a "total" self in ways that deny what they find when they face their everyday lives. Just as with beauty rhetoric that explains a need for women to unite their two "selves" and yet maintains that the body remains a thing unto itself, rhetoric sent forth from a world that asks women to be effective public citizens who thrive in the workforce and simultaneously to be perfectly maintained, traditionally feminine females is, in a word, crazymaking. The ambivalence with which the mind and body have been divided by cultural practices returns tenfold when the two reunite into one awkward being.

The same skepticism launched toward Nigella Lawson as a public figure is caricatured in Fielding's novel. The life outlined for Bridget is likely not far off from the lives of many women of her relative generation: women raised during the 1970s upon equal parts second-wave feminism and glamor-laced media. "I am," says Bridget, "a child of *Cosmopolitan* culture, have been traumatized by supermodels and too many quizzes and know that neither my personality nor my body is up to it if left to its own devices" (59). Although Bridget is wise enough to analyze the rhetoric of popular culture and its effects upon her being, she is nonetheless unable to shake off the fetters of a world thrust upon women through mass media. Though she self-consciously fashions herself from the accumulation of cultural attitudes toward women and their desires for romance, for career, for family, she does not always master her own narrative. Rachel Blau DuPlessis explains, "The plot of courtship as social and gender reconciliation begins to break by the latter half of the nineteenth century. The contradiction between love and vocation in plots centering on women is accentuated, and romance [...] is less able to be depicted as satisfying the urgencies of [...] self-development, desire for useful work, ambition, and public striving" (15). Interestingly, this plot breaks just as the insurgence of auto-objectifying literatures begins, indicating that as women grew by degrees more able to confront the plots that they were handed, their desires were increasingly policed by beauty writers and other perpetuators of the myths attached to the quest for physical perfection in the name of courtship. A century later, Bridget, whose plot is still caught up in this contradiction, cannot remove herself from its confines and is caught between the poles of satisfaction via the male partner and satisfaction via self and vocation. Because Bridget cannot fit either mode of being, though, she emerges as a figure both comic and a bit pathetic. Because of our collective cultural training, Bridget's desire to become a part of the romance plot is the easiest aspect of her characterization to consider, rather than her simultaneous ability to critique the culture from which she emerges. Readers still rest most comfortably with figures that can be easily defined, with women who fit certain generic qualifications, and so Fielding's protagonist has too often been miscategorized as a whining single woman in search of a mate instead of a woman well aware of her position in the culture.

Although she is a product of our culture, Bridget is hardly a character from any known plot because she defies the extremes with which she is presented. The narrative admits, at times, to its complicity in the ubiquitous romance plot, but for Bridget that plot is foiled by her inability to accept a permanent role in such a plot structure. Even as the point of origin for many of her impulses is the desire to be a part of a heterosexual love relationship, she is not wholly able to give way to the demands that the plot of courtship and marriage is wont to place upon her. Bridget is caught between the two avenues that women are supposed to choose between, and, indeterminate, she is presented as a median point on the spectrum of contemporary feminist thinking. She proclaims herself to be a feminist, but in a way that has not rung true for some critics and members of Fielding's reading audience because of her inability to adopt some party line. Kelly A. Marsh assesses Bridget's detractors, explaining that "criticisms are based upon two questionable premises: that the self can be remade in such a way that one is in control, and that control is ultimately achievable by anyone" (52–3). It is the lack of "control" that is at the center of Bridget's subject formation in the midst of cultural change, though, and that is at the heart of her characterization. Fielding acknowledges in Bridget the absolute inability to be in control, and for readers who are unable to see that unique subject construct, its comedy falls flat. Bridget's lack of "control" indicates not simply that she does not have it all together, but also that she defies the strictures of modern auto-objectifying principles. She is far more challenging to cultural norms than she might appear at first glance. Her inability to land squarely within one feminist camp or another, too, simply underscores Bridget's confusion over what it means to be a woman in what Peggy Orenstein calls a "half-changed world," as well as her defiance toward fitting into a prescribed role that does not take into account her many, sometimes conflicting impulses.

Bridget's character is flanked by those of her two best female friends, Jude and Sharon, each of whom represents a more typically constructed version of femininity at the close of twentieth century: Jude is attached to "Vile Richard," her "self-indulgent commitment phobic" (19) boyfriend whose infractions take up much of Jude's mental energy. Sharon, "the nearest thing to a feminist mouthpiece in the novel" (Whelehan, *Fielding's* 29), coins the term "emotional fuckwit" as a way to succinctly wrap up the shortcomings of the men with whom the cohort comes into contact. Compared with Jude, who is caught up in self-help guides to romance and who returns time and again to her partner even when he might leave a little something to be desired, Bridget does not take the traditional route, even though she does scrutinize it for potholes and unforeseen twists in its course. Jude and Bridget both revel in ideal images of Jane Austen's Mr. Darcy, and for Bridget, "Darcy and Elizabeth [...] are my chosen representatives in the field of shagging, or, rather, courtship" (246). The rough edges of romance lie in Bridget's full view; however, unlike Jude, who chooses to ignore the vile defects of her Richard, Bridget meets those rough patches head-on, even when she meets them awkwardly. There is enough of Sharon's anti-sexism within Bridget for her to push against the confines of a traditional feminized story line. Bridget has internalized not only the traditions of culture to which Jude has succumbed, but also a bit of the attitude embraced by the woman who refuses to silence her beliefs and desires: "They exist in a total Culture of Entitlement," Sharon fumes about men. "Pass me one of those mini-pizzas, will you?" (125).

Bridget balances between the two extremes and attempts to integrate her position vis-à-vis feminist thought much in the same way as she does her understandings of herself as both a social agent and an embodied, sexual female. She is battered by "fears of dying alone and being found three weeks later half-eaten by an Alsatian" (20), but simultaneously resolves to "develop inner poise and authority and sense of self as woman of substance, complete *without* boyfriend"; troublingly, though, the latter is noted as "best way to obtain boyfriend" (2). Orenstein outlines this conflict: "In their professional lives, their personal lives, and their dreams of the future, young women face a series of interlocking dilemmas, a dizzying combination of external obstacles and internal contradictions that push them simultaneously toward autonomy and dependence, modernity and tradition" (40). These types of dilemmas are the same as those that I have described as part and parcel of the mind/body problem that philosophers and theorists have banged their heads against for a very long time. Most adult women at the turn of the millennium struggle with the inscriptions of culture upon always resistant flesh and with the trials of a modernity that asks them to write off the aspects of experience in order to give primacy to the mental realm that runs the modern show. As an example of the problems that arise when women cannot align themselves with a known version of femininity or womanhood, Bridget has been hailed by many as not quite right, or as little but fodder for a good laugh. She is, however, representative of the space left between the parts of an imperfectly divided female subject, one who must claim the physical vehicle of her social agency, but who has long been acculturated to position her "self" at least an arm's reach from the body that must remain in a submissive posture.

The form that Fielding has chosen for her novel—the diary and all of its attendant emotional and personal baggage—provides a vehicle for Bridget's problematic relationship with herself as a woman who desires to maintain a career path and an ideal body shape. Her New Year's resolutions include moratoria on behaving "sluttishly around the house" and falling for "emotional fuckwits or freeloaders, perverts," as well as desires to be "more confident" and "more assertive" and to "[e]at more pulses" (2–3). Her diary entries recount each day's caloric intake, the number of alcoholic beverages consumed and cigarettes smoked, and any number of other everyday details that denote Bridget's attempts to obtain cultural and social normativity. Bridget's diary is a good collection of what many women of her relative generation rack up as they pass through their own days, and according to Whelehan, "our relationship with Bridget is one of complicity [...] . *Bridget Jones's Diary* depends on that sense of a shared female discourse" (*Feminist* 180). Like the wisdom imparted from woman to woman in cookery books and housekeeping manuals, this narrative of shared experience allows readers to identify with Bridget through common connections to women's popular culture. The cultural impulse toward guilt and confession, as well as toward the paralyzing normativizing demands upon the physical component of the subject, is evident within Fielding's novel and is key to maintaining readerly empathy. The trends set out in mass culture and documented by the fictitious Bridget are very much a part of the everyday lives of many, if not most, women in contemporary culture.

One of the most notable normativizing projects taken up by the novel is that of Bridget's quest for physical perfection and an ideal weight. Bridget is concerned with her body weight in a manner not unlike that prescribed in any number of maintenance manuals written throughout the twentieth century, and "the body is represented as chaotic and in need of policing" (Whelehan, *Fielding's* 48). What is most striking about her proportions, though, is that they fall right in the center of those weights prescribed for the ideal British woman. Though she obsesses daily about her weight and her food consumption, Bridget's weight at the beginning of the novel and that at its end are but one pound different, and at 9 st. 2 lb. (128 pounds) she "embodies" the ideal that she is so certain eludes her. Unless she is of a height that is not average (and if she were, then she would likely bemoan that fact, making it more than obvious to readers), then Bridget Jones actually exemplifies the body type outlined by those height-weight charts examined previously in Chapter 1 and sought by so many women for more than a century. Fielding parodies the constant conflict between appearance and reality that typically results from cultural standardizations, and she emphasizes this cultural irony through her depictions of Bridget's inability to view herself in terms other than those set out for her within the pages of glossy periodicals and six-hundred-page beauty books. "One of the key ironies of the book," argues Whelehan, "is in the reader's acknowledgement that Bridget is not really fat, and the book therefore offers a study in women's skewed relationships to their own bodies" (*Fielding's* 74). Part of Fielding's farce also rests upon the reality that although Bridget and countless others willingly follow the prescriptions set forth in popular media, they rarely are able to conform to any ideal beyond those set forth by the criteria of their own flesh. On Christmas Day, Bridget writes, "9 st 5 (oh God, have turned into Santa Claus, Christmas pudding or similar)" (300). The ironic humor of the novel is captured in Bridget's holiday statement: over the course of her diary year she has gained 5 st. 2, but lost 5 st. 3. The efforts put into following the elusive quest for perfection are a large component of what makes Bridget both slightly pathetic and altogether real for those readers who themselves share in such quixotic attempts.

The humor and pathos of Fielding's novel are lost on many, however, as has been evident in the fuss made over actress Renée Zellweger's much publicized weight gain as she prepared to portray a Bridget described as "chubby" in the film adaptation of the novel. Interestingly, in Zellweger's case, the weight gain was viewed as a matter of will because it was meant to further her career and craft: "This method-acting zeal to *become* the character by gaining 17 lbs to get to 9 st 3 lb [...] extends to her commitment to getting the English accent right as well as getting some experience working in a publisher's office" (Whelehan, *Fielding's* 74). While Bridget the character is maligned for her inability to "control" her weight, and thus her flesh and her embodied agency, the actor who portrays her avoids the same accusations because what she exhibits through the weight gain (and subsequent quick and well-publicized loss) is the ability to conform to cultural expectations to manipulate one's body. In the novel, Fielding actually characterizes and pokes fun at the very sort of frenzy that the media have focused upon during the filming of both *Bridget Jones's Diary* and its sequel, *Bridget Jones: The Edge of Reason*. The gap between the real and perceived Bridget not only lies within her own fictional head, but has been received intact by a culture that cannot decipher the fact that if Bridget is less than ideal, then she is so only by standards that she has adopted from mass media that in turn have wondered over Zellweger's milkshake-and-doughnut diets on her way to playing a Bridget that is significantly different from the one outlined in Fielding's prose. This case of mistaken reading (and misadaptation) helps to illustrate the ways in which Bridget, as a representative of contemporary culture, has come to exhibit such behaviors, as well as the ways in which the culture perpetuates itself.

Fielding's Bridget, though, is not only caught up in the project of modern auto-objectification; she also attempts to round out her intellectual capacities on her way to becoming a "whole" female subject. Her foray into popular self-help, though, only muddles her attempts to locate a sense of self beyond the troubled one found for women in the mass media. A book read by Bridget tells her that when times get tough, "[w]hat you have to do is be a heroine and stay brave, without sinking into drink or self-pity and everything will be OK" (195). Such agency-producing wisdom for the modern female subject, however, is in direct conflict with that wisdom which drives Bridget to diet her way toward a version of success in which the goal is matrimony and not necessarily a career or a version of the self strengthened by intellectual improvement. At times, Bridget merely looks for ways beyond such lax behavior as lying "fully dressed and terrified under the duvet, chain-smoking, glugging cold *sake* out of a beaker and putting on make-up as a hysterical displacement activity" (89). At other junctures, she uses her amalgamation of Zen-like philosophies and other appeals to "inner poise" to navigate the treacherous terrain of office parties. Regardless, Bridget is one of the number of women for whom Kay Cooke advises, "full control over your life is an impossible enough goal without expecting that you can control your hip shape as well" (6). The struggle for personal achievement or fulfillment accorded Bridget in one text is negated by the numerous other cultural messages that she receives. Though Bridget can be seen as simply one example of what it can mean to be a late-twentieth-century woman, she has, however, often been viewed with a shake of the critical head when not with scorn. Her neurotic obsession with men and with her physical appearance, when combined with her real ability to be economically and socially independent, may not strike chords of truth for Bridget's readers unless they are, like she is, thirty-something singletons at the mercy of millennial women's culture. To some she seems unlikely, unrealistic. But Bridget Jones is, perhaps, one of the best examples of an embodied mind that can be produced during an age in which social and cultural mandates still hand down ambivalent messages to women.

Like Bridget Jones, the title character of Rachel Cusk's novel *Saving Agnes* is "riddled with terminal caprice" (2). Her whimsy, however, eventually takes on more serious proportions than does that with which Bridget is afflicted. Like Bridget, Agnes is an educated woman, but unlike Fielding's protagonist, who obtained her credentials at one of the red bricks, Cusk's is a graduate of Oxford, "beautiful *and* brainy" (4, original italics). Her educational credentials, however, do not exempt Agnes from a keen susceptibility to accepted standards of feminine beauty. Agnes Day, Cusk explains, "painted her face and starved herself; she shaved her legs and plucked her eyebrows and scrubbed the gravelly flesh on her thighs with a mitt of similar texture" (17) in the name of standardized beauty, and according to the text Agnes is indeed attractive. Her innate physical appearance, though, does not mollify her, and so Agnes searches for the sort of "authentic," contrived beauty prescribed for women in Kenton's guide to 1990s beauty. She views herself as falling so short of the ideal for female beauty that she feels the need to strive "not to please others but merely not to disgust them" (18). Try as Agnes might to project herself as the ideal of a "thrusting young professional running on a tight schedule," she nevertheless declares herself a "failure *extraordinaire*" (12). Just as countless women have searched for ways to eradicate bacteria from their homes in the face of such an impossibility, Agnes searches for bodily perfection and indeed builds her self-image from the theories that tell her that this can be achieved.

The dueling facts that perfection is not possible and that, if impossible, such ideology leaves no foundation for Agnes's sense of subjectivity create the crisis that lies at the center of the novel. Agnes not only must learn, but also must accept the fact that perfection is only relative to an ever-shifting culture of the moment, and this lesson, although ultimately achieved, leaves Agnes as a citizen of a realm that has not yet manifested. Agnes is a composite of messages that insist that women take charge of their lives, but that at the same time insist that such control is the domain of a higher self and is exercised over the shell of the body. Judith Newman, in a coffee-table volume of beauty prescriptions simply titled *Body*, illustrates this message in her discussion of how everyday stress affects women: "Powerlessness often is the major culprit. Stress reduction is about gaining control of your environment, and moving from victimhood to empowerment" (171). Here the rhetoric of feminism is superimposed over the project of modern auto-objectification, and women such as Agnes Day are asked to consider issues of control and power from within the context of pages of considerations of ways in which one's physical body can and should be controlled. The message, as it is in the other contemporary beauty books discussed above, is ostensibly positive, but the undercutting contradiction of its delivery creates a rhetorical outcome for readers that is complicit in the division of a woman into physical and psychical selves. The twisted logic of the culture of auto-objectification remains steadily in charge of the world that Cusk describes, and, even as Agnes learns to overcome her own misguided notions of selfhood and empowerment, Cusk has underscored the reality of a society still resting on age-old theories that leave an enlightened Agnes almost completely disenfranchised.

Throughout the novel, Agnes runs ragged while attempting to construct herself in an image that she does not quite fit; as with Bridget Jones, Agnes Day discovers that gap between the realities of the physical world and the rhetoric of mass culture. Agnes is shown to have been susceptible, even as a young girl, to the ideologies of feminine perfection, and she brings with her into adulthood the growing list of ways in which she feels that she should accommodate the world at large. There are few aspects of Agnes's self-image—of her body/image—that are not conditioned by either cultural messages or by the desires of others. With a clear understanding that the foundation of cultural femininity is an abject female body that defies standardization, and thus that begs for normativization, Agnes accepts the fact that "legitimacy could be attained at the cost of a little bloodshed" (45). In order to join the ranks of what she imagines to be legitimate womanhood, an adolescent Agnes "committed the felony of false menstruation" (45), and for two years feigns the female rite of a monthly period. The natural rhythms and schedules of her endocrine system mean nothing to Agnes in the face of feeling as if she is less than what standards might call for and, though she does not menstruate until age fifteen (46), she endures the troubles of the ruse long before she needs to in order to feel herself a part of the "normal" world. At an early age she has internalized the codes of the system around her and capitulates to a degree that creates in Agnes a picture of the Foucauldian docile body. The inscriptions of culture, even down to the enactment of menses, mark Agnes and draw her to the center of standardization. The fight to maintain such a position, though, is a long fight, one that eventually leaves her in a state of cultural (as well as emotional) breakdown.

In addition to the insidious messages for women gleaned from mass culture, messages from others who perpetuate the mythology of feminine perfection are part of what Agnes, in the position of total object, of full docility, succumbs to in her quest for normalcy. The theories of Paul Schilder, as explored in the previous chapter, are applicable to Agnes, whose own body image waxes and wanes in response to the bodies of others, as well as to their suggestive discussions of her physical appearance. In Cusk's characterization of Agnes, the social qualities of body images exceed sympathetic responses and emerge to demonstrate her lack of resistance, her capitulation to standardization, particularly to the sorts of standards for beauty that are supposed to (the stories tell us) bring with them bona fide love and happiness ever after. Her college beau and the man to whom Agnes seems to have lost any shred of selfhood is described as "indubitably diminutive" (22), and as Agnes recalls her fall into love with him, she also recalls having physically shrunk in order to become *his* ideal. "Through sheer love, it seemed, he had made her his perfect match. It did not occur to her to wonder why," Cusk's narrator wryly notes, "he had not succeeded instead in making himself taller" (23). The lengths that a fully auto-objectified Agnes can and will go to in order to norm herself to the standards that promise her a life at the heart of the romance plot indicate the extent of the damage that can be done by the codes for bodily maintenance. John, her boyfriend, provides the norming standards with his own height, and Agnes, much like Schilder's patient whose hands "grew" upon suggestion, morphs her own body/image in order to suit his shape. Rather than provide Agnes with any true sense of empowerment, as promised by Newman's beauty book, the kind of "control" over herself that Agnes exhibits is a *reaction to* the control of a system of which she is the objectified victim, and thus is no true source of empowerment. "She wondered," we find, "when exactly in her life she had ceased to act, had ceased to be effective" (167). For Agnes, Cusk hints, that moment lies far back in time; socialization begins, perhaps, in the womb, if not soon after we make our entrance into the world. The vehicle of the body, a necessary aspect of agency and subjectivity, has been sacrificed at the altar of normativity. Though Agnes has followed the path of modern intellectualism—a path that has throughout the twentieth century been rhetorically connected to social agency for women—without the resistance of the physical body and an acknowledgment of the agency of the flesh, Agnes seemingly cannot be effective: cannot effect change, cannot resist the mechanisms of standardization, cannot control herself in ways that are productive rather than reductive.

The epitome of Agnes's ability to conceive of herself as pure object lies in her recollection of a time during her relationship with her diminutive lover when, rather than actively refuse sexual overtures, she chose to "lay inert, as if on a marble slab" while John "gasped and sighed above her" (159), engaging in intercourse with an unwilling partner whose lack of agency prohibits saying "no." Though Agnes notes that she had "imagined" that John was raping her, what she fails to recognize is that she was figuratively raping herself through a negation of her physical body as a part of that "self." She "tasted resentment, oppression and rage on her tongue" (159), but could not surpass her docility and turn those tastes into fighting words. Her full capitulation to the codes of bodily maintenance are symptomatic of a greater, and more devastating, illness that Agnes has contracted: she has no framework for a selfhood that will allow her to exhibit her femininity and a subjectivity imbued with the agency necessary to detach from destructive behaviors done in the name of acceptance and love.

Eventually, Agnes cannot maintain her auto-objectifying behavior, and as she works to tear down the codifications of social and cultural prescriptions that cloak any "true," integrated self, her inability to identify with anything but cultural standards leads to an emotional numbness that is near a nervous breakdown. During her break from the traditions of beauty she "[lets] herself go," and, although the "phrase did imply a certain freedom from imprisonment [...] its effects were far from captivating" (138). The brazen quality of letting oneself go is at once freedom and bleak no-woman's-land. As a woman who has "surrendered her brush and palette" and become "that which she had always feared [...] she already was, underneath" (138), Agnes faces that fear but is unsure of what lies beyond the slim range of femininity that she has allowed herself to navigate. Unadorned, Agnes cannot be sure of the wiles on which she had previously relied and finds that men look at her as either "an object of admiration or studied avoidance" (170). As she begins to alter her appearance—and, by extension, her body image, the way in which she can conceive of herself as an embodied social agent—Agnes faces the same contradictions of tradition and modernity, of old and new social roles for women, as does Fielding's Bridget Jones. In order for either character to allow both her physical and psychical selves to share equal billing within the makeup of her subjectivity, she must also be willing to allow for the unexpected, the unscripted to occur as she negotiates territory that has not yet been formed by the old ways of thinking about selfhood. For a woman such as Agnes, who leaves nothing to chance prior to her fall from the center of normativity, this new world offers her little consolation. Cast adrift into a world for which she has not been properly socialized—that real world where lived experiences deny the separation of mind from body—Agnes can seemingly do little but "cry and claw at her body with rage" (138).

Just as Bridget Jones is cast at the center of a continuum of thought and experience, Agnes Day finds that in her new state—neither adored feminine nor radically masculinized—she can find comfort in a "hermaphrodite sensibility" (138). In her home Agnes contrasts with both Nina, her housemate who is both adamantly feminist and traditionally beautiful, and Merlin, their male housemate. On the job, as well, Agnes shifts from being an editorial assistant on the verge of getting the sack to a woman who "became expert at locating errors and discrepancies," who "wrote an article for the magazine and was surprised to find it accepted" (139); she presides in this context between Greta, her obtuse Canadian coworker, and Jean, her efficient superior. As Agnes allows for her physicality to present itself beyond the confines of auto-objectification, she finds balance within the other areas of her life. Cusk positions Agnes in a way that indicates how difficult the half-changed world at the end of the twentieth century is for women *and* the fact that although that balance might be precarious, it is a potentially possible balance to strike. Unlike Bridget Jones, whose wavering has made her a questionable representation of contemporary female experience, Agnes walks the tightrope of femininity, commanding a certain amount of dignity and integrity. Even as she leaves behind what many might consider the trappings of her "civilization," Agnes does so as an escape on a way to a more complex and, one must imagine, more integrated existence. Cusk has allowed for the truly numbing effects of auto-objectification to emerge as far more tragic or pathetic than weight gain and a "distinct whiff of human flesh" (138). Because readers can identify the ways in which Agnes has limited her emotional and physical experiences vis-à-vis her objectification of her own being, her fall into mind/body totality, although perhaps troubling in its turn from social and cultural ritual, can hardly be viewed as less desirable than the life lived by Agnes beforehand. There may not be a map of this world, but it can't be worse than the one in which Agnes has lived before tossing away her lipstick.

By drawing a parallel between her protagonist and the homeless who wander London's Camden Town, Cusk underscores the notion that Agnes is a cast-out in the world that she has abandoned. Without the noticeable currency of dress and makeup, Agnes does not have a place within the "respectable" side of this borough of the city, a cultural borderland between abject poverty and genteel living. She can be too easily mistaken for one of the "alternatives" who mill about the underground station, looking for a place to sleep for the night (174). Without literal currency, too (having given her last pound to a homeless woman with whom she has a brief encounter), Agnes cannot command a place in a society constructed for the self-sufficient; she cannot even pay her fare on the underground. Agnes imagines that it is "obvious what kind of person" she is, but then regards herself in the metal of the station wall: she "looked scruffy and old" and not much different from the street people gathered in the station (175). Appearances are what they convey, and Agnes in her new state represents to others yet another individual who has chosen to live at the margins of society. In Agnes's case, those margins are only figurative—she still has a home, a job—but the metaphor is clearly drawn: in a culture that prizes the drawn outline rather than the experiences that fill in the center of its figure, no one who defies the norm can be a full-fledged citizen.

The station guards mistake her for just another bit of social detritus, as do those whom she attempts to busk for tube fare home, but in effect, Agnes is social excess. Even though she has chosen a path that will serve her more readily than that which she has previously walked, Agnes meets a fate similar to that explored forty years earlier by Barbara Pym when she cast Prudence Bates as an unwitting figure of sexual and cultural excess. The world has changed by degrees, but the excess of the world—that which does not fit within its boundaries for proper codes and behaviors—remains displaced. When Agnes realizes that the man who gives her two pounds in an embarrassed exchange is actually John, her old lover who does not recognize her, she can understand the changes that she has undergone and the fact that those changes have inevitably altered who Agnes Day is at all. As a child Agnes may have "enjoyed frequent changes of identity" (13), but at this juncture in her early adulthood, Agnes's identity is severed from any earlier self subjugated to a perfectionist's ideals of success and privilege. As Agnes allows herself to live within her body, rather than to play upon her body as if it were an inert object, she must face the fact that the female body will conjure up a variety of possibilities for those who interact with it. Most of those possibilities, however, remain for Western culture tinged with the same anxieties long cast toward female embodiment.

Neither Bridget Jones nor Agnes Day represents that seamless figure of mind/body totality depicted by Woolf in her vision of Ellen Terry; however, both do illustrate the ways in which an embodied female subjectivity can be depicted at the turn of the twenty-first century. Modernity might have become simply a chronic state of process and progress, but the driving force of modernity—that prized and rational mind—has failed all of the women writers discussed in this project. The quiet but ultimately important knowledge of a body granted the freedom to rejoin its mental complement is what should mark a new stage of the modern, of an enlightenment that returns human subjects, but especially female subjects, to a state of integration that has been understood as natural by philosophers, cognitive scientists, and others, but that remains just beyond our frameworks for understanding. Fielding and Cusk both are able to navigate the issues of mind/body duality more thoroughly than have the women discussed in other chapters whose representations of the binary led to divided protagonists, even if the women whom they have configured remain outcasts in a world still bound to the same prescriptions dealt to women for over a century in periodicals, beauty guides, and other volumes that detail the processes of auto-objectification. As writers and readers can more fully conceive of ways past the rigid normativity of defined qualities of the female body, then that "body" in all of its various shapes, classes, races, and abilities can begin to emerge not as an entity that should produce anxiety and social tensions, but that can showcase the fact that in order for one to approach the world on two feet, those feet necessarily must be real feet and not simply metaphors for the stability of the intellect. Readers might shudder at Agnes and laugh at Bridget Jones, but those characterizations, even if they are uncomfortable and maligned, might come closest to the real lives of those who turn the pages of their texts. As the simple facts of embodiment become more often aligned and equated with a subjectivity that has for so long denied its physical aspects, then as a culture we will, hopefully, be more willing to accept into our fold the half-breeds formed of embodied minds, the "alternatives" to a divided world.

Bibliography

Ackley, Katherine Anne. "'All This Reading': The Importance of Literature in the Novels of Barbara Pym." Lenckos and Miller: 33–46.

Adam, Jill. *Beauty Box: A Book for Women about Bodies, Faces, Make-Up, Let-Downs*. London: Kingsway Reproductions, [1940].

Adams, Carol J. *The Sexual Politics of Meat*. New York: Continuum, 1990.

Adolph, Andrea. "Luncheon at 'The Leaning Tower': Consumption and Class in Virginia Woolf's *Between the Acts*." *Women's Studies: An Interdisciplinary Journal* 34 (2005): 439–59.

Anderson, T. McClurg. "Housework with Ease." Wheatcroft: 32–9.

Armstrong, Nancy and Leonard Tennenhouse, ed. *The Ideology of Conduct: Essays on Literature and the History of Sexuality*. New York and London: Methuen, 1987.

The Art of Beauty: A Book for Women and Girls (By a Toilet Specialist; Edited by "Isobel" of Home Notes*)*. The Isobel Handbooks. No. 7. London: C. Arthur Pearson Limited, 1899.

The Art of Being Beautiful: A Series of Interviews with a Society Beauty (By S— G—).London: Henry J. Drane, [1902].

Aslett, Don. *Is there Life after Housework?* 1982. Watford, UK: Exley, 1983.

Baker, Niamh. *Happily Ever After?: Women's Fiction in Postwar Britain, 1945–60*. New York: St. Martin's, 1989.

Bal, Mieke. *Narratology: Introduction to the Theory of Narrative*. Second ed. Trans. Christine van Boheemen. 1980. Toronto: U of Toronto P, 1985.

Barker, Francis. *The Tremulous Private Body: Essays on Subjection*. 1984. Ann Arbor: U of Michigan P, 1995.

Barr, Ann and Paul Levy. *The Official Foodie Handbook*. New York: Arbor House, 1984.

Barthes, Roland. *S/Z: An Essay*. Trans. Richard Miller. New York: Hill and Wang-Farrar, Strauss, Giroux, 1974.

Bayley, John. "Barbara Pym as Comforter." Lenckos and Miller: 166–72.

de Beauvoir, Simone. *The Second Sex*. Trans. H. M. Parshley. 1949. New York: Bantam, 1965.

Beeton, Mrs. [Isabella Mary]. *Mrs. Beeton's Cookery Book: All About Cookery, Household Work, Marketing, Trussing, Carving, Etc. New Edition*. London: Ward, Lock, & Co., 1909.

Belenky, Mary Field, et al. *Women's Ways of Knowing: The Development of Self, Voice, and Mind*. New York: Basic Books, 1986.

Bell, Mrs. J. N. *The ABC of Housekeeping; or Mistress and Maid*. London: Henry J. Drane, [1902].

Bennett, Sir Thomas. "Planning Houses for a New Town." Wheatcroft: 40–46.

Benson, James. Letter to M. Lyster. 3 July 1951. Mass Observation *Bulletin* 42, May/June 1951. Mass Observation Archives. University of Sussex.

Bloom, Ursula. *The Housewife's Beauty Book*. London: Robert Hale Limited, [1941].

———. *Me—After the War: A Book for Girls Considering the Future*. London: John Gifford, Ltd., 1944.

———. *Wartime Beauty*. London: Bantam, 1943.

Booth, Wayne C. *The Rhetoric of Fiction*. Second ed. Chicago: U of Chicago P, 1983.

Bordo, Susan. *Unbearable Weight: Feminism, Western Culture, and the Body*. Berkeley: U of California P, 1993.

Bourdieu, Pierre. *Distinction: A Social Critique of the Judgement of Taste*. Trans. Richard Nice. Cambridge: Harvard UP, 1984.

Bourne, Aleck. *Health of the Future*. Harmondsworth: Penguin, 1942.

Bowlby, Rachel. *Just Looking: Consumer Culture in Dreiser, Gissing, and Zola*. New York: Methuen, 1985.

Brent, Eve. "She is Britain's Champion Housewife." *Sunday Pictorial* November 2, 1941: 7+.

Brontë, Charlotte. *Jane Eyre*. 1847. Ed. Beth Newman. Case Studies in Contemporary Criticism. New York: Bedford-St. Martin's, 1996.

Brooks, Peter. *Body Work: Objects of Desire in Modern Narrative*. Cambridge: Harvard UP, 1993.

Butler, Judith. *Bodies that Matter: On the Discursive Limits of "Sex."* New York: Routledge, 1993.

———. *The Psychic Life of Power: Theories in Subjection*. Palo Alto: Stanford UP, 1997.

Carter, Angela. *The Magic Toyshop*. 1967. London: Virago, 1981.

de Certeau, Michel. *The Practice of Everyday Life*. 1974. Trans. Steven Rendall. Berkeley: U of California P, 1984.

Chadwick, Edwin. *Report on the Sanitary Condition of the Labouring Population of Great Britain*. 1842. Ed. and intro. M. W. Flinn. Edinburgh: Edinburgh UP, 1965.

Chatman, Seymour. *Story and Discourse: Narrative Structure in Fiction and Film*. Ithaca and London: Cornell UP, 1978.

Chatterton, Lydia. *Win-the-War Cookery*. London: Weldon's, Ltd., 1939.

Chernin, Kim. *The Obsession: Reflections of the Tyranny of Slenderness*. New York: Harper Colophon, 1981.

Cleland, John. *Beauty for You*. London: Paul Hamlyn, 1965.

Conran, Shirley. *Superwoman: Everywoman's Book of Household Management*. 1975. London: Penguin, 1977.

Cooke, Kay. *Real Gorgeous: The Truth about Body and Beauty*. 1994. London: Bloomsbury, 1995.

"Cookery Demonstrations." "Gert and Daisy Food Talks." [Elsie and Doris Waters] *Kitchen Front*. 23 December 1940. Transcript. Microfilm 629/630. BBC Written Archives Center.

The Council of Scientific Management in the Home. *Meals in Modern Homes*. London: COSMITH, 1955.

"Cover Girl Calorie Chart." London: Health and Beauty Bureau, 1941.

Cox, Muriel. *The Good Housekeeping Beauty Book*. London and Chesham: Gramol Publications, 1946.

Cusk, Rachel. *Saving Agnes*. London: Picador, 1993.

David, Elizabeth. *A Book of Mediterranean Food*. London: John Lehmann, 1950.

Davidson, Phyllis. *Home Management*. London: B. T. Batsford, Ltd., 1960.

Davison, Irene. *Etiquette for Women: A Book of Modern Manners and Customs*. London: C. Arthur Pearson, Ltd., 1928.

Deutsch, Felix, ed. *On the Mysterious Leap from the Mind to the Body: A Workshop Study on the Theory of Conversion*. New York: International Universities P, 1959.

Donato, Deborah. *Reading Barbara Pym*. Madison and Teaneck, NJ: Farleigh Dickinson UP, 2005.

Douglas, Mary. *Natural Symbols: Explorations in Cosmology*. 1970. New York: Vintage, 1973.

———. *Purity and Danger: An Analysis of the Concepts of Pollution and Taboo*. 1966. London and Henley: Routledge and Kegan Paul, 1978.

Dunlap, Barbara J. "Reading Charlotte M. Yonge into the Novels of Barbara Pym." Lenckos and Miller: 179–93.

Dunmore, Helen. *Talking to the Dead*. 1996. Boston: Back Bay, 1998.

DuPlessis, Rachel Blau. *Writing Beyond the Ending: Narrative Strategies of Twentieth-Century Women Writers*. Bloomington: Indiana UP, 1985.

Epstein, Marcy J. "Consuming Performances: Eating Acts and Feminist Embodiment." *The Drama Review* 40 (Winter 1996): 20–36.

Everett, Barbara. "*Excellent Women* and After: The Art of Popularity." Lenckos and Miller: 64–75.

Eyles, Leonora. *Feeding the Family: Hints for the Intelligent Housewife*. London: Grant Richards and Humphrey Toulmin, 1929.

"Family Failings." Review of *Jane and Prudence*, by Barbara Pym, *The Wier*, by Jane Gillespie, and *Anne Fitzalan*, by Marguerite Steen. *Times Literary Supplement* 2 Oct. 1953: 625.

Felski, Rita. *The Gender of Modernity*. Cambridge: Harvard UP, 1995.

Fielding, Helen. *Bridget Jones's Diary*. London: Picador, 1996.

Flynn, Elizabeth A. *Feminism Beyond Modernism*. Carbondale: Southern IL UP, 2002.

Forty, Adrian. *Objects of Desire: Design and Society 1750–1980*. London: Thames and Hudson, 1986.

Foucault, Michel. *Discipline and Punish: The Birth of the Prison*. Trans. Robert Hurley.1975. New York: Vintage, 1995.

———. *The History of Sexuality, Volume One*. Trans. Robert Hurley. 1976. New York: Vintage, 1980.

Gent, Helena. *Health and Beauty for Women and Girls*. London: Health & Strength, Ltd., [1909].

Glowinski, Michal. "On the First-Person Novel." *New Literary History* 9 (1977): 103–14.

Good Housekeeping Institute. *Fish, Meat, Egg and Cheese Dishes*. London and Chesham: Good Housekeeping, [1944].

———. *Good Housekeeping's 100 Recipes for Unrationed Meat Dishes*. London: Good Housekeeping, 1940.

Great Britain. Ministry of Food. *Bulletin*. No. 530. 21 January 1950.

———. Ministry of Food. *How Britain Was Fed in Wartime: Food Control 1939– 1945*. London: HMSO, 1946.

———. Ministry of Food. *Retail Price List*. Sixteenth ed. 7 Nov. 1949.

———. Ministry of Food. *Retail Price List*. Sixteenth ed. Supplement F. 24 April 1950.

Grosz, Elizabeth. *Volatile Bodies: Toward a Corporeal Feminism*. Bloomington and Indianapolis: Indiana UP, 1994.

Hard-Time Cookery. London: The Association of Teachers of Domestic Subjects, 1940.

Hardyment, Christina. *From Mangle to Microwave: The Mechanization of Household Work*. London: Polity, 1988.

Harrison, Brian. "The Kitchen Revolution." *Consuming Passions: Food in the Age of Anxiety*. Sian Griffiths and Jennifer Wallace, ed. Manchester: Mandolin-Manchester UP, 1998. 139–49.

Hart, Alan. "Tim couldn't fix it." *Woman's Own* July 16, 2001: 12–13.

Herbert, S. Mervyn. *Britain's Health*. Harmondsworth: Penguin, 1939.

The Holy Bible. King James Version. Cleveland and New York: The World Publishing Co., n.d.

Horsfield, Margaret. *Biting the Dust: The Joys of Housework*. 1997. New York: Picador, 1999.

Household Management: Being a Guide to Housekeeping; Practical Cookery; Pickling and Preserving; Household Work; Dairy Management; the Table and Dessert; Cellarage of Wines; Brewing and Wine-Making; the Boudoir and Dressing-Room; Travelling; Stable Economy; Gardening Operations, Etc.; Forming therefore a Handbook of the Duties of the Housekeeper, Cook, Lady's-Maid, Nursery-Maid, Butler, Valet, Footman, Coachman, Groom, and Gardener (by an Old Housekeeper). Weale's Rudimentary, Scientific, and Educational Series. No. 149. London: Crosby Lockwood & Co., 1877.

Humble, Nicola. *Culinary Pleasures: Cookbooks and the Transformation of British Food*. London: Faber and Faber, 2005.

Kelsall, Helen M. *The National Society's Training College of Domestic Subjects Who's Who 1893–1957*. London: n.p., [1957].

Kingsford, Anna, M. D. *Health, Beauty, and the Toilet: Letters to Ladies from a Lady Doctor*. London and New York: Frederick Warne and Co., 1886.

Kino, Carol. Review of *Talking to the Dead*, by Helen Dunmore. *The New York Times* 1 June 1997, late ed., sec. 7: 24.

Kristeva, Julia. *Powers of Horror: An Essay on Abjection*. Trans. Leon S. Roudiez. New York: Columbia UP, 1982.

Lakoff, George and Mark Johnson. *Philosophy in the Flesh: The Embodied Mind and Its Challenge to Western Thought.* New York: Basic-Perseus, 1999.

Langland, Elizabeth. *Nobody's Angels: Middle-Class Women and Domestic Ideology in Victorian Culture.* Ithaca: Cornell UP, 1995.

Lanser, Susan Snaider. *Fictions of Authority: Women Writers and Narrative Voice.* Ithaca: Cornell UP, 1992.

Lawson, Nigella. *How to Be a Domestic Goddess: Baking and the Art of Comfort Cooking.* London: Chatto & Windus, 2000.

———. *How to Eat: The Pleasures and Principles of Good Food.* Ed. Arthur Boehm. New York: John Wiley and Sons, 2000.

Lears, Jackson. *Fables of Abundance: A Cultural History of Advertising in America.* New York: Basic Books-HarperCollins, 1994.

Leigh, Michelle Domingue. *The New Beauty: East-West Teachings in the Beauty of Body & Soul.* Tokyo and New York: Kodanshe Intl., 1995.

Lenckos, Frauke Elisabeth and Ellen J. Miller, ed. *"All This Reading": The Literary World of Barbara Pym.* Madison, NJ: Farleigh Dickinson UP, 2003.

The Living Bible. Paraphrased. Self-help ed. Wheaton, IL: Tyndale House, 1982.

Mace, C. A. "Satisfaction in Household Work." Wheatcroft: 17–27.

Macherey, Pierre. *A Theory of Literary Production.* 1966. Trans. Geoffrey Wall. London: Routledge and Kegan Paul, 1978.

The Man-Who-Sees. "Worldly and Unworldly." *My Home* Aug. 1945: 26+.

Marin, Louis. *Food for Thought.* 1986. Trans. Mette Hjort. Baltimore: Johns Hopkins UP, 1989.

Marsh, Kelly A. "Contextualizing Bridget Jones." *College Literature* 31.1 (2004): 52–72.

Mass Observation. *Future Outlooks 1946.* Bulletin 1 (March/April 1946).

———. *The Housewife's Day.* Bulletin 42 (May/June 1951).

———. *Our Daily Bread.* Bulletin 24 (January 1949).

Mass Observation Archive. Topic collection 67 (Food). 2/B (Food Questionnaire December 1940). University of Sussex.

———. Topic collection 67 (Food). 2/C (Cafés 1940). University of Sussex.

———. Topic collection 67 (Food). 3/C (Rationing 1941). University of Sussex.

———. Topic collection 67 (Food). 5/D (Menus 1948). University of Sussex.

———. Topic collection 67 (Food). 5/E (Menus 1950). University of Sussex.

McNeil, Steve. "She Knew What She Wanted." *Woman's Own* July 6, 1950: 9+.

Mendelson, Anne. "An Original Sin." *Gourmet* August 2000: 150.

Merleau-Ponty, Maurice. *The Phenomenology of Perception.* Trans. Colin Smith. 1962. New York and London: Routledge, 1998.

———. *The Visible and the Invisible.* 1964. Ed. Claude Lefort. Trans. Alphonso Lingis. Evanston: Northwestern UP, 1968.

Michie, Helena. *The Flesh Made Word: Female Figures and Women's Bodies.* New York: Oxford UP, 1987.

Monk's House Papers. Ms. B.4. Fragments. University of Sussex.

———. Ms. B.5. Working Drafts. University of Sussex.

My Home. January 1943.

―――. February 1943.

Newman, Judith. *Body*. London: Thames and Hudson, 1994.

O'Hara, Daniel T. "Why Foucault No Longer Matters." *Reconstructing Foucault: Essays in the Wake of the 80's*. Ed. Ricardo Miguel-Alfonso and Silvia Caporale-Bizzini. Amsterdam: Rodopi, 1994.

Oliver, Kelly. "Nourishing the Speaking Subject: A Psychoanalytic Approach to Abominable Food and Women." *Cooking, Eating, Thinking: Transformative Philosophies of Food*. Ed. Deane W. Curtin and Lisa M. Heldke. Bloomington and Indianapolis: Indiana UP, 1992. 68–84.

―――. *Subjectivity Without Subjects: From Abject Fathers to Desiring Mothers*. Lanham, MD: Rowman and Littlefield, 1998.

Orenstein, Peggy. *Flux: Women on Sex, Work, Love, Kids, and Life in a Half-Changed World*. New York: Anchor: 2000.

Philips, Deborah and Ian Haywood. *Brave New Causes: Women in British Postwar Fictions*. Leicester and Washington: Leicester UP, 1998.

Pizzey, Erin. *The Slut's Cookbook*. London: Macdonald & Co., Ltd., 1981.

Poovey, Mary. *Making a Social Body: British Cultural Formation, 1830–1864*. Chicago: U of Chicago P, 1995.

Punday, Daniel. *Narrative Bodies: Toward a Corporeal Narratology*. New York: Palgrave Macmillan, 2003.

Pym, Barbara. *Excellent Women*. 1952. New York: Plume, 1978.

―――. *A Glass of Blessings*. 1958. London: Jonathan Cape, 1977.

―――. *Jane and Prudence*. 1953. New York: Dutton, 1981.

―――. *A Very Private Eye: An Autobiography in Diaries and Letters*. Ed. Hazel Holt and Hilary Pym. New York: Dutton, 1984.

Receipt Book. Add. ms. 46171. British Lib., London.

"Regency furniture." *Encarta* (online). 15 January 2002 <www.encarta.com>.

Roberts, Elizabeth. *Women and Families: An Oral History, 1940–1970*. London: Blackwell, 1995.

Rosenblatt, Louise M. *The Reader, the Text, the Poem: The Transactional Theory of the Literary Work*. Carbondale: Southern IL UP, 1978.

Rossen, Janice. *The World of Barbara Pym*. London and Basingstoke: Macmillan, 1987.

Rubenstein, Helena. *My Life for Beauty*. London: The Bodeley Head, 1965.

Rupert, Mrs. Anna. *A Book of Beauty*. London: n.p., 1892.

Ryan, Marie-Laure. "Immersion vs. Interactivity: Virtual Reality and Interactivity." *Postmodern Culture* 5.1 (1994): 39 pars. 27 December 2000 <http://jefferson.village.virginia.edu/pmc/text-only/issue.994/ryan.994>.

―――. *Narrative as Virtual Reality: Immersion and Interactivity in Literature and Electronic Media*. Baltimore: Johns Hopkins UP, 2001.

Sage, Lorna. *Bad Blood*. 2000. London: Fourth Estate-HarperCollins, 2001.

Scarry, Elaine. *The Body in Pain: The Making and Unmaking of the World*. Oxford: Oxford UP, 1985.

————. *Dreaming by the Book*. New York: Farrar Straus Giroux, 1999.

Sceats, Sarah. *Food, Consumption, and the Body in Contemporary Women's Fiction*. Cambridge: Cambridge UP, 2000.

Schabert, Ina. "Habeus Corpus 2000: The Return of the Body." *European Studies* 16 (2001): 87–115.

Schilder, Paul. *The Image and Appearance of the Human Body*. 1935. New York: International Universities P, 1950.

Schofield, Mary Anne. "Well-fed or Well-loved? Patterns of Cooking and Eating in the Novels of Barbara Pym." *The Windsor Review* 18.2: 1–8.

Sillitoe, Helen. *A History of the Teaching of Domestic Subjects*. London: Methuen, 1933.

Smith, Delia. *Delia Smith's Cookery Course*. Part One. 1978. London: BBC, 1979.

Smith, Patricia Juliana. "'The Queen of the Waste Land': The Endgames of Modernism in Angela Carter's *Magic Toyshop*." *Modern Language quarterly* 67.3 (2006): 333–61.

Spacks, Patricia Meyer. *Gossip*. New York: Knopf, 1985.

Stallybrass, Peter and Allon White. *The Politics and Poetics of Transgression*. Ithaca: Cornell UP, 1986.

Steedman, Carolyn Kay. *Landscape for a Good Woman: A Story of Two Lives*. 1986. New Brunswick: Rutgers UP, 1992.

Streatfeild, Noel. *Saplings*. 1945. London: Persephone, 2000.

Summerfield, Penny. "Women in Britain since 1945." *Understanding Post-War British Society*. Ed. James Obelkevich and Peter Catterall. London and New York: Routledge, 1994. 58–2.

Swift, Rachel. *Fabulous Figures or How to Be Utterly, Uniquely Gorgeous*. London: Pan-Macmillan, 1995.

Terry, Ellen. *Ellen Terry's Memoirs*. 1908. Preface, etc. Edith Craig and Christopher St. John. London: Victor Gollancz, Ltd., 1933.

Tompkins, Jane P., ed. and intro. *Reader-Response Criticism: From Formalism to Post-Structuralism*. Baltimore and London: Johns Hopkins UP, 1980.

Travis, Molly Abel. *Reading Cultures: The Construction of Readers in the Twentieth Century*. Carbondale: Southern Illinois UP, 1998.

Tyler, Anne. Foreword. *Excellent Women; Jane and Prudence; An Unsuitable Attachment*. By Barbara Pym. New York: Quality Paperback, 1984.

Weld, Annette. *Barbara Pym and the Novel of Manners*. New York: St. Martin's, 1992.

Wheatcroft, Mildred, ed. and intro. *Housework with Satisfaction*. London: National Council of Social Service, 1960.

————. "The Home Industry." Wheatcroft: 13–16.

Whelehan, Imelda. *The Feminist Bestseller: From* Sex and the Single Girl *to* Sex and the City. Houndmills, UK: Palgrave Macmillan, 1995.

————. *Helen Fielding's* Bridget Jones's Diary. New York and London: Continuum, 2002.

Whitaker, Ruth. *Modern Developments in Domestic Science Training*. London: J. M. Dent & Sons, Ltd., 1937.

Woman's Own. April 27, 1940.

———. September 14, 1940.

———. February 5, 1943.

———. July 6, 1950.

Woolf, Virginia. *Between the Acts*. 1941. New York: Harcourt Brace Jovanovich, 1985.

———. "Ellen Terry." *Collected Essays*. Vol. Four. New York: Harcourt, Brace, and World, 1967. 67–72.

Wyatt, Jean. "The Violence of Gendering: Castration Images in Angela Carter's *The Magic Toyshop*, *The Passion of New Eve*, and *Peter and the Wolf*." *Women's Studies: An International Journal* 25.6: 549–70.

Wyatt-Brown, Anne M. *Barbara Pym: A Critical Biography*. Columbia: U of Missouri P, 1992.

Young, Mary Evans. *Diet Breaking: Having It All Without Having to Diet*. London: Hodder and Stroughton, 1995.

Zweiniger-Bargielowska, Ina. *Austerity in Britain: Rationing, Controls, and Consumption 1939–1955*. Oxford: Oxford UP, 2000.

———. "Housewifery." *Women in Twentieth-Century Britain*. Ed. Ina Zweiniger-Bargielowska. Essex: Longman-Pearson, 2001. 149–64.

Index

the abject, 11, 12, 54, 91
abstinence, 92, 94; *see also* purity
Adam, Jill, 72
    Beauty Box, 20–21, 59–60
Adams, Carol J., 94
Adolph, Andrea, 30
advertisements, 46, 47, 48, 78–9
agency, 15–19, 22, 28–9, 65–7, 73, 119,
        121–5, 136, 144–50, 160, 165–6
alcohol consumption, 65n6, 84–5
ambivalence, 16, 19, 21–2
appearance, 53, 54
appliances, 45–8
Armstrong, Nancy, 24, 64
The Art of Beauty, 58
The Art of Being Beautiful, 19–20, 55
Aslett, Don, 49
the Association of Teachers of Domestic
        Subjects, *Hard-Time Cookery*, 79
austerity, 31, 69–104
authority, 27–8, 138–44
auto-objectification, 68, 105–6, 134–5,
        150, 154–6, 159, 163–7; *see also*
        objectification
    body maintenance and, 54–64
    mind/body duality and, 18–26, 31, 33
    regimentation and, 35–6, 42–3, 47

Baker, Niamh, 103
Bal, Mieke, 27
Balenky, Mary, 74
Barker, Francis, 2, 25
    The Tremulous Private Body, 12–13
Barthes, Roland, 107, 126–7, 136
Baudrillard, Jean, 15–16
BBC, 70–71
beauty, 154–5
    rhetoric of, 61
    standardization of, 19–21, 54–64
beauty manuals, 24–5, 29, 54–64, 65–6,
        80–81, 154–5

Beauvoir, Simone de, 37, 45
Beckham, Victoria, 63
Beeton, Mrs., 24, 51, 74, 86, 156
Bell, Mrs. J. N., 47
Bell, Vanessa, 114n1
Benson, James, 41, 42
bio-power, 16, 43–4
blood, 11
Bloom, Ursula, 56, 59, 60
    The Housewife's Beauty Book, 60–61
    Me—After the War, 50, 61
    Wartime Beauty, 80, 80n2
the body, 1n1, 4, 7, 9–10, 12, 108; *see
        also* body image; body/image;
        embodiment; mind/body duality
    appearance of, 53
    auto-objectification and, 54–64
    consumption and, 64–8, 78–80, 94,
        102, 127, 130
    discourses on, 49–54
    as a "gestalt," 4, 128–9, 133
    housework and, 46–7
    knowledge and, 6, 106, 128–30,
        132–3, 151
    language and, 128–9
    maintenance of, 23–4, 49–68; *see also*
        regimentation
    minds and, 107
    narrative and, 26–8
    readers and, 127–8, 131–5
    reading and, 127–8
    regimentation of, 49–54, 64–8
    representation of, 132–3
    textuality of, 5–7, 105–50
body image, 3–4, 3n2, 5, 11, 32, 105–6,
        126–30, 132, 134, 141, 144–5,
        164–5; *see also* body/image
body-image dysphoria, 15
    language and, 130–31
    visuality of, 130–31, 133–4
    in written texts, 130–31

body/image, 3n2, 5, 106, 126, 126–7, 134, 135, 141–3, 164; *see also* body image
Booth, Wayne, 134
Bordo, Susan, 6, 52, 53
    Unbearable Weight, 6
Bourdieau, Pierre, 30
Bowlby, Rachel, 15–16
Bridget Jones's Diary (film), 162
Bridget Jones: The Edge of Reason, 162
British Medical Association, 50
Brontë, Charlotte, *Jane Eyre*, 120–21n2
Brooks, Peter, 141–2
Butler, Judith, 8–9, 8n3, 13, 14, 21
    Bodies that Matter, 8n4, 9
    Gender Trouble, 8n4, 9
    The Psychic Life of Power, 16

capitalism, 19
Carter, Angela, 25
    The Magic Toyshop, 32, 107, 108, 117–26, 120–21n2, 127, 135–8, 144–50, 145n7
castration, 11
Certeau, Michel de, 16–18, 23, 28, 29, 75–6, 127–8, 132
Chadwick, Edwin, 41
    Report on the Sanitary Condition of the Labouring Population of Great Britain, 40–42
characterization, 25, 26–8, 33, 81–6, 107–26, 140, 150, 168
Chatman, Seymour, 26
Chatterton, Lydia, 74–5, 76, 79, 95–6n4
    Win-the-War Cookery, 73–4
Chernin, Kim, 59
cinema, 62, 162
citizenship, 71; *see also* austerity
Cixous, Hélène, 8n3
class, 30–31, 39–42, 53–54, 90–92, 107; *see also* the middle class; the working class
cleanliness, 23–4, 35–49; *see also* household maintenance; hygiene
Cobb, Stanley, 1
commodification, 19; *see also* objectification
conduct manuals, 23–4, 23n7
confession, 44–5

conformity, 23, 42–3; *see also* standardization
Conran, Shirley, 46
consumerism, 13–17
consumers, 17, 25, 127
consumption, 9–10, 15–17, 25, 27–30, 64–8; *see also* consumerism; eating disorders
    agency and, 65–7, 124–5
    beauty manuals and, 65–6
    the body and, 64–8, 78–80, 94, 102, 105–50
    characterization and, 81–6, 107–26
    class and, 107
    control of, 69–104, 95–6n4
    cultural attitudes toward, 107–8
    femininity and, 29, 92–3, 113–17
    from a femnist perspective, 14–15
    hygiene and, 66
    as masculine, 95–6
    maternity and, 10–11
    moral hygiene and, 66
    regimentation and, 64–8
    sexuality and, 66, 84–5, 92–3, 94–102, 107–26
    transgression and, 113–17
consumption relations, 13–15
control, 163–4
Cooke, Kay, 57–8, 63, 163
    Real Gorgeous, 154
cooking, 28, 29, 123–4, 156
    cooking shows, 155–7
    the culinary revolution, 123
cooking manuals, 51–2, 74–7, 81, 155–7
I Corinthians, 91, 92
Council of Scientific Management in the Home, 48–9
"Cover Girl" chart, 61n3
Cox, Muriel, 59, 60, 61
culture, 35, 37; *see also* women's culture
    cleanliness and, 35–8, 42
    consumption and, 107–8
Cusk, Rachel, 25, 33
    Saving Agnes, 163–8

danger, 38, 144–7
David, Elizabeth, *A Book of Mediterranean Food*, 93–94
Davidson, Phyllis, 49, 50
desire, 4–5, 15, 141

dietary prohibitions, religious, 22, 91, 92
dirt, 35–6, 38–40, 45, 54
disease, 51
disembodiment, 26–8, 67–8, 117–19, 140–41
disempowerment, 15
disinfection, 50
docility, 6, 66, 164–5
domestic help, 36
domesticity, 36–7, 43, 46–7, 153
domestic sciences, 40–41, 48–50, 54,
    55, 72–3
Donato, Deborah, 86
Dors, Diana, 62
Douglas, Mary, 25, 28, 38, 39, 42, 53–4
    Purity and Danger, 35, 43–4
dress, 54
duality, 35, 37; *see also* mind/body duality
Dunmore, Helen, 25, 112
    Talking to the Dead, 32, 107, 108–17,
        114n1, 123, 125–6, 127, 135–44,
        147, 149–50, 156
DuPlessis, Rachel Blau, 158–9

eating disorders, 15, 22, 29
education, 40–41, 49–50, 54, 72–3
Education Act of 1870, 49–50
Education Act of 1944, 72–3
egalitarian feminism, 8n3
embodiment, 4–6, 9–12, 18–19, 21, 67–8,
        117, 128–34, 151, 154–56, 160,
        167–8; *see also* the body; mind/
        body duality
    characterization and, 26–8
    feminist thought on, 8–9, 8n3
    literacy of, 105–6
    mind/body duality and, 144–50
    modernity and, 151–2
    narrative and, 134–5, 137
    narrative authority and, 138–44
    reader response and, 138–43
    representation of, 131–5
    sexuality and, 14–15, 69–104
    subjectivity and, 12–13, 14–15, 154–5
    women writers and, 134–5
Epstein, Marcy J., 10, 15, 19
Etiquette for Women, 64–5
exercise, 56
Eyles, Leonora, 95

fashion magazines, 86–7; *see also*
    women's magazines
fashion models, 62
Felski, Rita, 15
femininity, 21, 37, 43, 71, 94, 138–9, 156,
    159–60
    consumption and, 113–17
    domesticity and, 36–7, 123–4
    food and, 29
    self and, 165–8
    self-denial and, 83–4
    during World War II, 72–4
feminist discourses, 8, 8n3, 29, 126,
    159–61
Fielding, Helen, 25, 33
    Bridget Jones's Diary, 158–63, 167, 168
flappers, 62
Flynn, Elizabeth, 126
food, 10–12, 15, 29; *see also* consumption;
        cooking; rationing
    language of, 120–21, 156
    power and, 123
    subjectivity and, 29–30
Food Advice Division, 71
Food and Nutrition, 70–71
Food Flashes, 70
Forever Summer, 155
Forty, Adrian, 48, 50
Foucault, Michel, 5–6, 13, 14, 28, 53, 66
    Discipline and Punish, 6, 44
    The History of Sexuality, Volume One,
        42, 43–4
Fox, Henry M., 1, 2
Freud, Signund, 1, 10, 11

gas ovens, 47
genre development, 25
Gent, Helena, 57
    *Health and Beauty for Women and
        Girls*, 56
George IV, 96
germs, 49, 50, 51, 54
germ theories, 49
Girls' Own Paper, 36
Glover, Gordon, 99n5
Good Housekeeping, 59
Good Housekeeping Institute, *Fish, Meat,
        Egg and Cheese Dishes*, 75

Good Housekeeping's 100 Recipes for Unrationed Meat, 76
Grosz, Elizabeth, 8n3, 11, 13
    Volatile Bodies: Toward a Corporeal Feminism, 8

Hardyment, Christina, 49
Harrison, Brian, 123
Head, Henry, 3n2
health
    discourses on, 49–54
    health science, 54
health manuals, 24–25, 154–5
Hollywood, 62
homosexuality, 97–8
Horsfield, Margaret, 37, 46
household maintenance, 23–4, 35–7, 56
    the body and, 46–7
    evolution of, 45–9
    modernity and, 45–9
    morality and, 38–45
    rhetoric of, 46, 48–9, 50
household receipt books, 51–2
housekeepers, 38–9; *see also* housewives
housekeeping manuals, 24–5, 35–7, 49,
    51–2, 154–5
The Housewife's Day, 41
housewives, 36–9, 41, 41n1, 45–7, 48, 49,
    50–51, 54–64, 76–7, 78
housework; *see* household maintenance
How Britain Was Fed in Wartime, 69
Humble, Nicola, 74, 156
hygiene, 38–42, 49–54, 53–4, 66, 95–6;
    see also cleanliness

identity, 12, 14; *see also* self
imagination, 128, 131–3
immersion, 133–5, 136, 141–2, 144–5
infancy, 10–11
interactivity, 133–5
interpretation, 16–17, 106–7, 126–8; *see
    also* reading

Johnson, Mark, 2, 22, 25–6

Kelsall, Helen M., 41
Kemsley Newspapers, 41
Kennedy, Mrs., 48
Kenton, Leslie, *The New Joy of Beauty*, 155

Kingsford, Anna, *Health, Beauty, and the
    Toilet*, 55–6, 151–2
Kino, Carol, 149
the Kitchen Front, 69, 70, 71, 73–4, 76, 78, 80
Kitchen Front, 70
kitchens, 50–51
Klein, Melanie, 10
knowledge, 3–4, 21, 22, 128–30
Kristeva, Julia, 9, 11, 12, 14–15, 22, 54, 91

lactation, 11
Lakoff, George, 2, 22, 25–6
Langland, Elizabeth, 23–4
language, 1, 1n1, 2, 13–14, 37, 120–23,
    128–9, 130–31, 132, 134, 150
Lawson, Nigella, 155–8
    How to Be a Domestic Goddess, 155–6
    How to Eat, 115, 155–6, 157
League of Nations, 61n3
Lears, Jackson, 52
Leigh, Michelle, 58, 155
Levitican laws, 91
liberal feminism, 8n3
London Health and Beauty Bureau, 61n3

Mace, C. A., 48
Macherey, Pierre, 137
Magazines; *see* women's magazines
Manuals; *see specific kinds of manuals*
"The Man-Who-Sees," 71–2, 85, 155
Marin, Louis, 11
Marmola Antifat Tablets, 59
Marsh, Kelly A., 159
masculinity, 43, 94–102
Massé, Michelle, 135n6
Mass Observation, 41, 49, 79–80, 91
    The Housewife's Day, 81
maternity, 10, 10–12, 113
"matter out of place," 53–4
McNeil, Steve, "She Knew What She
    Wanted," 81–3
Meals in Modern Homes, 48–9
meaning, 22, 25, 132
meat, 95, 98
    in I Corinthians, 91–2
    masculinity and, 95–6, 98
    rationing of, 90–92
    during World War II, 90–92
mechanization, 45–9

medicine, discipline of, 52–3, 54
men, shortages of after World War II, 87
Mendelson, Anne, 156
menstruation, 11
Merleau-Ponty, Maurice, 2–3, 128, 129
MetLife insurance charts, 60
Michie, Helena, 66
the middle class, 24, 30–31, 39–40, 42, 46, 48, 49, 53, 81
   household maintenance and, 36–7
   rationing and, 76–7
milk, 11
mimesis, 132, 133–4
mind/body duality, 1–33, 107, 117–20, 126, 151, 155
   attempts to transcend, 155–8
   body maintenance and, 63–4
   embodiment and, 144–50
   female characterization and, 33
   female subjectivity and, 154–7
   narrative and, 135–50
   as a trope, 25–6
   women and, 71–3
   women writers and, 30–32, 154, 168
   Woolf and, 30–31
Ministry of Agriculture, 71
Ministry of Food, 69–71, 73, 74–5, 76, 77, 78, 79, 80, 90, 91, 94, 95–6n4
Ministry of Supply, 71
Modernism, 148
modernity, 30, 31, 51
   embodiment and, 151–2
   female subjectivity and, 151–2, 168
   housework and, 45–9
   hygiene and, 49–54
monogamy, 42–3
moral codes, 43–4
moral hygiene, 38–45, 95–6
   food consumption and, 66
morality
   class and, 40–42
   cleanliness and, 38–45
   sexuality and, 42–4
motherhood; *see* maternity
motility, 4–5, 29, 132
Ms. magazine, 19n6
My Home, 69–72, 83–4, 87, 104

narrative, 26
   the body and, 26–8

characterization and, 26–8
embodiment and, 134–5, 137
mind/body duality and, 135–50
narrative authority, 27–8, 138–44
narrative conventions, 137
narrative voice, 25
sensory perception and, 136–7
nature, 37
neuropsychology, 22
the "New Look," 86–7
Newman, Judith, *Body*, 164, 165
Nigella Bites, 155, 156
nonverbal communication, 105
nurturing, 112–13

objectification, 21, 105, 106; *see also* auto-objectification
O'Hara, Daniel T., 13
Oliver, Kelly, 12, 14
orality, 121–3
order, 23–4
Orenstein, Peggy, 159

pain, 144–5
Panter-Downes, Mollie, *One Fine Day*, 32, 77–8
Paul, 91, 92, 94
Pearson, C. Arthur, 21
Pender, Lisa, 62–3, 62n4
Perception; *see* sensory perception
perfection, 163–5; *see also* standardization
la perruque, 76
physical education, 54
Physical Training and Recreation Act, 54
Pizzey, Erin, *The Slut's Cookbook*, 113–21
plastic surgery, 22
pleasure, 127–8, 156
pollution, 43; *see also* dirt
Poovey, Mary, 40, 53
postmodernity, 13
postural model, 3n2
power, 43–4, 123, 163–4; *see also* agency
the private realm, 35–68
proportions, 59–63, 61n3; *see also* weight
psychoanalysis, 10–11
Public Health Act of 1848, 40
Public Health Commissions, 41
publishing, 51–2, 53; *see also specific kinds of manuals*; women's magazines

Punday, Daniel, 133
  Narrative Bodies, 26–7
purity, 38–9
Pym, Barbara, 25, 99n5, 108
  Excellent Women, 85–6, 87, 87n3, 93,
    94, 97
  A Glass of Blessings, 96–8, 100
  Jane and Prudence, 31–2, 85–104,
    95–6n4, 112, 167
Pyrhönen, Heta, 145n7

rationing, 31, 69, 73–4, 75, 82–3, 91, 92,
    95–6n4, 96
reader response, 105–50
  danger and, 144–7
  embodiment and, 138–43
  sensory perception and, 144–5
  sexuality and, 141–3, 144–7
  theories of, 126, 136, 137, 141–3
readers, 107, 126–8, 131–5; *see also* reader
    response; reader/text dyad; reading
reader/text dyad, 126–7, 136
reading, 17, 105–50; *see also* reader
    response
  aesthetic, 136–7
  the body and, 127–8
  efferent, 136, 137
  "fat" vs. "thin" ways of, 135–6, 144, 150
  as mimesis, 132
  as performance, 132, 134
  as resistance, 127–8
  sensory perception and, 136
Receipt Book, 52
refrigerators, 47
regimentation, 23–4, 43–4, 49–54, 55–6;
    see also standardization
Roberts, Elizabeth, 45–6, 48
Rosenblatt, Louise, 107, 126
  The Reader, the Text, the Poem, 136, 137
Rossen, Janice, 94
Rubenstein, Helena, 57
Rupert, Anna, 57
Ryan, Marie-Laure, 133–4, 133n5, 136, 141

Sage, Lorna, 24, 39, 41, 45, 57, 81
  Bad Blood, 12
Salisbury, Lord, 20
sanitation, 41, 50, 53
Scarry, Elaine, 128, 142

  The Body in Pain, 132–3, 144–5
  Dreaming by the book, 131–3
Sceats, Sarah, *Food, Consumption, and the
    Body in Contemporary Women's
    Fiction*, 10–11
Schabert, Ina, 4, 9, 27
Schilder, Paul, 3n2, 4, 5, 32, 106, 129–32,
    134, 142, 144, 164–5
  *The Image and Appearance of the
    Human Body*, 3
secretions, 11
security, 43
self, 12–14, 18, 20–22, 25, 45, 52, 68,
    72, 106, 154–5, 165–8; *see also*
    identity; subjectivity
self-denial, 78–9, 82–4, 102–3, 116–17
self-improvement books, 21, 53, 162
seminal fluid, 11
sensory perception, 130–34, 136–7, 144–5, 156
servants, 36, 46, 47, 49
sex manuals, 66
sexual difference, 8, 8n3, 9
sexuality, 10, 11, 13–15, 73, 94, 138–41,
    144–50, 151, 160
  cleanliness and, 37
  consumption and, 66, 84–5, 92–3,
    94–102, 107–26
  cooking and, 156
  embodiment and, 14–15, 69–104
  as masculine, 94–9
  morality and, 42–4
  reader response and, 141–7
  self and, 14
  self-denial and, 82–3
  sexual excess, 69–103
  subjectivity and, 13–15
sexual revolution, 123
sexual threat, 144–7; *see also* danger
Sloane Square, 62
slums, 39, 40–41
Smith, Delia, 157
Smith, Patricia Juliana, 148
social code, 54
social constructionism, 8n3, 9
social order, 23, 43–4, 55–6; *see also*
    regimentation
solidarity, 74–5
Spivak, Gayatri, 8n3
standardization, 19–21, 23, 24, 33, 54–64,
    161–5; *see also* regimentation

Steedman, Carolyn, 42, 46, 87
strategies, 16–17, 18
Streatfeild, Noel, *Saplings*, 32, 83–85, 98
subjectivity, 12–15, 18, 30–31, 66–7,
     165–8; *see also* self
    auto-objectification and, 18–19, 20–25, 47
    body maintenance and, 63–4
    confession and, 44–5
    consumerism and, 15–16
    embodiment and, 12–15, 154–5
    food and, 29–30
    mind/body duality and, 154–7
    modernity and, 151–2, 168
    morality and, 44–5
    self-denial and, 78–80
    sexuality and, 13–15
    tactical nature of, 18
    women writers and, 32–3
subject/object duality, 18–19
suburbs, 48
Summerfield, Penny, 81
Swift, Rachel, 60

tactics, 16–17, 18, 23, 29, 75–6
Terry, Ellen, 33, 152–4, 168
    A Story of My Life, 153
Terry, Josephine, *Food without Fuss*, 74
texts, 106–7, 126–7; *see also* reader/text dyad
textual codes, 137
textuality, 105–50
Times Literary Supplement, 88
Tompkins, Jane, 107
traits, 26–7
transgression, 113–17, 123, 136, 138–9, 155
Travis, Molly, 66, 127

the Utility Scheme, 87

vacuum cleaners, 45, 47
virtual reality (VR), 133–4
Vogue, 86, 87

washing machines, 45, 48
Waters, Doris, 70

Waters, Elsie, 70
weight, 58–63, 61n3, 161–2
well-being, 59
Wheatcroft, Mildred, 41n1
    Housework with Satisfaction, 48
Whelehan, Imelda, 156, 158, 161, 162
Whitaker, Ruth, 41
will, 22
Woman's Own, 59, 62–3, 62n4, 70, 78–9,
    81–3, 88
women; *see also* women writers
    consumption and, 29, 92–3
    food and, 10–12, 15, 29, 92–3
    meat and, 92–3
    mind/body duality and, 71–3
women's culture, 81–3, 154–5; *see also*
    women's magazines
Women's League of Health and Beauty, 54
women's magazines, 19–21, 19n6, 29, 49,
    59, 62–3, 62n4, 69–71, 78–9, 81–4,
    86–8, 93, 98, 104
women's programming, 81
women writers, 25
    embodiment and, 134–5
    female subjectivity and, 32–3
    mind/body duality and, 30–32, 154, 168
Woolf, Virginia, 32–3, 168
    Between the Acts, 30–31, 114n1, 152,
    153, 154
    "Ellen Terry," 152–4
    Freshwater, 153
    "The New Biography," 30
Woolton, Lord, 69, 70, 71, 74–5, 78, 96
the working class, 36, 39–40, 46, 77
World War II, 31, 69–104
Wyatt, Honor, 99n5
Wyatt, Jean, 147, 148
Wyatt-Brown, Anne M., 87, 97, 98

Young, Mary Evans, *Diet Breaking*, 154–5

Zellweger, Renée, 162
Zweiniger-Bargielowska, Ina, 69, 76, 79